Daily Reading Comprehension

GRADE 6

The following illustrations were created by the artists listed (provided through Shutterstock.com) and are protected by copyright: Bipsun (page 9); Denis Cristo (pages 9, 10); Norwayblue (page 10)

Writing: Bonnie Brook Communications
Editorial Development: Marilyn Evans, Debra Housel, James Spears
Copy Editing: Carrie Gwynne, Cathy Harber
Art Direction: Cheryl Puckett
Cover Design: Cheryl Puckett
Design/Production: Carolina Caird, Arynne Elfenbein, Yuki Meyer, Jessica Onken, Olivia Trinidad

EVAN-MOOR Educational Publishers

EMC 3616

Visit *teaching-standards.com* to view a correlation of this book.

Correlated to Current Standards

Congratulations on your purchase of some of the finest teaching materials in the world.

For information about other Evan-Moor products, call 1-800-777-4362, fax 1-800-777-4332, or visit our website, www.evan-moor.com.

10 Harris Court, Suite C-3, Monterey, CA 93940-5773. Printed in India.

009

CPSIA: Manipal Technologies Limited, Manipal, India [3/2025]

Contents

How to Use *Daily Reading Comprehension*

Daily Reading Comprehension provides a unique integration of instruction and practice in both comprehension strategies and comprehension skills.

Strategies—such as visualizing or asking questions—are general, meta-cognitive techniques that a reader uses to better understand and engage with the text. **Skills**—such as finding a main idea or identifying a sequence of events—focus on particular text elements that aid comprehension. See page 6 for a complete list of strategies and skills covered in *Daily Reading Comprehension.*

The first six weeks of *Daily Reading Comprehension* introduce students to comprehension strategies they will apply throughout the year. Weeks 7–30 focus on specific skill instruction and practice. All 30 weeks follow the same five-day format, making the teaching and learning process simpler. Follow these steps to conduct the weekly lessons and activities:

STEP 1 The weekly teacher page lists the strategy or skills that students will focus on during that week and provides a brief definition of the strategy or the skills. Read the definition(s) aloud to students each day before they complete the activities, or prompt students to define the skills themselves. You may also wish to reproduce the comprehension skill definitions on page 8 as a poster for your classroom. Then reproduce the strategy visual aids on pages 9–14 and distribute them to students.

STEP 2 The teacher page provides an instructional path for conducting each day's lesson and activities. Use the tips and suggestions in each day's lesson to present the skills and introduce the passage.

STEP 3 Each student page begins with directions for reading the passage. These directions also serve as a way to establish a purpose for reading. Help students see the connection between setting a purpose for reading and improving comprehension.

STEP 4 Because much of reading comprehension stems from a reader's background knowledge about a subject, take a moment to discuss the topic with students before they read a passage. Introduce unfamiliar phrases or concepts, and encourage students to ask questions about the topic.

STEP 5 After students have read a passage, two comprehension activities give students an opportunity to practice the strategies and skills. In weeks 1–6, the first activity is an open-ended writing or partner activity that encourages students to reflect on the reading process, applying the weekly strategy. The second activity provides three constructed response items that practice the week's skills in a test-taking format.

In weeks 7–30, students complete the constructed response activity before practicing the strategy activity. The teacher page for these weeks offers suggestions for teaching the skills and gives tips for reminding students of the strategy(ies). Throughout the week, encourage students to refer to the strategy visual aids. Use the Student Record Sheet on page 15 to track student progress and to note which skills or strategies a student may need additional practice with.

Weekly Teacher Page

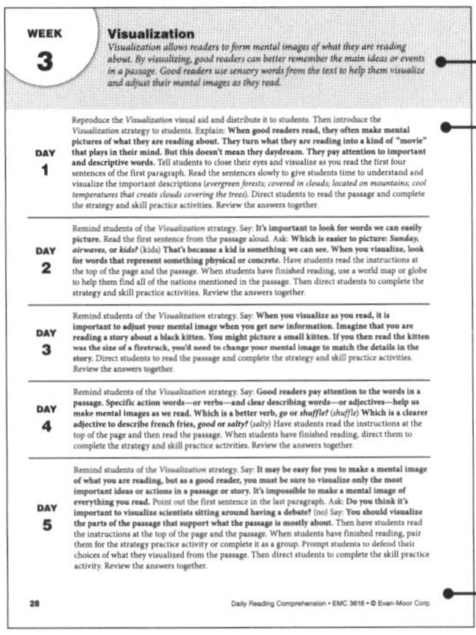

Weekly skills are explained at the top of each teacher page.

The daily instruction path provides suggestions for modeling the skill and guiding students through the passage and activities.

Strategy Visual Aid

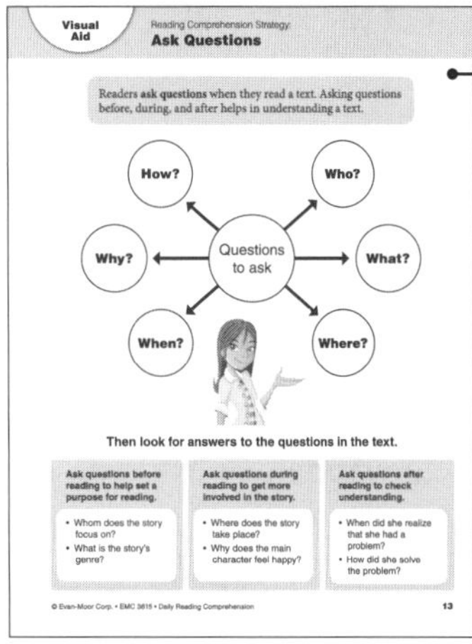

A definition and graphic image for each strategy help students to understand the concept and provide a reference as they complete the activities.

Daily Student Pages

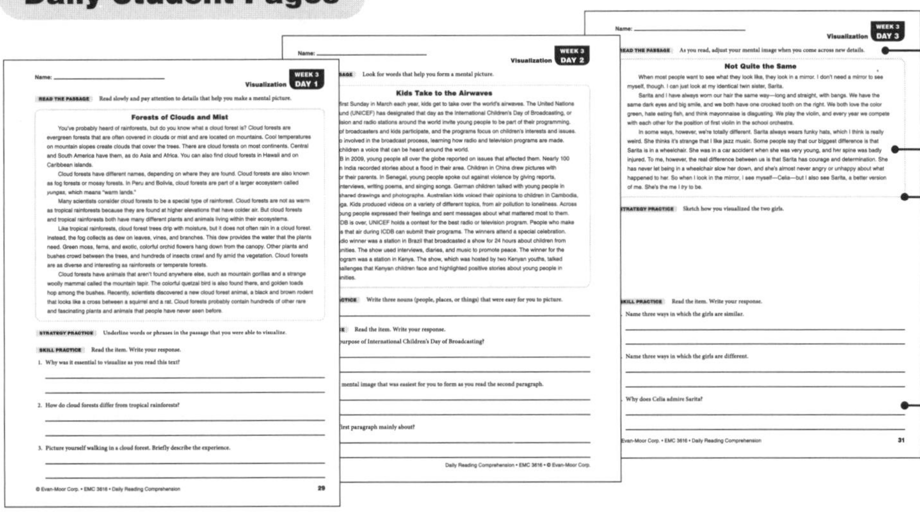

Activity directions help students establish a purpose for reading.

Grade-appropriate text supports comprehension.

Each passage is followed by three constructed response items, practicing specific comprehension skills, as well as an open-ended strategy-based activity. In weeks 1–6, the strategy activity precedes the skill activity.

Student Record Sheet

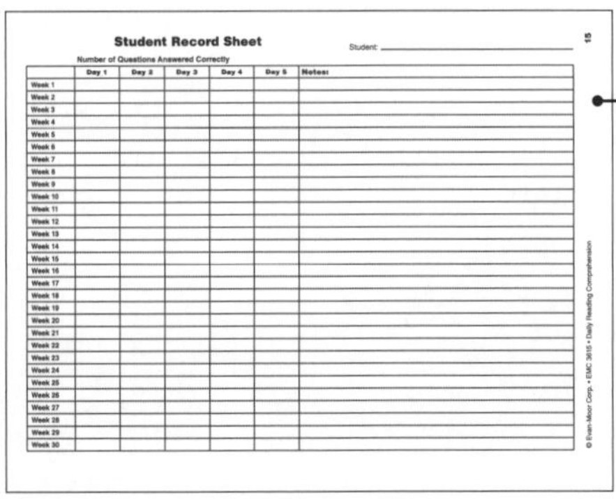

The record sheet allows you to record students' progress and identify areas in which individuals need improvement.

Comprehension Strategies and Skills

In *Daily Reading Comprehension*, students learn and practice the following commonly tested comprehension strategies and skills, all proven to increase students' abilities to read and understand a wide range of text types. Reproduce and post the strategy visual aids on pages 9–14. You may also wish to post or distribute copies of page 8, which provides a student-friendly list of skills and helpful questions that students can ask themselves as they read.

Strategies

Make Connections
Students make connections to the text to aid their comprehension. Connections can be made to personal experiences or to things the students have seen or read.

Visualization
Students make mental images of what they are reading. They learn to look for vivid language, including concrete nouns, active verbs, and strong adjectives.

Organization
Students learn to find the organizational pattern of a text. This allows them to anticipate what they are reading and helps them focus on the author's central message or important ideas.

Determine Important Information
Students learn to categorize information based on whether it supports an author's central message or is important for a specific purpose.

Ask Questions
Students learn to ask questions before reading to set a purpose for reading, during reading to identify when their comprehension breaks down, or after reading as a way to check their understanding of a passage.

Monitor Comprehension
Students learn to pay attention to their own reading process and notice when they are losing focus or when comprehension is breaking down. They then can employ another strategy to help them overcome their difficulty.

Skills

Main Idea and Details
Students identify what a passage is mostly about and find important details that support the main idea.

Sequence
Students look for the order in which things happen or identify the steps in a process.

(Skills, continued)

Cause and Effect
Students identify what happens (effect) and why it happens (cause).

Evaluate Evidence
Students study an author's claims and the evidence that the author gives to support those claims.

Compare and Contrast
Students note how two or more people or things are alike and different.

Make Inferences
Students use their background knowledge and clues from the text to infer information.

Character and Setting
Students identify who or what a story is about and where and when the story takes place.

Theme
Students look for the moral or lesson in a fiction story or an author's view about the world in nonfiction.

Author's Purpose
Students determine why an author wrote a passage and whether the purpose is to entertain, to inform, to persuade, or to teach.

Prediction
Students use their background knowledge and clues from the text to figure out what will happen next.

Nonfiction Text Features
Students study features that are not part of the main body of text, including subheadings, captions, entry words, and titles.

Visual Information
Students study pictures, charts, graphs, and other forms of visual information.

Scope and Sequence

	Comprehension Strategies						Comprehension Skills											
	Monitor Comprehension	Make Connections	Visualization	Organization	Determine Important Information	Ask Questions	Main Idea and Details	Sequence	Cause and Effect	Evaluate Evidence	Compare and Contrast	Make Inferences	Prediction	Theme	Character and Setting	Author's Purpose	Nonfiction Text Features	Visual Information
Week 1	●						●						●					●
Week 2		●										●		●	●			
Week 3			●				●		●		●							
Week 4				●				●	●	●								
Week 5					●					●							●	●
Week 6						●					●			●		●		
Week 7	●		●				●	●										
Week 8					●	●			●	●								
Week 9		●		●							●	●						
Week 10	●		●											●	●			
Week 11		●				●							●			●		
Week 12				●	●												●	●
Week 13	●		●				●	●										
Week 14					●	●			●	●								
Week 15	●	●									●	●						
Week 16	●		●											●	●			
Week 17		●				●							●			●		
Week 18				●	●												●	●
Week 19	●		●				●	●										
Week 20					●	●			●	●								
Week 21		●		●							●	●						
Week 22	●		●											●	●			
Week 23		●				●							●			●		
Week 24				●	●												●	●
Week 25	●		●				●	●										
Week 26					●	●			●	●								
Week 27		●		●							●	●						
Week 28	●		●											●	●			
Week 29		●				●							●			●		
Week 30				●	●												●	●

How to Be a Good Reader

Ask yourself these questions to help you understand what you read:

Main Idea and Details	What is the story mostly about? What tells me more about the main idea?
Sequence	What happens first, next, and last? What are the steps to do something?
Cause and Effect	What happens? (the effect) Why did it happen? (the cause)
Evaluate Evidence	What claims is the author making? What evidence supports these claims?
Compare and Contrast	How are these people or things the same? How are these people or things different?
Make Inferences	What clues does the story give? What do I know already that will help?
Prediction	What clues does the story give? What do I know already that will help? What will happen next?
Character and Setting	Who or what is the story about? Where and when does the story take place?
Theme	What lesson does this story teach? How does the author feel about this topic?
Author's Purpose	Does the story entertain, inform, try to persuade me, or teach me how to do something?
Nonfiction Text Features	What kind of text am I reading? What does it tell me?
Visual Information	Is there a picture, chart, or graph? What does it tell me?

Reading Comprehension Strategy:

Make Connections

Readers **make connections** between the text and themselves, the world around them, or other things they have read and seen.

The Best Vacations TV show advertised an amusement park with six roller coasters.

This guy reminds me of my uncle, who loves to ride roller coasters.

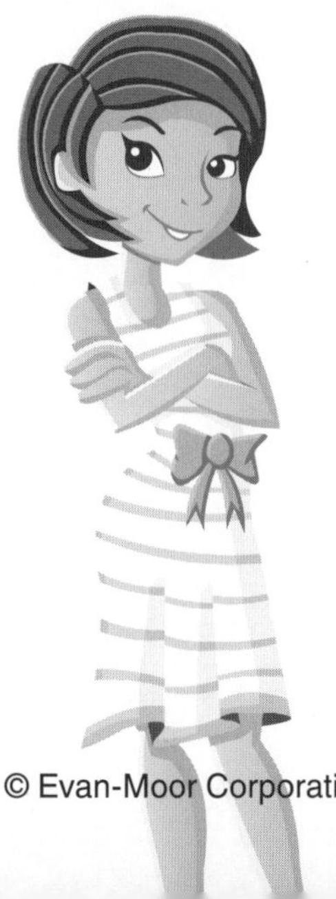

I read something about a wakeboarding contest in Santa Cruz, CA.

I bet wakeboarding is kind of like snowboarding...

Reading Comprehension Strategy:

Visualization

Readers use **visualization** to understand a text. Visualization is using details to create pictures in the mind and imagine what is happening in the text.

To use visualization, look for words that **describe**, such as adjectives, action verbs, adverbs, and concrete nouns.

When you read...

Mr. Flannery opened the box and said, "They have big heads and round bodies. And they sure do squeal like pigs."

Mr. Morehouse could not believe his ears. "But they are not pigs!" he insisted.

You may picture...

Reading Comprehension Strategy:

Organization

Readers use the **organization** of a text to understand what the text is about. Organization is the way an author chooses to share information.

To know a text's **organization**, pay attention to the words the author uses.

This text has a question-and-answer organization.

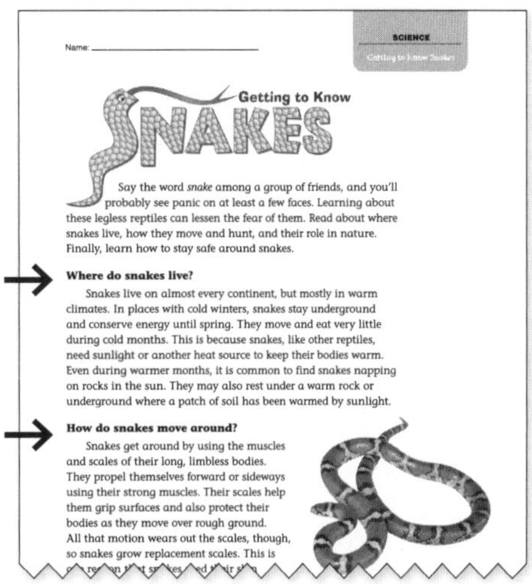

Name: ______________________

SCIENCE

Getting to Know SNAKES

Say the word *snake* among a group of friends, and you'll probably see panic on at least a few faces. Learning about these legless reptiles can lessen the fear of them. Read about where snakes live, how they move and hunt, and their role in nature. Finally, learn how to stay safe around snakes.

Where do snakes live?

Snakes live on almost every continent, but mostly in warm climates. In places with cold winters, snakes stay underground and conserve energy until spring. They move and eat very little during cold months. This is because snakes, like other reptiles, need sunlight or another heat source to keep their bodies warm. Even during warmer months, it is common to find snakes napping on rocks in the sun. They may also rest under a warm rock or underground where a patch of soil has been warmed by sunlight.

How do snakes move around?

Snakes get around by using the muscles and scales of their long, limbless bodies. They propel themselves forward or sideways using their strong muscles. Their scales help them grip surfaces and also protect their bodies as they move over rough ground. All that motion wears out the scales, though, so snakes grow replacement scales. This is

Organization of Text	Key Words and Phrases to Look for
Cause and Effect	leads to, result, cause, effect, impact, outcome
Sequence	first, second, third, fourth, etc..., next, then, after, before, last, finally
Compare and Contrast	like, alike, in contrast, similarly, different, unlike, on the other hand
Main Idea and Details	for example, also, one reason is, for instance, specifically
Question and Answer	who, what, where, when, why, how

Determine Important Information

Readers **determine important information** in a text. Determining important information is figuring out the main topic and staying focused on details related to that topic.

To **determine important information**, have a purpose for reading and look for information related to that purpose.

Identify a purpose for reading.

Do you have an activity to complete that is related to the text? Or do you need to get information from the text for any specific reason?

Begin by scanning a text for words or features that stand out.

What stands out when you look at the page? Are any words or phrases repeated? Are there any bold words or headings? These are clues that point to important ideas in the text.

Look for information related to your purpose for reading.

Find information that is related to the text that will help you complete the activity or help you get the information you need.

Identify the main topic of the text.

Look at headings, topic sentences, captions, and bold text.

Find details that relate to the main topic.

Look for key words that relate to the main topic.

Identify details that are not as important for understanding the main topic.

Avoid being distracted by unimportant details in the text.

Visual Aid

Reading Comprehension Strategy:

Ask Questions

Readers **ask questions** when they read a text. Asking questions before, during, and after helps in understanding a text.

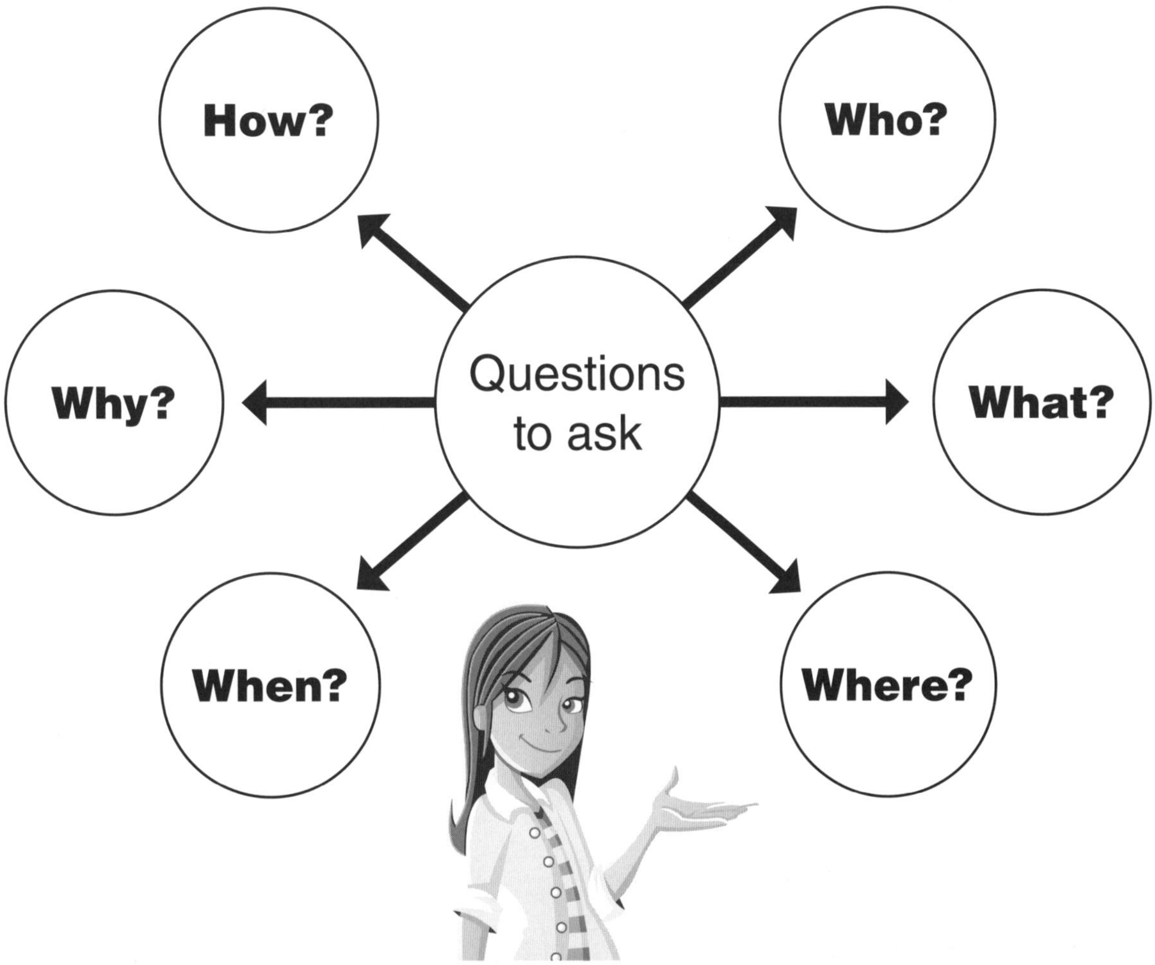

Then look for answers to the questions in the text.

Ask questions before reading to help set a purpose for reading.

- Whom does the story focus on?
- What is the story's genre?

Ask questions during reading to get more involved in the story.

- Where does the story take place?
- Why does the main character feel happy?

Ask questions after reading to check understanding.

- When did she realize that she had a problem?
- How did she solve the problem?

Reading Comprehension Strategy:

Monitor Comprehension

Readers **monitor comprehension** when they read a text. Readers who monitor comprehension keep track of how well they understand the text.

To **monitor comprehension**, think about the text while reading it.

As Dad parked the car, I noticed people holding signs and shouting in the grocery store parking lot. It was a protest, and one of the signs had the words: "Unfair Pay, Unfair Treatment of Farm Workers" written on it. Another sign read, "Boycott California Grapes in 1966."

Use visualization. Create mental pictures and imagine what is happening in the text.

"The fields have no protection from the sun, so the farm workers get very hot while working," Dad said. "They're also expected to work long hours with no break. Usually, there's no bathroom facility. And it's exhausting, back-breaking work."

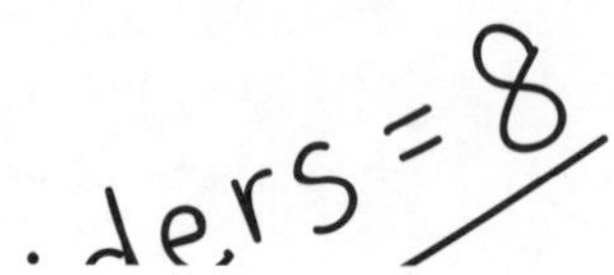

Make notes about the text. Use the margin of the text, a sheet of paper, or a device to write details that you think are important.

Break the text into chunks. Pause after every paragraph and think about what the paragraph is saying.

TIP: Compare reading a text to eating an apple. We don't eat a whole apple at once. We take one bite at a time and chew it before taking another bite. Monitoring comprehension is like taking one bite at a time.

Student Record Sheet

Student: ______________________

Number of Questions Answered Correctly

	Day 1	Day 2	Day 3	Day 4	Day 5	Notes:
Week 1						
Week 2						
Week 3						
Week 4						
Week 5						
Week 6						
Week 7						
Week 8						
Week 9						
Week 10						
Week 11						
Week 12						
Week 13						
Week 14						
Week 15						
Week 16						
Week 17						
Week 18						
Week 19						
Week 20						
Week 21						
Week 22						
Week 23						
Week 24						
Week 25						
Week 26						
Week 27						
Week 28						
Week 29						
Week 30						

WEEK 1

Monitor Comprehension

When students monitor their comprehension, they keep track of how well they understand the material and identify when their understanding breaks down. Related activities include asking questions, taking notes, and paraphrasing what has been read.

DAY 1

Reproduce the *Monitor Comprehension* visual aid and distribute it to students. Explain that ancient Egyptians lived in 2500 BCE. Then have students read the passage independently, and then introduce the *Monitor Comprehension* strategy. Explain: **Good readers monitor their comprehension by paying attention to how well they understand what they are reading.** Model the strategy: **As I was reading, I realized I didn't understand exactly who Edwin Smith was. I reread that part of the passage slowly and figured out he was a man who bought antiques.** Direct students to complete the strategy practice activity, and then have them share their responses. Then direct students to complete the skill practice activity. Review the answers together.

DAY 2

Remind students of the *Monitor Comprehension* strategy, and point out the instructions at the top of the page. Ask: **How would pausing after each paragraph help you monitor comprehension?** (It gives you a chance to think about the paragraph to make sure you understand it.) When students have finished reading the passage, model the strategy: **I didn't understand what the author meant when she said Isadore spent his time streaming world music. I reread and figured out that it meant Isadore used the Internet to listen to music on his computer.** After students complete the strategy practice activity, have them share their responses. Then direct students to complete the skill practice activity. Review the answers together.

DAY 3

Remind students of the *Monitor Comprehension* strategy. Then build background by helping students pronounce words they may find difficult and explaining more about the Mayan culture and civilization, if necessary. When students have finished reading, direct them to complete the strategy practice activity. Ask volunteers to share their responses, and discuss their answers as a group. Then direct students to complete the skill practice activity. Review the answers together.

DAY 4

Remind students of the *Monitor Comprehension* strategy, and build background by pointing out on a map where the different places mentioned in the passage are located. When students have finished reading, explain: **One good way to monitor our comprehension is to recall the main idea of each paragraph.** Assign students or small groups different paragraphs to focus on as they complete the strategy practice activity. Ask volunteers to share their responses and discuss how recalling the main idea helped them understand the paragraph better. For the skill practice activity, direct students to answer the items independently. Review the answers as a group.

DAY 5

Remind students of the *Monitor Comprehension* strategy. Then point out the timeline on the page and say: **Sometimes a passage will have a visual element, such as a timeline, that accompanies it. It's important that we understand both the main passage and the timeline.** When students have finished reading, direct them to complete the strategy and skill practice activities. Review the answers together.

Name: ______________________________

READ THE PASSAGE Read slowly. Reread any section you do not understand.

Medical Practices in Ancient Egypt

Learning About the Human Body

Today's medical examiners study the body parts of deceased people to learn about things that can be harmful and to help prevent illnesses. Ancient Egyptians also performed examinations on bodies to help understand causes of illness. Examinations helped ancient Egyptians learn about the human body. By comparing the hearts of people who were different ages, for example, Egyptians could determine what a young, healthy heart was supposed to look like.

Keeping a Written Record

The Egyptians not only studied the human body, but they also kept detailed records of what they discovered. They wrote and drew their observations on papyrus, a form of paper. The papyrus records became the medical textbooks of that time. Their observations allowed Egyptian doctors to share their knowledge, including how to treat various diseases.

Edwin Smith Papyrus

In 1862, an American named Edwin Smith purchased a medical papyrus in Luxor, Egypt. Smith was not a medical expert, but he knew a lot about old documents. He knew that what he had found was valuable. The papyrus turned out to be an ancient textbook on surgery. The papyrus was probably written around 1600 BC, but it was based on information from a thousand years before that. The papyrus presents the information as case studies, including an analysis of whether patients survived.

STRATEGY PRACTICE How did examinations help ancient Egyptians learn about the human body?

____

____

SKILL PRACTICE Read the item. Write your response.

1. What is this text mostly about?

____

____

2. What is the purpose of the headings?

____

____

3. What are doctors in 3020 most apt to learn from a medical textbook published in 2020?

____

____

Name: ______________________________

READ THE PASSAGE Think about how the brothers behave.

Ishmael and Isadore

Brothers Ishmael and Isadore were complete opposites. People who knew them both could hardly believe they were from the same planet, let alone the same family. The boys were not unkind toward one another, but their personalities were so different that it was difficult for them to reach a decision they both liked. Their mother frequently played the referee in their disagreements.

Ishmael, the older brother, was tall and athletic, and he loved sports. He played baseball, football, and basketball. Isadore, the younger brother, hated sports. He was quieter and less active than his brother. He preferred spending his time on the computer, making short videos and writing blog entries.

The brothers' taste in music was completely different, too. Ishmael loved classic rock. He listened to bands like the Beatles, the Who, and the Rolling Stones. Isadore didn't care much for those bands. He preferred spending his time streaming world music, especially music from Central Africa. Luckily for their parents, both boys enjoyed listening to music through headphones.

One other thing the brothers did agree on was that they wanted a pet. Mom had resisted getting one, but after both brothers had pleaded and begged, she finally agreed.

"We can get a pet, as long as you two take care of it," she said. "That means you do the feeding, you do the training, and if it needs to be walked, you do the walking."

"No problem, Mom," Ishmael and Isadore said together.

"Good, we all agree," Mom said. "Now, what kind of pet are we going to get?"

STRATEGY PRACTICE Was there any part of the passage that you didn't understand right away? How did you figure it out?

____

____

SKILL PRACTICE Read the item. Write your response.

1. What is the main idea of this text?

____

____

2. Predict what will happen next. Why do you think so?

____

3. If the brothers choose a dog, who is most apt to take the dog running? Explain.

____

____

Name: ______________________________

READ THE PASSAGE Underline or make notes about words you do not understand.

Mayan Calendars

The Maya were an influential people living in what is now Guatemala, Belize, Honduras, El Salvador, and parts of southern Mexico. The ancient Maya developed sophisticated systems of agriculture, architecture, science, mathematics, and writing. One of the most important Mayan developments was the creation of calendars.

The ancient Maya had three calendars. Two of them were the Tzolkin (ZOL-keen) calendar, which was tied to religious beliefs, and the Haab (hayb) calendar, which was based on the length of a year.

Understanding astronomy helped the Maya accurately measure days, months, and years. A year had 365 days by Mayan calculations, as it does in our own calendar. The Mayan year, though, was made up of 18 months, and each month had 20 days. An extra 5 days were added to complete the calendar year. These days rounded out the calendar nicely, but the Maya thought they were unlucky.

One of the most unusual Mayan calendars was actually a pyramid. Around AD 1050, the Maya built the Pyramid of Kukulkan (KO-KUL-kan) at Chichén Itzá (CHEE-chen EET-sah). The pyramid had a stairway on each of its four sides. Each stairway had 91 steps. Counting the platform at the top, there were 365 steps, the same number of days in the calendar year.

STRATEGY PRACTICE List one or two words you found confusing and describe how you figured out their meanings.

____

SKILL PRACTICE Read the item. Write your response.

1. What is the second paragraph mostly about?

____

____

2. Why did the author include a map?

____

____

3. Cite the part of the sentence that supports the idea that the Pyramid of Kukulkan was a calendar.

____

____

Name: ____________________

READ THE PASSAGE Read slowly and think about the main idea of each section.

Ancient and Modern Chinese Characters

In the Beginning

When people write in English, they use letters of the alphabet. People who write in Chinese, however, use characters that stand for words or ideas. Historians believe Chinese writing began as early as 1500 BC. The earliest forms were called "oracle bones." These were animal bones marked with pictures and symbols. In addition to writing on bones, the Chinese also made marks on turtle shells. By 1400 BC, the Chinese writing system had become more complex. It had more than 2,500 characters. Around 200 BC, Chinese characters became standardized. This means that everyone used the same characters.

Then and Now

Many modern Chinese characters are similar to those from 2,000 years ago. For example, the character that means *man* in the Lishu system from 200 BC is similar to the character that means *man* from the Jiantizi, or modern simplified system, of the twentieth century.

A Simpler System

People have made efforts to change Chinese characters over the centuries. The most important changes happened in the twentieth century. The Chinese government simplified many characters so that more people could learn to read. Both this simpler system and traditional characters are now used in different areas. Even with these changes, Chinese writing from 2,200 years ago is still understood today.

STRATEGY PRACTICE Did you understand the main points the writer makes? Why or why not?

____

SKILL PRACTICE Read the item. Write your response.

1. How do the headings in this text help the reader?

____

____

2. What is the main idea of the text?

____

____

3. Which fact from the text supports the idea that ancient and modern Chinese characters are similar?

____

____

Name: ______________________________

READ THE PASSAGE Read slowly and pause after each paragraph.

Colossus of Rhodes

The Colossus of Rhodes, a giant bronze statue, was one of the Seven Wonders of the Ancient World. Other ancient civilizations also built large statues, but the Colossus of Rhodes was one of the tallest. At more than 105 feet (32 meters) tall, it was twice as big as most of the other colossi (kuh-LOSS-eye), or giant statues, of ancient times. The Statue of Liberty, its modern counterpart, is only slightly taller.

The Colossus of Rhodes was designed and built by the sculptor Chares (CHAR-eez) of Lindos. It showed the sun god Helios. The people of the Greek island of Rhodes had it built to celebrate the defeat of Demetrius I in 305 BC. Chares and the artists in his workshop began building the statue in 292 BC. The Colossus was completed twelve years later. It welcomed friends and warned foes as they approached the island's harbor.

Unfortunately, the statue stood for only 56 years. In 224 BC, a powerful earthquake hit Rhodes. The quake damaged the Colossus, and it fell to the ground in giant pieces. The statue's parts lay on the ground for hundreds of years, and travelers came from all over to see these impressive ruins.

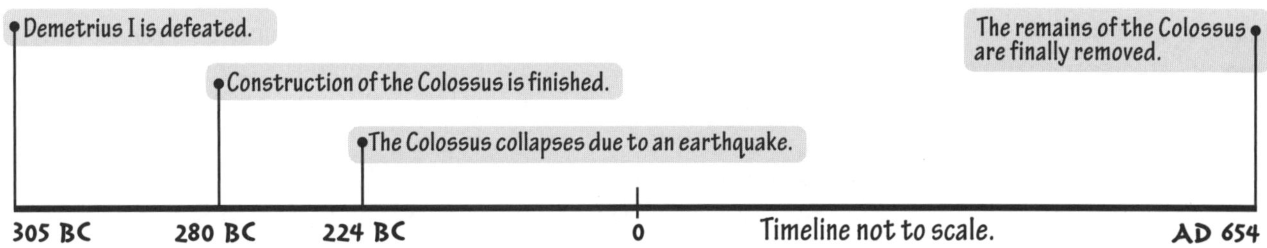

STRATEGY PRACTICE List two important facts about the Colossus of Rhodes.

____

____

SKILL PRACTICE Read the item. Write your response.

1. In what year was the Colossus of Rhodes completed? How do you know?

____

____

2. Why was the Colossus of Rhodes one of the Seven Wonders of the Ancient World?

____

____

3. What information does the timeline give you that the text does not?

____

WEEK 2

Make Connections

This strategy helps students put what they are reading into context by helping them see the connections between the text and themselves, the world around them, and other things they have read or seen.

DAY 1

Reproduce the *Make Connections* visual aid and distribute it to students. Then introduce the *Make Connections* strategy to students and explain: **When good readers read, they often will be reminded of something they have seen, done, or read before. This helps them better understand the situation, the details, or the feelings involved in what they are reading. But it is important to stay focused on the text and not be distracted by the connections you make.** Have students read the instructions at the top of the page and the passage. When students have finished reading, model a connection you made with the text (e.g., Say: "Like the narrator, I was nervous the first time I rode a horse."). Direct students to complete the strategy and skill practice activities. Review the answers together.

DAY 2

Remind students of the *Make Connections* strategy and ask them if they have ever done something that was disgusting but important. (cleaning the bathroom, taking out the trash, etc.) Say: **You can use that experience to make a connection with this passage.** Have students read the passage. When students have finished, direct them to complete the strategy practice activity. Ask volunteers to share their responses, and have students discuss how they answered the question based on their own experiences. Then direct students to complete the skill practice activity. Review the answers together.

DAY 3

Tell students that making a connection is often good practice when reading about events or things from the past. Point out the instructions and say: **Even if the time and place of what we are reading is unfamiliar, we can often understand more about a topic by connecting it to what we know to be true today.** Have students read the passage. Then direct students to complete the strategy practice activity. Invite volunteers to share their responses, and point out the connections they found between natural disasters in the past and today. Finally, direct students to complete the skill practice activity. Review the answers together.

DAY 4

Remind students of the *Make Connections* strategy, and then point out the instructions and the title. Say: **As good readers, we connect what we are reading to other things that we have read or seen before.** Then elicit from students common traits of folk tales. (talking animals; a moral; set in ancient times; etc.) Have students read the passage. When students have finished the strategy practice activity, have volunteers share their responses. Discuss responses that include other folk tales or myths. Then direct students to complete the skill practice activity. Review the answers together.

DAY 5

Remind students of the *Make Connections* strategy. Tell students they are going to read about a group of boys who changed the way newspapers were sold. Then have students read the passage. When students have finished, direct them to find two details from the passage that describe a very different way of life from today. Ask students how making a connection to the life of a newsboy could help a reader better understand the passage. (e.g., Being treated unfairly by others helps a reader understand what it was like for the newsboys to be cheated by the newspapers.) Direct students to complete the strategy and skill practice activities. Review the answers together.

READ THE MEMOIR Think about how the writer probably feels.

Up to the Mountaintop

I like challenges, but this one was almost too difficult. I had begged Mom to take me on a completely new adventure for my sixteenth birthday. Now, here we were, just Mom and me with our guide, Milo, standing on the shore of Lake Arenal in Costa Rica. Towering above the lake was Volcán Arenal, one of the active volcanoes in the region. I watched as the volcano spit out lava and coughed up big boulders. Luckily, we were headed in the other direction.

Milo greeted us in Spanish and helped us mount our horses. Getting on my horse was difficult, but controlling it was a little easier. We started on our tour. The guidebook said we'd cross three rivers. As we splashed through a stream, I asked, "Was that the first river?"

"I don't think so, Katie," Mom said wryly.

Soon enough, we came to the first river. There was no mistaking it. I felt sick to my stomach when I saw that the far shore was half a football field away! The 4-foot-deep (1.2 m) river flowed over boulders. So much for dry shoes—or jeans.

After two more rivers, the trail got even steeper and muddier. With each step of the horses' hooves, there were loud squishing and sucking sounds. The rainforest was magnificent and absolutely beautiful. But I wondered whether my horse could keep its balance in knee-high mud. What did I know about horses? I imagined my mare stumbling on rocks hidden beneath the sludge—and us crashing over a cliff and being swept away by lava.

Three terrifying hours later, we came to a corral. Were we stopping? To one side was a gorgeous view of the lake and volcano, and to the other, a brightly painted restaurant. "Okay," I laughed nervously. "That was terrifying, but I'm so glad we did it!"

STRATEGY PRACTICE Describe a personal experience that is similar to Katie's experience.

____

____

SKILL PRACTICE Read the item. Write your response.

1. Describe the setting of this memoir.

____

____

2. Draw an inference about Katie's experience riding horses.

____

3. Name two adjectives that describe Katie. Explain your choices.

____

Name: ____________________

READ THE PASSAGE Think about what Jeff Biggs does and how he feels about his job.

Dirty Job? Oh Yeah!

"You couldn't pay me to do that job!" Have you ever said that? Some occupations are so gross that most people would never be willing to do them.

Jeff Biggs has a job like that, but he likes it. He's the kind of guy who, as a kid, loved to slosh around in mud after a rainstorm; the kind of kid who loved squeezing oatmeal through his fingers.

Biggs's dirty job is being a sewer inspector. "Believe me," says Biggs, "gross doesn't come close to describing it. I creep, sometimes swim, through sewage all day." City sewers carry household wastewater and storm-drain runoff to water treatment plants. In addition to the unpleasant smells, sewer tunnels are home to creatures such as cockroaches and rats. And these creatures aren't shy.

What is it like to do a really disgusting job day after day? "Someone has to do it," says Biggs. "I seriously can't imagine sitting in an office all day, and I earn a good salary. At the end of my workday, I've accomplished something, and I've helped to keep our city's water clean and drinkable."

And after work? "I don't walk into the house right away," explains Biggs. "We installed the washing machine in the garage and put a shower stall in there, too. I toss my clothes into the washer, take a shower, and dress in clean clothes. Then I greet my family. Of course, sometimes, the clothes go into the trash, not the washer."

STRATEGY PRACTICE What would happen if no one performed jobs like the one Jeff Biggs has?

____

____

SKILL PRACTICE Read the item. Write your response.

1. Name two adjectives that describe Jeff Biggs's working environment. Explain your choices.

____

____

2. What did the author mean by the statement "And these creatures aren't shy"?

____

____

3. Describe Jeff Biggs's attitude toward his occupation.

____

____

Name: ______________________________

READ THE LETTER Think about how people today and from long ago have dealt with natural disasters.

A Letter from Antioch

Antioch, Syria
Saturday, May 23, AD 526

Dear Father,

I write to tell you the shocking news that has happened since your departure last month. On Wednesday, Antioch suffered a terrible earthquake. Mother and I are safe, and our house is damaged but still standing. However, over 220,000 people in the city have died, and officials expect even higher numbers as the survivors search the rubble for their loved ones. Hundreds are fleeing the city, carrying their few undamaged belongings on their backs.

Many of the familiar churches, markets, theaters, and monuments have been destroyed. Some buildings that withstood the initial quake collapsed during aftershocks. One of the saddest losses was the Great Church. Although it survived the aftershocks, it caught fire yesterday and burned.

Looters are going into collapsed buildings and stealing valuables. Thieves have attacked some people who are fleeing the city. But all hope is not lost. Just this morning, brave people rescued a young woman and her child from the ruins of a house. As I write, volunteers are retrieving many of our pieces of fine mosaic art. They are loading them into boats to transport them to other locations. And messengers arrived from Emperor Justin this morning. He has pledged to help us rebuild.

I wish you a safe journey and urge caution on your return.

Your son,
Simeon

STRATEGY PRACTICE **Do you think people in the past reacted any differently to disasters from the way people do today? Explain.**

____

____

SKILL PRACTICE **Read the item. Write your response.**

1. **How does Simeon feel about Antioch?**

____

____

2. **Why are people fleeing the city?**

____

3. **What two opposing realities are revealed in the third paragraph?**

____

____

Name: ______________________________

READ THE FOLK TALE Look for phrases or ideas that remind you of other folk tales.

The Elephant and the Hummingbird

Long, long ago—in the days when people could talk to animals and learn their stories—an elephant walked slowly beside the Yellow River. This was before animals were tamed, even before the first Chinese emperors ruled. That's how long ago it was.

The elephant was enjoying a peaceful stroll. Thick grasses and beautiful lotus flowers bloomed, and the water in the Yellow River made a pleasant swishing sound as it flowed past the elephant.

Noticing what appeared to be a hummingbird, the elephant stopped. Although they don't exist in China today, the elephant had seen hummingbirds before. He'd watched them hover above lotus flowers, their wings beating so quickly that they appeared only as a blur. The elephant sometimes wished he could move as quickly as a hummingbird. This one, however, was lying upside down, her wings motionless and her legs pointing toward the sky. Occasionally, the little bird would sigh heavily or grunt, as if working extra hard.

"What are you doing?" asked the elephant. He slowly walked around the hummingbird, trying to understand the odd behavior. "You look ridiculous, you know."

"I am holding up the sky," replied the hummingbird calmly. "I overheard that it might fall today."

The elephant raised his trunk and made a sound that today might pass as a deep laugh. "You're holding up the sky? Why, just look at it. The sky is bigger than I am, and I doubt you could hold me up. Even if the sky were going to fall, your tiny legs could not possibly do the job."

"Ah," said the hummingbird, "but these are the only legs I have. I might not be able to do it by myself, but I am doing what I can."

STRATEGY PRACTICE Describe a story, movie, or experience that this folk tale reminds you of.

____

____

SKILL PRACTICE Read the item. Write your response.

1. When and where does this folk tale take place?

____

____

2. What does the elephant think of the hummingbird's explanation? How do you know?

____

____

3. What is the lesson, or moral, of the text?

____

____

Name: ____________________

READ THE PASSAGE Look for descriptions of things or practices that have changed since 1899.

Newsies Strike New York

Today, people can buy a newspaper online, from a machine, or at a newsstand. But back in the 1800s, newsboys, or "newsies," were the principal sellers of newspapers. Newsies sold their newspapers, or "papes," on New York's streets. Newsies bought their newspapers from the companies that printed them. The newsboys then made their money by selling the newspapers to customers.

For two weeks in 1899, however, the newsies went on strike, refusing to sell papers. Boys from 5 to 15 years old united to make two newspaper companies reduce the price that they charged newsies for the newspapers. Striking newsboys held rallies, gave speeches, and chose leaders. One rally drew more than 7,000 striking newsies. Newsboys who continued to sell papers were harassed by the strikers. Some strikers threw the newspapers away, and others threatened to hurt the newsboys who wouldn't stop selling newspapers.

What started the strike? During the Spanish-American War, people were eager to read the news, so the *Journal* and *Evening World* raised the price that they charged for their newspapers. Newsies had to pay ten cents more for the papers. A dime made a difference to the kids who earned less than a dollar each day. Most newsies lived on the streets. Others used their earnings to help their struggling families. When the war ended, newsies expected newspaper companies to reduce their prices, but that did not happen.

Although the cost of papers to newsies never dropped, the strike was considered a success. The two offending newspaper companies agreed to buy back all unsold papers, and eventually this strike helped bring about child labor laws in the United States.

STRATEGY PRACTICE What does the newsies' strike of 1899 remind you of today?

____

____

SKILL PRACTICE Read the item. Write your response.

1. What lesson can you learn from the newsies' strike?

____

____

2. How do you think the strike helped to bring about labor laws?

____

____

3. Based on the information in the passage, name three common characteristics among newsboys.

____

____

WEEK 3

Visualization

Visualization allows readers to form mental images of what they are reading about. By visualizing, good readers can better remember the main ideas or events in a passage. Good readers use sensory words from the text to help them visualize and adjust their mental images as they read.

DAY 1

Reproduce the *Visualization* visual aid and distribute it to students. Then introduce the *Visualization* strategy to students. Explain: **When good readers read, they often make mental pictures of what they are reading about. They turn what they are reading into a kind of "movie" that plays in their mind. But this doesn't mean they daydream. They pay attention to important and descriptive words.** Tell students to close their eyes and visualize as you read the first four sentences of the first paragraph. Read the sentences slowly to give students time to understand and visualize the important descriptions (*evergreen forests; covered in clouds; located on mountains; cool temperatures that create clouds covering the trees*). Direct students to read the passage and complete the strategy and skill practice activities. Review the answers together.

DAY 2

Remind students of the *Visualization* strategy. Say: **It's important to look for words we can easily picture.** Read the first sentence from the passage aloud. Ask: **Which is easier to picture: *Sunday, airwaves,* or *kids?*** (kids) **That's because a kid is something we can see. When you visualize, look for words that represent something physical or concrete.** Have students read the instructions at the top of the page and the passage. When students have finished reading, use a world map or globe to help them find all of the nations mentioned in the passage. Then direct students to complete the strategy and skill practice activities. Review the answers together.

DAY 3

Remind students of the *Visualization* strategy. Say: **When you visualize as you read, it is important to adjust your mental image when you get new information. Imagine that you are reading a story about a black kitten. You might picture a small kitten. If you then read the kitten was the size of a firetruck, you'd need to change your mental image to match the details in the story.** Direct students to read the passage and complete the strategy and skill practice activities. Review the answers together.

DAY 4

Remind students of the *Visualization* strategy. Say: **Good readers pay attention to the words in a passage. Specific action words—or verbs—and clear describing words—or adjectives—help us make mental images as we read. Which is a better verb, *go* or *shuffle?*** (*shuffle*) **Which is a clearer adjective to describe french fries, *good* or *salty?*** (*salty*) Have students read the instructions at the top of the page and then read the passage. When students have finished reading, direct them to complete the strategy and skill practice activities. Review the answers together.

DAY 5

Remind students of the *Visualization* strategy. Say: **It may be easy for you to make a mental image of what you are reading, but as a good reader, you must be sure to visualize only the most important ideas or actions in a passage or story. It's impossible to make a mental image of everything you read.** Point out the first sentence in the last paragraph. Ask: **Do you think it's important to visualize scientists sitting around having a debate?** (no) Say: **You should visualize the parts of the passage that support what the passage is mostly about.** Then have students read the instructions at the top of the page and the passage. When students have finished reading, pair them for the strategy practice activity or complete it as a group. Prompt students to defend their choices of what they visualized from the passage. Then direct students to complete the skill practice activity. Review the answers together.

Name: ____________________

READ THE PASSAGE Read slowly and pay attention to details that help you make a mental picture.

Forests of Clouds and Mist

You've probably heard of rainforests, but do you know what a cloud forest is? Cloud forests are evergreen forests that are often covered in clouds or mist and are located on mountains. Cool temperatures on mountain slopes create clouds that cover the trees. There are cloud forests on most continents. Central and South America have them, as do Asia and Africa. You can also find cloud forests in Hawaii and on Caribbean islands.

Cloud forests have different names, depending on where they are found. Cloud forests are also known as fog forests or mossy forests. In Peru and Bolivia, cloud forests are part of a larger ecosystem called *yungas,* which means "warm lands."

Many scientists consider cloud forests to be a special type of rainforest. Cloud forests are not as warm as tropical rainforests because they are found at higher elevations that have colder air. But cloud forests and tropical rainforests both have many different plants and animals living within their ecosystems.

Like tropical rainforests, cloud forest trees drip with moisture, but it does not often rain in a cloud forest. Instead, the fog collects as dew on leaves, vines, and branches. This dew provides the water that the plants need. Green moss, ferns, and exotic, colorful orchid flowers hang down from the canopy. Other plants and bushes crowd between the trees, and hundreds of insects crawl and fly amid the vegetation. Cloud forests are as diverse and interesting as rainforests or temperate forests.

Cloud forests have animals that aren't found anywhere else, such as mountain gorillas and a strange woolly mammal called the mountain tapir. The colorful quetzal bird is also found there, and golden toads hop among the bushes. Recently, scientists discovered a new cloud forest animal, a black and brown rodent that looks like a cross between a squirrel and a rat. Cloud forests probably contain hundreds of other rare and fascinating plants and animals that people have never seen before.

STRATEGY PRACTICE Underline words or phrases in the passage that you were able to visualize.

SKILL PRACTICE Read the item. Write your response.

1. Why was it essential to visualize as you read this text?

____

____

2. How do cloud forests differ from tropical rainforests?

____

____

3. Picture yourself walking in a cloud forest. Briefly describe the experience.

____

____

READ THE PASSAGE Look for words that help you form a mental picture.

Kids Take to the Airwaves

On the first Sunday in March each year, kids get to take over the world's airwaves. The United Nations Children's Fund (UNICEF) has designated that day as the International Children's Day of Broadcasting, or ICDB. Television and radio stations around the world invite young people to be part of their programming. Thousands of broadcasters and kids participate, and the programs focus on children's interests and issues. Kids are also involved in the broadcast process, learning how radio and television programs are made. ICDB gives children a voice that can be heard around the world.

On ICDB in 2009, young people all over the globe reported on issues that affected them. Nearly 100 children from India recorded stories about a flood in their area. Children in China drew pictures with messages for their parents. In Senegal, young people spoke out against violence by giving reports, conducting interviews, writing poems, and singing songs. German children talked with young people in Serbia and shared drawings and photographs. Australian kids voiced their opinions to children in Cambodia, Fiji, and Tonga. Kids produced videos on a variety of different topics, from air pollution to loneliness. Across the world, young people expressed their feelings and sent messages about what mattered most to them.

After ICDB is over, UNICEF holds a contest for the best radio or television program. People who make the programs that air during ICDB can submit their programs. The winners attend a special celebration. The 2009 radio winner was a station in Brazil that broadcasted a show for 24 hours about children from poor communities. The show used interviews, diaries, and music to promote peace. The winner for the television program was a station in Kenya. The show, which was hosted by two Kenyan youths, talked about the challenges that Kenyan children face and highlighted positive stories about young people in their communities.

STRATEGY PRACTICE Write three nouns (people, places, or things) that were easy for you to picture.

____

SKILL PRACTICE Read the item. Write your response.

1. What is the purpose of International Children's Day of Broadcasting?

____

____

2. Describe the mental image that was easiest for you to form as you read the second paragraph.

____

____

3. What is the first paragraph mainly about?

____

____

Name: ___________________________

READ THE PASSAGE As you read, adjust your mental image when you come across new details.

Not Quite the Same

When most people want to see what they look like, they look in a mirror. I don't need a mirror to see myself, though. I can just look at my identical twin sister, Sarita.

Sarita and I have always worn our hair the same way—long and straight, with bangs. We have the same dark eyes and big smile, and we both have one crooked tooth on the right. We both love the color green, hate eating fish, and think mayonnaise is disgusting. We play the violin, and every year we compete with each other for the position of first violin in the school orchestra.

In some ways, however, we're totally different. Sarita always wears funky hats, which I think is really weird. She thinks it's strange that I like jazz music. Some people say that our biggest difference is that Sarita is in a wheelchair. She was in a car accident when she was very young, and her spine was badly injured. To me, however, the real difference between us is that Sarita has courage and determination. She has never let being in a wheelchair slow her down, and she's almost never angry or unhappy about what happened to her. So when I look in the mirror, I see myself—Celia—but I also see Sarita, a better version of me. She's the me I *try* to be.

STRATEGY PRACTICE Sketch how you visualized the two girls.

SKILL PRACTICE Read the item. Write your response.

1. Name three ways in which the girls are similar.

____

____

2. Name three ways in which the girls are different.

____

____

3. Why does Celia admire Sarita?

____

____

Name: ______________________________

WEEK 3 DAY 4

Visualization

READ THE PASSAGE Look for strong verbs and clear nouns and adjectives.

A Plane in the Hudson River

Some airplanes are made specifically to land on water, but US Airways Flight 1549 was not one of those planes. The plane took off from LaGuardia Airport on January 15, 2009, with 155 people on board. Just three minutes later, the pilot, Captain Chesley Sullenberger, radioed that the plane was in trouble. It had hit some large geese. The left engine had exploded in fire, smoke, and metal.

Captain Sullenberger quickly realized that the plane could not make it back to the airport. The aircraft was rapidly losing power and would soon be too slow to stay in the air. Sullenberger turned the plane toward the Hudson River, which flows between New York and New Jersey.

"Brace for impact!" Captain Sullenberger announced over the intercom. Many passengers were tense and scared, but the flight crew did their best to keep everyone calm. Most passengers lowered their heads and got ready for a rough crash landing.

After several tension-filled minutes, Captain Sullenberger landed the plane perfectly on the surface of the Hudson River. People watching from ferries that were traveling between New York and New Jersey were shocked at the sight. The plane's passengers climbed onto the wings as the plane began to fill with water and sink. Boats from both sides of the river rushed to aid the stranded passengers. The waters were icy cold, and the smell of gasoline filled the air. As passengers scrambled from the plane to the waiting boats, rescuers handed them blankets, coats, and life jackets to stay warm.

All 155 people were brought to safety, and Captain Sullenberger was celebrated as a hero. It was the first time a major aircraft had ever crash-landed in water with no deaths.

STRATEGY PRACTICE Underline the verbs and draw a box around the adjectives that helped you visualize the scene as you read.

SKILL PRACTICE Read the item. Write your response.

1. What caused the plane's left engine to stop functioning?

____

____

2. How did this emergency water landing differ from all others?

____

____

3. Why is it a good thing that this event happened in a busy city?

____

____

Name: ______________________

READ THE PASSAGE Make a mental image of the events described in the passage.

The World's Biggest Wave

A tsunami is a giant ocean wave. It is usually created by an earthquake on the seafloor and can travel hundreds or even thousands of miles across the ocean. The biggest local tsunami ever to hit land happened on July 9, 1958, when an earthquake shook the undersea fault near Lituya Bay, Alaska. Lituya Bay is part of Alaska's Glacier Bay National Park. The magnitude 8.0 earthquake shook 40 million cubic yards (31 million cubic meters) of dirt, rocks, and ice from a mountain at the head of the bay. The landslide fell 3,000 feet (914 meters) and hit the water with tremendous force, which created the enormous tsunami wave. The wave was more than 1,640 feet (500 meters) high and crashed over five square miles (13 square kilometers) of land, uprooting millions of trees.

There were no towns in the area, so unlike the deadly tsunami of 2004, in which more than 200,000 people in Indonesia and elsewhere were killed, the 1958 tsunami killed only two people. They were on a fishing boat anchored in the bay when the wave swamped them. Another boat, the Badger, was carrying William Swanson and his wife. The boat rode the wave inland before it began to sink. The Swansons were able to leap to a small skiff and were rescued a few hours later. A third boat, the Edrie, with Howard Ulrich and his seven-year-old son aboard, rode the wave over land and then back out to the bay. The Ulriches, amazingly, were unharmed.

For many years, scientists debated about what really caused the tsunami in Lituya Bay. Some scientists claimed the amount of debris that fell into the bay was not enough to cause such a massive wave. They thought that the earthquake itself triggered the wave. However, as our understanding of geology, earthquakes, and tsunamis has improved, most scientists now accept the rockslide as the true cause for the wave. No one disputes, however, that the wave was the largest ever recorded and will likely remain so for years to come.

STRATEGY PRACTICE Describe to a partner the parts of the passage you thought were the most important to visualize in order to understand the main idea of the passage.

SKILL PRACTICE Read the item. Write your response.

1. The average skyscraper is 350 feet (107 m) tall. How does knowing this fact help you envision the wave discussed in the text?

____

2. How did the 1958 and 2004 tsunamis differ?

____

____

3. Was the cause of the 1958 tsunami the typical cause? Explain.

____

____

WEEK 4

Organization

By looking at how a passage or selection is organized, students can better understand the author's intent, as well as predict what information is likely to appear later in the text. Texts are often organized sequentially, around main ideas and details, according to causes and effects, or by comparison and contrast.

DAY 1

Reproduce the *Organization* visual aid and distribute it to students. Then introduce the *Organization* strategy to students and explain: **By looking at the organization of a passage, we can get a better idea of what the author intended to tell us. Many of the same types of passages are organized the same way.** Explain to students that the passage they are about to read is a biography. Ask: **What do we usually see in biographies?** (dates, names, important events in a person's life, etc.) Then say: **I expect to see this passage organized sequentially around important dates in the life of this person.** Have students read the instructions at the top of the page and read the passage. When students have finished reading, direct them to complete the strategy practice activity. Ask volunteers to share their responses. Then direct students to complete the skill practice activity. Review the answers together.

DAY 2

Remind students of the *Organization* strategy, and point out that by knowing the organization of a passage, good readers can pay more attention to important details and don't have to work as hard to understand what the passage is about. Point out the bold heading in the first paragraph. Say: **This heading tells me that this paragraph will likely explain how water has been on our planet for a long time. The passage will probably be organized around main ideas and examples of those ideas.** Have students read the instructions at the top of the page and the passage. When students have finished reading, direct them to complete the strategy and skill practice activities. Invite volunteers to share their responses.

DAY 3

Remind students of the *Organization* strategy, and point out the instructions at the top of the page. Say: **Another way writers organize passages is by cause and effect. This passage tells the causes and effects of a snake problem in Florida. When we read these types of passages, we are looking for what happens and why it happens.** Explain that cause-and-effect signal words (*because, as a result, therefore,* etc.) can help them best understand this kind of text. Have students read the passage. When students have finished, direct them to complete the strategy and skill practice activities. Review the answers together.

DAY 4

Remind students of the *Organization* strategy, and have them recall the common ways a passage can be organized (by main idea, sequence, and cause and effect). Point out the instructions at the top of the page, and ask students to guess which way this passage is organized (sequentially). Say: **Not all passages organized by sequence go from first to last or earliest to latest.** Have students read the passage. When students have finished reading, direct them to complete the strategy practice activity and share their responses. Explain that writers will vary how they organize a passage in order to make it more interesting to the reader. Then direct students to complete the skill practice activity. Review the answers together.

DAY 5

Remind students of the *Organization* strategy and say: **Writers organize their stories in many ways. Some writers begin at the end of a story and then tell you what happened leading up to it. Other writers begin with the main problem a character faces and show how the problem is resolved. By understanding how the story is told, we can make sense of what we are reading.** Have students read the instructions at the top of the page and the passage. When students have finished reading, direct them to complete the strategy and skill practice activities. Review the answers together.

Name: ______________________

READ THE PASSAGE Look for important events in the life of Sarah Edmonds.

Soldier in Disguise

In April 1863, a Civil War soldier known as Franklin Thompson deserted from the Union Army. Thompson was sick with malaria but was afraid to go to an army hospital. What was Thompson so afraid of? His real name was Sarah Edmonds—and "he" was one of hundreds of women who pretended to be men so that they could fight in the Civil War.

Edmonds was born in Canada in 1841 and came to the United States in 1858. She disguised herself as Franklin Thompson and worked as a book salesman. In May 1861, one month after the Civil War began, she enlisted in the Second Michigan Infantry.

For two years, Edmonds served in the army as Private Thompson. The Second Michigan Infantry fought in some important and violent battles, including First Bull Run in July 1861, Antietam in September 1862, and Fredericksburg in December 1862. Edmonds kept her gender a secret by sleeping in her own tent and sneaking off to bathe privately.

Upon leaving the army, Edmonds resumed her real identity. She eventually revealed her service as Thompson in order to get a pension as a Civil War soldier. In 1886, the War Department recognized her as a female soldier who had served faithfully as a private during the war. She received the $12-a-month pension and was cleared of the desertion charge. When she died in 1898, Edmonds was buried with military honors.

STRATEGY PRACTICE How does adding dates to the passage help organize it?

____

____

SKILL PRACTICE Read the item. Write your response.

1. Why did Franklin Thompson desert from the Union Army?

____

____

2. What caused Edmonds to reveal the truth about her identity?

____

____

3. Why did Edmonds receive military honors at her funeral?

____

____

READ THE PASSAGE Think about how the author introduces each paragraph.

Facts About Water

Drink of the Dinos Water is as old as Earth itself. Look at a glass of water. It might contain the same drops that a dinosaur drank millions of years ago. It could have made up the first rainbow you ever saw or a river that your ancestors fished in. It could have snowed on the Alps or been part of a worm or a carrot. It could have carved a canyon or been pumped up from a well. Water constantly recycles itself as rain, vapor, ice, fog, or snow. Over a period of 100 years, a drop of water will spend 98 years as ocean, 20 months as ice, 2 weeks in a river or lake, and less than a week in the air. It will spend the rest of its time in living things.

Liquid for Life Earth is the only planet known to have liquid water on its surface. That is why life can exist here. The human body is about two-thirds water. You might guess that our blood is mostly water, but there is even water in our bones. An elephant is 70% water, and a tomato is 95% water. Water carries oxygen and breaks down food. It also carries waste out of our bodies. Plants use water to make food and move nutrients around. Over half of the world's plants and animals use fresh or ocean water as a home.

Power of Water Water shapes land more than anything else. Waves eat away coastlines. Glaciers cut valleys. Rivers break down mountains and carve canyons. Water's movement also provides power we can use. It flows through turbines, machines with blades. Water spins the blades, making electricity.

STRATEGY PRACTICE How does the author organize information about water?

____

____

SKILL PRACTICE Read the item. Write your response.

1. What would be a better title for this passage?

____

____

2. Why do you think water is sometimes called "liquid gold"?

____

____

3. Water can be liquid, solid, or gas. Which form do you think it is in the least often? Explain your thinking.

____

____

READ THE PASSAGE Look for the causes and effects of the python problem in Florida.

Florida's Python Problem

Sometimes pets are more than we can handle, like when a small puppy grows up to be a huge dog. People can usually find a new home for a big dog, but a giant pet snake is not so easy to give away. As a result, some people in Florida have released their pet pythons into the wilderness of the Florida Everglades. Problem solved? Only for the pet owners.

The snakes that are the biggest problem are Burmese pythons. These snakes are not native to the Everglades. Pet dealers originally brought them to the United States from Southeast Asia. Because Burmese pythons are not native, they disrupt the natural order of the Everglades' ecosystem.

The snakes' size and strength are also a problem. Burmese pythons can grow to be 20 feet (6 m) long. There are reports of terrifying battles between pythons and alligators in the Everglades. Even more worrisome is the impact on creatures that are no match for the monster snakes. For example, biologists have discovered endangered birds, bobcats, and wood rats in pythons' stomachs.

Another effect of python dumping is the spread of these snakes beyond the Everglades. Pythons swim well and can move more than a mile a day on land. In addition, one snake can produce nearly 100 eggs. Their wide range of movement and high rate of birth means that the snakes can quickly overrun a habitat.

As a result of this scary scenario, Florida park rangers, wildlife officials, and others are on "python patrol." They capture and kill Burmese pythons to try to keep the numbers under control. There is also a greater effort to teach people about the responsibilities of keeping a python.

STRATEGY PRACTICE Underline the words in the passage that signal cause and effect.

SKILL PRACTICE Read the item. Write your response.

1. How did Burmese pythons end up in the Florida Everglades?

____

____

2. What problems are pythons causing in Florida?

____

____

3. Why are pythons spreading beyond the Everglades?

____

____

Name: ______________________

READ THE PASSAGE Think about the order in which the events in the passage occurred.

Growing Good Examples at the White House

In 2009, people praised First Lady Michelle Obama for planting a vegetable garden soon after moving into the White House. The hope was that growing vegetables on the White House lawn would encourage Americans to eat more healthfully and motivate other families to grow fresh produce, too. It might seem like a new idea to plant a presidential garden to influence national behavior. However, earlier presidents and first ladies also used the White House grounds to set a good example.

In 1943, during World War II, First Lady Eleanor Roosevelt planted a "victory garden" at the White House. The goal was to get Americans to grow small gardens to feed themselves. That way, more food was available to send to American soldiers fighting overseas. Mrs. Roosevelt was widely admired, and her garden inspired many families to plant more food for themselves.

Twenty-five years earlier, during World War I, President Woodrow Wilson used the White House lawn to send a message to Americans. Wilson brought in a flock of sheep to cut the grass. It was a novel way to show how to use "natural resources" during wartime.

There was a time when a vegetable garden at the White House was simply practical. President John Adams planted the first garden in 1800. Adams didn't need to set an example, since most of the nation were already farmers. He just wanted food for his family and guests to eat!

STRATEGY PRACTICE Why do you think the author chose this way of organizing the passage?

____

____

SKILL PRACTICE Read the item. Write your response.

1. What evidence does the text offer that the former first family's influence on the nation's behavior was *not* a new idea?

____

____

2. What resource was conserved by using sheep to keep the White House lawn trimmed?

____

____

3. What was the purpose of the earliest White House garden?

____

____

Name: ______________________________

READ THE PASSAGE Think about how the author introduces each character and tells the events in the story.

Three Parts for Three Characters

Denzel could hear the sounds of the song "Follow the Yellow Brick Road" as he walked closer to the auditorium. He was relieved that the auditions weren't over. He really wanted to try out for the sixth-grade production of *The Wizard of Oz*. Waiting in the hall were his two best friends, Colin and Felipe. Colin was walking on his hands in a wide circle. Then he did a back flip, a cartwheel, and a backward leap into a handstand. Felipe was doing his favorite herky-jerky robot dance.

Just as Denzel reached the boys, there was a sudden boom outside. "What was that?" Denzel shouted. He had a voice that could be loud and strong one moment and drop to a whisper the next instant.

"It's thunder," Colin laughed. "You should audition for the role of the character who needs courage!"

"Come on!" Felipe urged with a stiff turn and bow to end his dance. "We'll miss our turns!"

The trio hurried inside the auditorium. A girl named Rachel, with hair teased like a lion's mane, was beginning her audition. The boys watched her. She pranced around the stage like a lion, but she spoke very quietly, and it was hard to hear her. When she finished, Felipe auditioned by dancing like a robot. Colin went next, showing his acrobatic skills. Denzel went last.

When the auditions ended, each boy had the perfect part for his talents. Colin was the Scarecrow, who is supposed to flop, slip, and slide all over the stage. Felipe's robot moves were just like the Tin Man in his rusty metal suit. And Denzel's booming roar and soft whisper made him the best Cowardly Lion the play could have.

STRATEGY PRACTICE If the author began the story by telling you what part each boy received, how would it change your reaction to the story?

____

____

SKILL PRACTICE Read the item. Write your response.

1. What is the purpose of these auditions?

____

____

2. How did Rachel probably feel at the end of the story?

____

____

3. How do Colin's words foreshadow the story's ending?

____

____

WEEK 5

Determine Important Information

When readers determine important information, they identify the type of text they are reading and then concentrate on finding the essential ideas, events, or details from that text. For nonfiction, determining the important information often means finding the main idea. For fiction, it means understanding essential plot points, themes, or character actions.

DAY 1

Reproduce the *Determine Important Information* visual aid and distribute it to students. Then introduce the *Determine Important Information* strategy to students. Explain: **Good readers look for information that helps them understand what they are reading or answers a question they have.** Ask: **If you wanted to know which players scored during a football game, what information would you look for in a newspaper story about the game?** (mention of the times that each team scored points) **Information about the coaches or weather would not help you find out what you wanted to know. The important information would be the part of the story that told you who scored touchdowns or kicked field goals.** Direct students to read the instructions at the top of the page, study the web page, and complete the strategy and skill practice activities. Review the answers together.

DAY 2

Remind students of the *Determine Important Information* strategy. Point out the graph and text on the page. Say: **When you see a graph or chart along with text, it's helpful to study the relationship between them. First, look for the information they have in common. Then you can look for the information that one tells you that the other does not. Consider what information is best presented in a graph. This graph shows the number of people who use the Internet. What else can you learn from looking at this graph?** (The number of people who use the Internet is increasing.) Have students read the directions at the top of the page. Then have students read the passage and study the graph. When students have finished, direct them to complete the strategy and skill practice activities. Review the answers together.

DAY 3

Point out the index on the page to students and ask: **Why do some books have an index?** (to help us find information in the book about a specific topic) **Would you expect to find a main idea statement or a character's description in an index?** (no) **When we read different kinds of text, the information that is important is often different. So, sometimes an index will be organized in a special way.** Point out the text to the left of the index. Say: **The text tells us how the index is organized. We should read the text first so that we make the best sense of the index as we study it.** Have students read the instructions at the top of the page. Then direct students to read the text and study the index. When students have finished, direct them to complete the strategy and skill practice activities. Review the answers together.

DAY 4

Remind students of the *Determine Important Information* strategy. Have students look at the newspaper column briefly, and then ask: **What did you notice first?** Allow volunteers to share their answers, and then say: **I noticed the title of the column first. This is important information because it tells me what I am reading. When I look through a newspaper, the headlines and column titles help me recognize what I am looking for.** Have students read the directions at the top of the page and the newspaper column. When students have finished reading, direct them to complete the strategy and skill practice activities. Review the answers together.

DAY 5

Remind students of the strategy. Ask students if they recognize the type of text on the page (a program or playbill). Allow volunteers to share their experiences attending a performance where a playbill might have been handed out. Say: **A playbill tells a lot about the play or show you're watching. It tells you things that you most likely cannot learn from just watching the play.** Have students read the instructions at the top of the page and then study the playbill. Then direct students to complete the strategy and skill practice activities. Review the answers together.

Name: ____________________

READ THE WEB PAGE Look at each section carefully to understand what the web page is about.

Welcome to the SPORT POD

Are you looking for up-to-date scores?

Do you want more information about your favorite players?

Would you like to connect with passionate fans just like you?

You've come to the right place! The SPORT POD is the only sports website you'll ever need.

The **SPORT POD** has more features than any other site out there, including:

- live scores from baseball, football, basketball, soccer, hockey, tennis, lacrosse, cricket, bowling, volleyball, table tennis, and other sports around the world
- pre-game predictions and post-game analysis by experts
- strategy hints and scoring tips that can help you improve your game
- message boards where you can exchange information with players and other fans
- personal home pages that allow you to track your favorite teams and players

You are just ONE CLICK away! Best of all, you can use the SPORT POD completely FREE.*

YES, sign me up right away!

No thanks, not right now.

*New users get free access for the first 90 days of their membership.

STRATEGY PRACTICE Describe what the SPORT POD is and what this web page is mostly about.

____

____

SKILL PRACTICE Read the item. Write your response.

1. What is the purpose of the phrases next to the handprints?

____

____

2. Why is the "yes" button highlighted?

____

____

3. Look at the asterisk at the bottom right corner of the web page. What does it explain?

____

____

Name: ____________________

READ THE PASSAGE Read the passage and study the line graph.

Internet Boom

Today the Internet is widely used in homes, schools, and businesses around the world. However, that hasn't always been the case. The Internet was first developed in the 1960s and 1970s by U.S. government scientists as a way of sharing information. The earliest version of the Internet was called ARPAnet, for Advanced Research Projects Agency network. In 1969, only four computers were connected to the ARPAnet. Just 20 years later, though, as computers became more commonly developed, over 80,000 computers were connected.

Use of the Internet has continued to grow dramatically. Experts estimate that about 1% of the world's population used the Internet in 1996. By 2016, that percentage grew to over 43%.

How do researchers count more than 1 billion users? Programs called web crawlers browse the Internet to monitor how many pages and users are out there. Web crawlers work automatically, collecting data once they are started. These programs are sometimes called "spiders" because they "crawl" around the web.

As the Internet continues to grow, an increasing number of spiders scurry invisibly, collecting and sending information 24 hours a day.

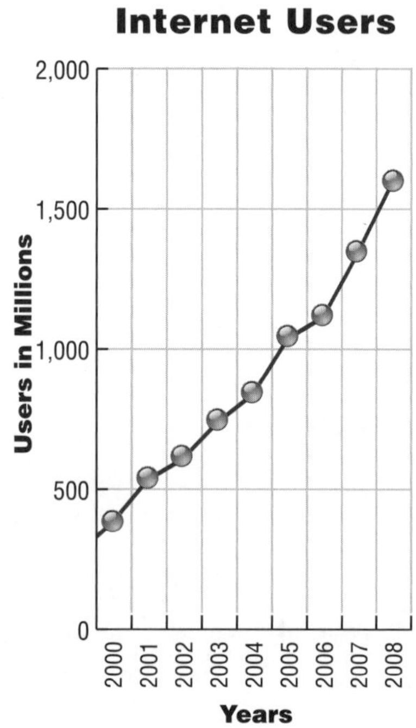

STRATEGY PRACTICE What trend about Internet users does the graph show?

____

SKILL PRACTICE Read the item. Write your response.

1. What is the purpose of the graph?

____

____

2. What information does the text give in the third paragraph that cannot be determined from the graph?

____

____

3. Why does the text mention billions of users in the third paragraph when the graph shows millions?

____

____

Name: ______________________________

READ THE INDEX Read the index and the passage from a book about planets and space.

Index to
The Planets and Beyond

Each entry in this index is followed by the page numbers where the entry is discussed. Page numbers in **boldface** type indicate pages on which entries are defined. Page numbers in *italic* type indicate pages on which illustrations or photographs appear. The abbreviation "**Pr**" indicates a page on which the entry is used in a project.

STRATEGY PRACTICE Describe the type of person who would need this book.

____

____

SKILL PRACTICE Read the item. Write your response.

1. On which page would you find the definition of a comet? How can you tell?

____

____

2. On which page(s) would you look to see an image of an aurora? How do you know?

____

____

3. What is the purpose of the first indented entry beneath "Atmosphere"?

____

____

Name: ______________________________

READ THE COLUMN Read the question carefully before you read the response.

ASK Dr. Science

Dear Dr. Science:
I couldn't sleep at all last night. My sister says it was because I ate a bowl of really spicy chili right before bedtime, but I think that's ridiculous. Can spicy foods at bedtime really affect your sleep?
—Sleepless in Secaucus

Dear Sleepless:
I know where you're coming from, as I often munch on jalapeño peppers before lights out. What does science say?
Researchers in Australia did an experiment to find out the effects of spicy foods on sleep patterns. They gave a group of people tasty late-night meals. Some nights, they got spicy meals with ingredients such as hot sauce and mustard. Other nights, their meals were mild.

It turns out that your sister is on to something. When participants ate spicy foods, their sleep patterns were changed. They took longer to fall asleep and they slept less overall, too.

Researchers aren't sure exactly how spicy foods change sleep patterns, but they have some theories. It could be due to simple stomach upset or indigestion. But they also suspect that body temperature plays a role. Spicy foods include a chemical that can raise the body's temperature. Other studies have connected increased body temperatures with poor sleep. So before you go to bed, put down the jalapeños and hot sauce!
—Dr. Science

STRATEGY PRACTICE If you were writing a research report about sleep studies, what part of this column would you refer to?

____

SKILL PRACTICE Read the item. Write your response.

1. Where might you find this type of text?

____

____

2. Why were the sleep study participants sometimes given mild late-night meals?

____

____

3. Summarize Dr. Science's response to *Sleepless in Secaucus*.

____

____

Name: ______________________________

READ THE PLAYBILL Think about how the information in the playbill is arranged.

STAGEONE PRODUCTIONS
presents

Oklahoma!

Book by	**Music by**	**Lyrics by**
Oscar Hammerstein II	Richard Rodgers	Oscar Hammerstein II

Based on the play *Green Grow the Lilacs* by Lynn Riggs

Starring

Robert Brown	Badra Owens	Celina Rodriguez
Mieka Morioka	Tiffany Pielman	Zack Wallace

Also with

Tabitha Brown	Heather Gold	Maria Jose Peña
Leslie Doherty	Reggie Hamner	James Siliman
Raul Espinosa	Willis Hitchens	Paula Tish

Settings by	**Costumes by**	**Lighting by**	**Sound by**
Lina Owens	Bradley Archer	Kalani Faralan	Jonna McCarthy

Choreography by	**Directed by**
Agnes De Mille	Layne Tish

STRATEGY PRACTICE Why are the actors in the musical listed in two different sections on the playbill?

____

____

SKILL PRACTICE Read the item. Write your response.

1. Name the songwriter(s) for *Oklahoma!* How did you determine this information?

____

____

2. Where would you find the name of a person who has a minor singing or acting role in this musical?

____

____

3. How did Agnes De Mille contribute to this production?

____

WEEK 6

Ask Questions

By asking questions, readers can set a purpose for reading or make sure they understood what they have read. Good readers ask questions to involve themselves with the text and often ask questions before, during, and after reading.

DAY 1

Reproduce the *Ask Questions* visual aid and distribute it to students. Then introduce the *Ask Questions* strategy to students. Explain: **One way good readers stay engaged and check their understanding is to ask questions. You can ask questions before, during, or after reading. When we ask questions before we read, we set a purpose for reading. The questions we ask can guide our reading.** Tell students they will read about a man who some people think created the Bigfoot legend. Prompt students to think of questions about what they might read. Model by saying: **I want to know who this person is. I also want to know a little more about Bigfoot.** On the board, write: "Who created the Bigfoot legend? Where is Bigfoot supposed to have lived?" Tell students they will look for these answers as they read. Then prompt students to think of a question they want to know the answer to and write it in the space provided for the strategy practice activity. Then direct students to read the instructions and passage before completing the strategy and skill activities. Review the answers together. If students have asked a question that cannot be answered by the passage, brainstorm ways of answering the question (looking up the topic; on the Internet; etc.).

DAY 2

Remind students of the *Ask Questions* strategy. Say: **When we ask questions during reading, we are monitoring our comprehension and focus. Asking a question while reading keeps us engaged with the text and sometimes alerts us to information in the text that we don't understand.** Have students read the instructions at the top of the page. Tell students to think of a question as they read the first paragraph. Direct students to write their question in the space provided for the strategy practice activity before they finish reading the passage. Have students read the rest of the passage, and then invite volunteers to share their questions. Discuss which questions helped students focus and those that signaled being confused by information in the passage. Then direct students to complete the skill practice activity. Review the answers together.

DAY 3

Remind students of the *Ask Questions* strategy. Tell students that asking a question after they read is a good way to check that they understood what they have read. Say: **When we ask questions after we read, we are reviewing what we have read to make sure we understand it. We ask ourselves the types of questions that we find on tests or in our textbooks.** Have students read the instructions at the top of the page and the passage. Then direct students to complete the strategy practice activity in pairs or as a group. Have students ask each other questions. Finally, direct students to complete the skill practice activity independently. Review the answers together.

DAY 4

Remind students of the *Ask Questions* strategy. Then ask: **When you read, when should you ask questions, and why?** (before reading to set a purpose for reading, during reading to stay engaged and identify areas of confusion, and after reading to check comprehension) Tell students they are going to read about modern tigers and smilodons, or saber-toothed tigers. Have students read the instructions at the top of the page and the passage. When students have finished, direct them to complete the strategy and skill practice activities. Review the answers together.

DAY 5

Remind students of the *Ask Questions* strategy. Tell students they are going to read about building physical endurance through exercise. Then have students read the instructions at the top of the page and the passage. When students have finished, pair students or complete the strategy practice activity as a group. Then direct students to complete the skill practice independently. Review the answers together.

Name: ______________________________

READ THE PASSAGE Think of a question about the topic of Bigfoot. As you read, look for the answer.

Ray Wallace's Bigfoot Hoax

For decades, people have heard about sightings of a gigantic creature in the forests of the Pacific Northwest. According to the stories, the creature always left huge footprints. A logger named Ray Wallace helped popularize these stories about the creature known as Bigfoot.

In 1958, one of Wallace's workers told a newspaper about spotting the creature's tracks. Wallace explained that his workers were scared of the beast. The story spread, and some people connected the creature to other legendary monsters, especially the Abominable Snowman, or Yeti, said to live in the mountains of Nepal. Wallace had pictures and film footage of a huge furry primate to back up his story. He also tried to sell castings of giant footprints and recordings of the creature's cries.

But in 2002, after Ray Wallace died, his family members had their own story to tell. They said that Wallace was a prankster and made the giant footprints himself. Wallace's wife admitted dressing up in a Bigfoot costume as part of the hoax. Apparently, Ray Wallace enjoyed fooling people. He told his Bigfoot stories for decades. However, Wallace certainly was not responsible for all the other reported sightings of Bigfoot. In fact, some people continue to report seeing the monster. Despite some people's belief that Bigfoot exists, when Ray Wallace passed away, his own son said, "Bigfoot is dead."

STRATEGY PRACTICE Write a question you have about the passage. Then write the answer you found.

____

____

SKILL PRACTICE Read the item. Write your response.

1. What is the author's purpose for writing this text?

____

____

2. How does the author allow for the possibility that Bigfoot is real?

____

____

3. Why did the author include the quotation from Wallace's son at the end of the text?

____

____

Name: ______________________

READ THE PASSAGE Think of one question you have about each paragraph.

Ephesus

Although tourists might think the best place to view Roman ruins would be the modern city of Rome, they would be mistaken. There is one city that helps visitors understand better than any other what it must have been like to live in the ancient Roman world. That city, in western Turkey, is Ephesus (EF-ih-sus). In Ephesus, visitors find fabulous ruins from around AD 100, such as the magnificent library and a theater that once seated 24,000 audience members. The ruins are among the best-preserved in the world and include houses, temples, and baths. Tourists can also visit ancient residences, complete with marble floors and frescoes painted on the walls.

Ephesus used to serve as an important trading center for the Roman Empire because it had access to the Aegean Sea. However, the river that led to the Aegean filled with silt, and today Ephesus is miles inland. The city was deserted in the Middle Ages. Visitors to Ephesus can walk down a Roman road and see buildings that the ancient Romans saw. They can appreciate feats of engineering that are still impressive, such as the incredible acoustics in the huge open-air theater. Here, Roman audience members once listened to classical plays and watched gladiators fight. At Ephesus today, tourists can experience the ancient Roman Empire in its most inspiring form.

STRATEGY PRACTICE Write a question you thought of while reading the first paragraph.

____

____

SKILL PRACTICE Read the item. Write your response.

1. What is the author's opinion of Ephesus? Cite text evidence in your response.

____

____

2. What can you learn about the Roman Empire by visiting Ephesus?

____

____

3. Is this text written to entertain, inform, or persuade? Explain your response.

____

____

Name: ______________________________

READ THE PASSAGE Think of a question that can be answered with information from the passage.

Taking Action

At Seven Oaks Middle School, Daniela Carrera was searching for a club to join. There was a dance club, a choir, an exercise club, and an action club that found creative ways to raise money for other people. Daniela was thinking about joining the dance club because she loved dancing.

Then Daniela's friend Ciara told her about the action club's new project. At first, Daniela was skeptical. "Why would people in a nursing home want a video-game console?" she asked Ciara.

"This would be a specific kind of console that plays fitness games. The games help people who need to exercise and move around but who can't get to a gym or exercise safely outdoors. Besides, everybody loves video games, don't they?" Ciara replied.

"Not my great-grandmother," Daniela said, laughing. But she agreed to go to the club meeting the next day.

At the meeting, Mr. Washington, the club's advisor, explained to Daniela and the others how fitness video games help motivate people to move. He described how the consoles can even help distract people who suffer from severe pain. That was all Daniela needed to hear.

"How can I help?" she asked as she signed up for the club.

"We're selling raffle tickets. With the money we raise, we'll buy two fitness consoles. We'll give one to the winner of the raffle. We'll give the other console to the nursing home," explained Mr. Washington.

"Great! Let's get started. I'm motivated to sell some tickets today!" said Daniela.

STRATEGY PRACTICE Write a question about information from the passage. Then ask a partner to answer it.

____

SKILL PRACTICE Read the item. Write your response.

1. How does the action club differ from the other clubs that Daniela has considered joining?

____

____

2. What is the author's purpose for writing this text?

____

____

3. Why is one console going to the student who wins the raffle?

____

____

READ THE PASSAGE Ask yourself questions to make sure you understand what you read.

The Smilodon and the Tiger

Although the now-extinct smilodon is also known as the saber-toothed tiger, it was not a close relative of the modern tiger. The more scientists study the two big cats, the more differences they find.

Tigers travel by themselves and run fast while chasing their prey. The smilodon, on the other hand, probably lived in packs. With much shorter tails than today's tigers, the smilodon did not have the balance to run at top speeds. It probably caught its prey by hiding quietly until an animal came near. Then the smilodon would surprise its prey.

Another main difference between today's tiger and the smilodon is the size of the smilodon's teeth. It is known as a "saber-toothed" cat because of two enormous teeth that grew from the top of its jaw. These teeth grew up to seven inches (18 cm) long and were surprisingly fragile. The smilodon probably used the teeth to bite into soft parts of its prey's body, such as its stomach. A modern tiger's teeth are much smaller, but they are stronger.

The smilodon lived in North and South America from about two million years ago until about ten thousand years ago. Tigers, of course, still exist today and live in eastern and southeastern Asia. No one knows for sure why the smilodon became extinct. However, scientists do know that many of today's tiger species are in danger of becoming extinct because of loss of habitat and human activity.

STRATEGY PRACTICE Write a question you had while reading. If you learned the answer, write it down.

____

____

SKILL PRACTICE Read the item. Write your response.

1. What is the author's purpose for writing this text?

____

____

2. Name three similarities between smilodons and modern tigers.

____

____

3. Name three ways in which smilodons and modern tigers differ.

____

____

Name: ____________________

READ THE PASSAGE Write questions about the parts of the passage you find difficult to understand.

Exercise and Endurance

Endurance is the body's physical ability to do an exercise for an extended period of time. The more endurance you have, the longer you can do the exercise. Endurance is about time, as opposed to strength, which measures your power against resistance, such as weights. Athletes build up endurance by training. They plan their exercise ahead of time. Then they gradually increase the amount of exercise. For example, some people increase it a little more every week.

Exercise can strengthen your heart and other muscles. There are two main types of endurance: cardiovascular endurance and muscular endurance. Cardiovascular endurance is the ability of your heart and lungs to pump blood filled with oxygen to your muscles and the rest of your body. Oxygen acts as a fuel for your muscles to help them work better. Muscular endurance is how continuously your muscles can work without getting tired out.

Your body needs more than just oxygen to fuel itself and build endurance. Water is one kind of fuel. Food is another. Food provides energy, which is measured in calories. Your body needs energy to work. Even breathing requires energy. Your body needs even more energy when you exercise.

You do not have to be an athlete to build physical endurance. Anyone can do it! Doing exercise on a regular basis and slowly increasing the amount of time you exercise will build endurance. Endurance isn't important only for sporting events. It can help you do any physical activity longer and more easily, including activities that we do in our daily lives.

STRATEGY PRACTICE Write a question about something that confused you in the passage. Discuss it with a partner.

____

SKILL PRACTICE Read the item. Write your response.

1. How is strength different from endurance?

____

____

2. Write three activities that require endurance more than strength.

____

____

3. Is the author's purpose to inform about endurance or to persuade the reader to build endurance? Explain.

____

____

WEEK 7

Main Idea and Details

Students look for the central idea or message of a passage or story. They also find details that best support the main idea.

Sequence

Students look for the order of events or steps in a process.

DAY 1

Tell students that reading comprehension almost always involves looking for the *Main Idea and Details*. Explain: **Each passage has a main idea, and each paragraph in a passage has a main idea. Also, within each paragraph, there are important details that support the main idea of the passage or paragraph. Good readers can distinguish between ideas that support the main idea and those that are extra information.** Have students read the instructions at the top of the page. Then remind them of the *Monitor Comprehension* strategy (Week 1). Tell students to read slowly and think about what they are reading. Then direct students to read the passage and complete the skill practice activity. Review the answers together. For the strategy practice activity, pair students or complete it as a group.

DAY 2

Ask students to recall what a main idea is and what details are. (The main idea tells what something is mostly about, and details are additional information that supports the main idea.) Tell students that fictional stories can have a main idea, just as nonfiction passages do. Then remind students of the *Visualization* strategy (Week 3). Say: **As you read, make a mental image of what is happening in the story. This will allow you to recall the important details more easily.** Have students read the instructions at the top of the page and the passage. When students have finished, direct them to complete the skill and strategy practice activities. Review the answers together.

DAY 3

Introduce the *Sequence* skill to students. Say: **Sequence can refer to the order of things in a series, the order of things based on when they happen, or the order of steps or instructions that need to be followed.** Tell students they will read about a pond ecosystem. Say: **As you read, pay attention to when things happen.** Then remind students of the *Monitor Comprehension* strategy. Say: **As you read, you may wish to make notes in the margin to help you remember what happens first, second, and so on, in a pond.** Have students read the instructions at the top of the page and the passage. When students have finished, direct them to complete the skill and strategy practice activities. Review the answers together.

DAY 4

Remind students of the *Sequence* skill. Then say: **The passage you are about to read contains dates. When good readers see dates in a passage, they often pay attention to these dates and the events that are connected to them.** Draw a timeline on the board. Say: **If you read something that contains many dates, a timeline is a good way to organize information you are reading.** Then remind students of the *Visualization* strategy. Say: **You can also make a mental image of the event that is described for each date. This will help you remember the date better.** Have students read the instructions at the top of the page and the passage. Then direct students to complete the strategy practice activity. Next, invite volunteers to use their own answers to fill in the timeline that you drew. Then direct students to complete the skill practice activity. Review the answers together.

DAY 5

Tell students they will practice both the *Main Idea and Details* and *Sequence* skills. Remind students of the *Monitor Comprehension* strategy. Say: **Read each item in the skill practice activity before you read the passage. Then, as you are reading the passage, you can look for the information that you need to answer the questions.** Have students read the instructions at the top of the page and read the passage. Then direct students to complete the skill and strategy practice activities. Review the answers together.

Name: ____________________

READ THE PASSAGE Pause after each paragraph and consider what that paragraph was mostly about.

Prometheus

In ancient Greek mythology, Prometheus was a Titan, one of the most powerful gods. Yet even though he was a god, he found humans interesting. Zeus, the ruler of all the gods, did not care about human struggles, but Prometheus wanted to help mortals.

According to the myths, Prometheus looked for ways to help humans solve their problems. For example, he taught people how to make bricks to build homes, how to tell the seasons by looking at the stars, and how to navigate their ships. Humans, with the help of Prometheus's knowledge, began to advance. They became more independent.

Zeus ordered Prometheus not to help the humans, but Prometheus continued. After Prometheus stole fire from Zeus and gave it to people, Zeus grew incredibly angry. Until then, Zeus alone had controlled fire. By giving it to the humans, Prometheus was offering them the final power they needed to grow and prosper without the help of the gods.

Zeus was furious. "You dared to defy me?" cried Zeus. "You brought fire to those too foolish to use it properly. Now you must be punished!" Zeus chained Prometheus to a mountain and kept him bound there for years.

Finally, Heracles, a brave warrior and one of Zeus's sons, could no longer stand to see Prometheus suffer. Heracles set Prometheus free.

SKILL PRACTICE Read the item. Write your response.

1. Summarize this myth in one sentence.

____

____

2. Why and how did Zeus punish Prometheus?

____

____

3. What would have happened to Prometheus if Heracles had not taken action? Write your prediction.

____

____

STRATEGY PRACTICE Summarize what you learned about Prometheus for a partner.

Name: ______________________________

READ THE PASSAGE Look for details that support each paragraph's main idea.

A Diagnosis

Every Sunday at exactly 11:00 AM, my whole family gathers in the lobby of the Oak Valley Manor for Senior Citizens. That's when my parents, my brother Phillip, and I join my great-grandmother June for Sunday brunch, a spectacular buffet of omelets, pancakes, French toast, and all the other foods people don't usually have time to prepare or get to eat during the school week.

Something different about Sunday brunch lately was the change in Dr. Shepard, a friend of my great-grandma, who eats brunch with us. When I first met Dr. Shepard, he used a walker to get around but still stood straight and tall and always smiled. Lately he seemed to move more slowly, hunched over his walker, and rarely smiled.

Recently, our dog Scout had been tired and hadn't wanted to play. Since pets are allowed in the Manor on Sundays, we decided to bring Scout along. As we walked in, we heard someone holler, "Come, Scout!" From a nearby chair, Dr. Shepard reached out his arms. Scout ran to him, her tail wagging wildly. He scratched behind Scout's ears and gently rubbed her belly.

"Dogs are the best!" he said. "And I should know. I used to be a vet."

"Wow, you were that kind of doctor? Maybe you can figure out what's wrong with Scout."

Dr. Shepard chuckled. "Maybe I can!" And with a huge smile he added, "Go ahead and join your family. I'll stay right here with Scout and see if I can make a diagnosis."

SKILL PRACTICE Read the item. Write your response.

1. What change had the narrator noticed in Dr. Shepard prior to this visit?

____

____

2. Why is Dr. Shepard so delighted to see Scout?

____

____

3. What is the main idea of this text?

____

____

STRATEGY PRACTICE Describe the part of the passage that was easiest for you to visualize.

____

____

READ THE PASSAGE Pay attention to the details of what happens in a pond and the order in which things happen.

The World in a Pond

An ecosystem is a community of living and nonliving things that work together. Organisms, light, heat, soil, water, and the atmosphere are all parts of an ecosystem. Any alteration to an ecosystem—such as changes in temperature, the kinds of animals living there, or pollution—can affect all parts of it. This can be especially obvious in the small, enclosed ecosystem of a pond.

In a pond, sunlight helps tiny plants called algae grow. Algae release oxygen, which fish need in order to breathe. Algae are also food for other tiny organisms. Fish eat the organisms and give off carbon dioxide, which plants use to grow.

Imagine what would happen, however, if something changed in the pond. For example, if sunlight didn't reach the pond because of thick pollution, or if the temperature of the water grew colder or warmer, the algae wouldn't grow. Without algae, there would first be less oxygen. Tiny organisms would starve. Fish would then die from the lack of oxygen. Plants would die without the carbon dioxide that fish give off. Then larger animals that eat the plants and smaller animals would not get enough food. Even humans, who eat the plants, fish, and larger animals, would feel the impact. The whole ecosystem would suffer.

SKILL PRACTICE Read the item. Write your response.

1. If algae stopped growing in a pond, what living thing would be the first affected?

____

____

2. How would the decline of tiny organisms affect fish?

____

____

3. How are pond plants dependent upon fish?

____

____

STRATEGY PRACTICE Make a numbered list telling the sequence of events that occur after algae disappear from a pond.

____

____

____

____

Name: ______________________________

Sequence **WEEK 7 DAY 4**

READ THE PASSAGE Pay attention to the dates and events described in the passage.

The Cliff Dwellers

Mesa Verde, which means "green table" in Spanish, is a high plateau in Colorado. Made of sandstone and shale, this plateau rises almost 2,000 feet (610 m) above surrounding land. The mesa has many canyons with streams and rivers running through them. At the tops of the rocky canyon walls, there are many overhangs and cave-like alcoves that have formed from water seeping into the sandstone.

People first came to Mesa Verde sometime around AD 550. These early inhabitants dug into the floors of the alcoves, creating what are now called pit houses. Around AD 750, people moved out of the pit houses in the canyon walls and built above-ground houses from mud and stone. Then, around the year 1200, they returned to the alcoves in the canyon walls.

Nobody knows why the people returned to the cliff pit houses. They may have feared attack from other groups and believed the alcoves offered better protection. They may have wanted better shelter from the wind and blistering sun. Whatever the reason, the cliff dwellers stayed less than a hundred years in the pit houses after they had moved back.

By 1300, the cliff dwellings had been abandoned, probably because of a severe drought in the area. It wasn't until over four hundred years later that cowboys, trappers, and prospectors began to visit and photograph Mesa Verde, astonished by the sight of hundreds of cliff houses built into the walls of the canyons.

SKILL PRACTICE Read the item. Write your response.

1. Describe the types of homes that the first Mesa Verde inhabitants created.

____

____

2. When did the Mesa Verde people leave their above-ground homes and where did they go?

____

____

3. When and why do archaeologists think that Mesa Verde inhabitants left the area?

____

____

STRATEGY PRACTICE Describe how you visualized the cliff dwellings of the Mesa Verde people.

____

____

Name: ____________________

READ THE PASSAGE Think about the main events described in the passage and when they happened.

Marching to the Sea

On March 12, 2005, several hundred people marched 240 miles (386 km) from the city of Ahmedabad (AH-mud-uh-BAHD) to the village of Dandi on the seacoast of India. They were reenacting Mahatma Gandhi's Salt March of 1930. Gandhi was an Indian whose nonviolent protests, or civil disobedience, led to India's independence from Great Britain. His program of civil disobedience began with the Salt March.

In 1930, India was a colony of Great Britain. The British had imposed a tax on salt in India to raise money. Salt was vitally important to Indians of every class and income level because it helped them preserve food and stay healthy in the country's intense heat. Gandhi and 78 followers decided to protest the tax by walking 240 miles (386 km) to the sea.

The journey lasted 23 days. Every town Gandhi passed emptied as the inhabitants ran out to watch the march. By the time Gandhi reached the sea, thousands of people had joined him. People all over India bought and sold salt illegally. The protests grew to include peaceful defiance of other laws and taxes. Gandhi was arrested and jailed by the British, but he had achieved his goal of bringing the plight of India to the world's attention. He had also started the movement that, 17 years later, would end in India becoming an independent nation.

SKILL PRACTICE Read the item. Write your response.

1. Write the main idea of the text in a single sentence.

____

____

2. What happened to Gandhi at the end of the march?

____

____

3. Which detail in the text lets the reader know that the Indian people supported Gandhi?

____

____

STRATEGY PRACTICE What was the reason for Gandhi's Salt March to the sea?

____

____

WEEK 8

Cause and Effect

Students practice identifying cause-and-effect relationships by looking for what happens (the effect) and why it happens (the cause).

Evaluate Evidence

Students practice evaluating evidence by identifying the author's main idea and examining the evidence the author uses to support that idea.

DAY 1

Introduce the *Cause and Effect* skill to students. Say: **When something happens, it is the *effect*. The thing that makes it happen is the *cause*.** Model by walking to the light switch and turning off the lights. Ask: **What caused the lights to go out?** (flipping the switch) **What is the effect of flipping the switch?** (The lights went out.) Say: **Often a writer will use causes and effects to explain a problem or a chain of events. The passage you will read is about wildfires. As you read, look for cause-and-effect relationships in the text.** Then remind students of the *Determine Important Information* strategy (Week 5). Point out that identifying important information helps you find causes and effects. Then have students read the instructions at the top of the page and the passage. When students have finished reading, direct them to complete the skill and strategy practice activities. Review the answers together.

DAY 2

Remind students of the *Cause and Effect* skill. Say: **Fiction writers often use cause-and-effect relationships to create a problem for the characters in their story or to start a chain of events that moves the plot forward. Understanding what happens and why it happens in a story is important for good comprehension.** Then remind students of the *Ask Questions* strategy (Week 6). Say: **As you read, ask yourself questions to find the causes and effects in this passage.** Then direct students to read the passage before completing the skill and strategy practice activities.

DAY 3

Introduce the *Evaluate Evidence* skill to students. Say: **When writers write nonfiction, they usually do so to tell us more about something, to try to persuade us about a topic, or to teach us how to do something. When we read, we must figure out why an author wrote something and evaluate the evidence that the author provides for the claims he or she makes.** Tell students the passage they will read is about interesting rock formations in Utah. Point out the second sentence in the second paragraph. Say: **The writer is making the claim that water is responsible for the rock formations. In order to support this claim, the writer will likely explain how the water makes the rock formations.** Then remind students of the *Determine Important Information* strategy. Say: **As you read, think of each claim the author is making, and look for the important information that supports that claim.** Then direct students to read the passage before completing the skill and strategy practice activities.

DAY 4

Remind students of the *Evaluate Evidence* skill. Say: **When a writer gives a main idea, he or she will give you details that support the main idea. These details are evidence that support the author's claims.** Read the third sentence of the first paragraph. Say: **This is the main idea. What evidence would you expect to see to support this main idea?** (the properties of gold that make it valuable) Then remind students of the *Ask Questions* strategy. Say: **As you read, ask questions about the main ideas that the writer gives in the passage. Look for the supporting details in the passage.** Then direct students to read the passage and complete the skill practice activity. Pair students for the strategy practice activity, or complete it as a group.

DAY 5

Tell students they will practice both the *Cause and Effect* and *Evaluate Evidence* skills. Tell students they will read about a woman named Shirley Chisholm. Say: **As you read, think about what Shirley Chisholm does and why she does these things. Also look for the claims that the writer is making and the evidence he gives to support these claims.** Then direct students to read the passage and complete the skill and strategy practice activities. Review the answers together.

Name: ______________________________

READ THE PASSAGE Look for the effects of wildfires listed in the passage.

Wildfires in Washington

Wildfires take place with alarming frequency in the drier areas of the United States, especially in the western states. Not only do the fires cause immediate damage by killing plants and animals in their path, but they can also have long-term effects that harm the ecosystem.

At the Hanford Reach National Monument in Washington State, different types of wildlife—such as the burrowing owl, the sagebrush vole, and the pygmy rabbit—abound. Visitors to Hanford Reach might also see elk, porcupines, and jack rabbits that live near the free-flowing Columbia River. The area is protected from development, which has helped these species thrive.

Over the last decade, several major wildfires have broken out at Hanford Reach. Thousands of acres have burned. One type of plant that has been severely damaged in the fires is sagebrush. This poses special problems for many of the species living in the park. First, animals such as the sage grouse depend on sagebrush as part of their natural habitat. It can take thirty years for sagebrush to grow large enough to provide shelter for these animals. Second, after the sagebrush burns, an invasive species called cheat grass can grow quickly in its place. Unfortunately, cheat grass burns more easily and at higher temperatures than sagebrush. That means that after sagebrush is destroyed, wildfires can occur more frequently and be even more devastating.

SKILL PRACTICE Read the item. Write your response.

1. How are species protected at the Hanford Reach National Monument?

____

____

2. What is the biggest issue facing animals that survive a wildfire?

____

____

3. How does cheat grass pose a problem after a wildfire?

____

____

STRATEGY PRACTICE Write a sentence explaining why sagebrush is such an important plant at Hanford Reach National Monument.

____

____

Name: ______________________

READ THE PASSAGE Think about the problem that Phil and Curtis face and what causes it.

Building a House of Cards

One day after school, Phil and Curtis were thinking of something fun to do. "Let's have a contest to see who can build the tallest house of cards," Phil suggested.

"Okay," said Curtis, "but you know I'm the house-of-cards champion."

"We'll see," Phil said as he took two packs of cards from his desk.

The two boys began working. Curtis first placed two cards so that they were touching each other at the top, making the shape of an upside-down V. Then he did the same thing with two more cards, placing them beside the first pair. Soon, he had a line of cards that looked like teepees. Next, he placed cards flat across the tops of the teepees to make the foundation for the next level.

Phil stood four cards on their edges to form a tall rectangle. Then he placed cards flat on top of the rectangle to make the foundation for his next level.

Now the brothers' troubles began. When Curtis tried to build his second level of teepees, he found that the cards on the bottom level would not stand. His teepees collapsed! When Phil tried to build his second level, the rectangle-shaped hut made of cards fell in a heap.

"Well, this is frustrating," said Phil.

"I have an idea," said Curtis. "Maybe my teepees would work better on top of your rectangle."

"Let's try it!" Phil said.

SKILL PRACTICE Read the item. Write your response.

1. Why did Phil and Curtis build houses with playing cards?

____

____

2. What happened when Curtis started building his second level?

____

____

3. What occurred after both brothers had difficulty creating their house of cards?

____

____

STRATEGY PRACTICE Write a question you had about what was happening in the passage. If you found the answer, write it.

____

____

Name: ____________________

READ THE PASSAGE Pay attention to the author's evidence for how hoodoos formed in the region.

Hoodoos in Bryce Canyon

Imagine the spires at the top of a sand castle—the kind you create by dripping layers of very wet sand. Hoodoos, a type of rock formation found primarily in Bryce Canyon, Utah, look something like wet sand, but they are made from colorful rock. Every year, millions of people come to Bryce Canyon to look at the pole-shaped hoodoos, which range from 5 to 150 feet (1.5 to 46 m) tall.

What caused these amazing formations? Scientists believe that water is responsible. Over millions of years, water and ice have shaped the limestone of the area, creating canyons, deep bowls, plateaus, and hoodoos. On many days in this region, the temperatures are freezing at night and much warmer during the day. The sun melts snow, and the resulting water flows into cracks in the limestone. When the water freezes at night, it expands and causes the cracks to widen and pull the rock apart. This is called frost wedging. Another way that water shapes the hoodoos is simply through rainfall. The rain contains a small amount of acid, which causes the soft limestone to dissolve. Some layers of rock in the hoodoos are harder than other layers, making parts of the hoodoos wear away more slowly. This gives hoodoos their unusual shapes and appearances.

Visitors to Bryce Canyon can hike through miles of natural mazes formed by hoodoos. However, to protect the fragile spires, visitors are asked to stay on the trails. If they were to climb on the hoodoos, they could damage the formations and rob future generations of the chance to see something that took eons to form.

SKILL PRACTICE Read the item. Write your response.

1. Why did the author mention sand castle spires at the beginning of the text?

____

____

2. *Hoodoos can form from very hard rock such as granite.* Prove this statement true or false using evidence from the text.

____

____

3. Can humans affect hoodoos? Use quotation marks to cite text evidence in your response.

____

STRATEGY PRACTICE What information from the passage would be important for writing a report about weathering in Bryce Canyon?

____

____

Name: ______________________________

READ THE PASSAGE Look for the evidence that the author gives to support each claim she makes.

The Value of Gold

People have treasured gold for thousands of years. But just what makes gold so valuable? Gold has several important properties that contribute to its value. First, it reflects light very well and has an attractive yellow color, making it ideal for use in jewelry. Second, it is very malleable, or easy to shape. Because gold is soft and easy to work with, it can be hammered into thin sheets that do not crack. These sheets can then be used to add decorative details to artwork or buildings. Third, it does not rust or wear away. It keeps its shape, which means that gold jewelry and art objects can pass from generation to generation and become more valuable over time. Fourth, gold is an excellent conductor of electricity, making it a good choice for electronics.

One of the most important reasons that gold is valuable, however, is that it is rare. Although gold exists in many places throughout the world, it is not easy to find or to mine. People who mine gold usually have to work very hard to get even tiny amounts of the precious metal. The fact that it is both beautiful and useful makes people want more of this precious metal than they can easily get, which drives up its price.

Finally, gold is valuable because people perceive it to be a symbol of wealth. Throughout recorded history, gold has been associated with wealth and power. Today we still value it for many of the same reasons that our ancestors did.

SKILL PRACTICE Read the item. Write your response.

1. What evidence did the author use to explain why gold is ideal for use in jewelry?

____

____

2. Why are small amounts of gold commonly used in electronics?

____

____

3. Quote the statement from the text that explains the primary reason why gold is valuable.

____

____

STRATEGY PRACTICE Write a question that can be answered with information from the passage. Then have a partner answer the question.

____

____

READ THE PASSAGE Think about why the author wrote the passage and how Shirley Chisholm was important.

Shirley Chisholm

"Aim high!" Shirley Chisholm told her political supporters, and she practiced what she preached. Born in 1924 in Brooklyn, New York, Chisholm spent part of her childhood in the island nation of Barbados. She returned to New York later, graduated from Brooklyn College, and earned a Master of Arts degree at Columbia University. Chisholm spent some time working in early childhood education before running for political office in the New York State Assembly.

After serving in the assembly, Chisholm ran for U.S. Congress in 1968 and became the first African American woman to be elected. Chisholm opposed the Vietnam War, and in her first speech in Congress, she promised to vote against any more spending on defense. "Our children, our jobless men, our deprived, rejected and starving fellows, our dejected citizens must come first," she said.

Aiming higher still, in 1972 Chisholm decided to run for president of the United States. She was the first African American to run as a candidate for the presidency in a major political party, and she was the first woman to run for president as a democrat. Ultimately, the democrats chose George McGovern as their candidate. McGovern later lost the presidential election to republican Richard Nixon. Afterward, Chisholm explained that she was tired of waiting for change to come someday in the future. "I ran because somebody had to do it first. I ran because most people thought the country was not ready for a black candidate, not ready for a woman candidate. Someday—it was time in 1972 to make that someday come."

SKILL PRACTICE Read the item. Write your response.

1. What two political offices did Shirley Chisholm hold?

____

____

2. Write two facts that demonstrate Chisholm's ideal of aiming high.

____

____

3. Why does the author include the quotation at the end of the text?

____

____

STRATEGY PRACTICE What information in the passage is most important for understanding Shirley Chisholm's political career?

____

____

WEEK

9

Compare and Contrast

Students practice comparing and contrasting by looking at the similarities and differences between two or more people or things.

Make Inferences

Students practice making inferences by using clues in a passage to understand what is being implied or inferred.

DAY 1

Introduce the *Compare and Contrast* skill to students. Say: **When we look at the similarities and differences between two or more things, we are comparing and contrasting.** To reinforce the concept, you may wish to draw a Venn diagram on the board and label the diagram "oranges" and "apples." Invite volunteers to list the similarities and differences between the fruits. Then tell students they are going to read about the eating habits of ancient Romans. Remind students of the *Make Connections* strategy (Week 2). Say: **As you read, make connections with the text in order to compare and contrast eating two thousand years ago with eating today.** Have students read the instructions at the top of the page and the passage. When students have finished reading, direct them to complete the skill and strategy practice activities. Review the answers together.

DAY 2

Remind students of the *Compare and Contrast* skill. Then tell students they are going to read two accounts of a whale-watching trip. Then remind students of the *Organization* strategy (Week 4). Say: **As you read, pay attention to how each account is organized.** Have students read the instructions at the top of the page and the passage. When students have finished reading, direct them to complete the skill and strategy practice activities. Review the answers together.

DAY 3

Introduce the *Make Inferences* skill to students. Say: **A writer doesn't tell us everything that happens, because doing so would make what we are reading uninteresting, or because the extra information is not necessary for us to understand the writer's main point. Instead, the writer relies on us to make inferences as we read. When we infer, we use clues from the text and our prior knowledge to figure out the information that is not included.** Then tell students they are going to read about a way of helping people in poor countries. Remind them of the *Make Connections* strategy. Say: **Whenever you make an inference, you have to make a connection with what you are reading. You can't make an inference without drawing upon your prior experience.** Direct students to read the passage and complete the skill and strategy practice activities. Review the answers together.

DAY 4

Remind students of the *Make Inferences* skill. Say: **When we make inferences, we use our background knowledge and clues from the text to fill in information that we haven't been told directly.** Then tell students they are going to read about wolves in Yellowstone National Park. Remind students of the *Organization* strategy and of the common ways a passage can be organized (main idea and details, fact and opinion, compare and contrast, cause and effect, and problem and solution). Say: **As you read, pay attention to how the writer organizes her ideas. Stop after you read each paragraph and think about what that paragraph was mostly about and how the writer organized the information.** Then have students read the passage. When students have finished reading, direct them to complete the skill and strategy practice activities. Review the answers together.

DAY 5

Tell students they will practice both the *Compare and Contrast* and *Make Inferences* skills by reading about an inspirational scientist who went to space. Build background on space exploration, if necessary, before students read the passage. When students have finished reading, direct them to complete the skill and strategy practice activities.

READ THE PASSAGE Compare the eating habits of ancient Romans to how people eat today.

Eating the Roman Way Today

It's hard to believe that there could be many similarities between the way we eat today and the diet and eating habits of ancient Romans. However, excavations at the ancient Roman towns of Pompeii and nearby Herculaneum have uncovered at least one significant parallel. Romans enjoyed convenient ways to get their food and ate on the go, just as we do today.

Buying baked bread is one example of a convenience in both the ancient and modern worlds. Most people today purchase bread in a store. There is evidence that Romans bought their bread, too, rather than baking it themselves. A large wall painting in Pompeii shows customers buying loaves of bread in a shop. Archaeologists have identified more than 30 shops that may have been bakeries. Signs on walls told Roman shoppers that certain vendors sold bread. In addition to these discoveries, archaeologists found that few homes in Pompeii had ovens, which suggests that most people did not bake at home.

Ancient Romans also had a version of take-out food. Pompeii is filled with shops that contain dishes to hold or display food. Many shops had built-in stoves that allowed them to cook and serve food. Types of foods that have been found in these shops include dates and lentils.

Archaeologists have also uncovered many houses with small barbecue grills. However, few of these houses had sets of dishes. Taken together, these pieces of evidence suggest that Romans frequently grabbed a quick bite to eat at home, right off the grill, or bought a meal to go. Sound familiar?

SKILL PRACTICE Read the item. Write your response.

1. What are two ways in which ancient Romans' diets were similar to our own?

____

____

2. Name two ways in which ancient Romans' eating habits differ from modern ones.

____

____

3. What is the most surprising fact in the article? How did you choose it?

____

____

STRATEGY PRACTICE Describe a common eating habit that you share with the ancient Romans.

____

____

Name: ____________________

READ THE PASSAGE Read each account and look for how they are similar and different.

The Whale Watch

Jeongsoo and Samuel went on a whale-watching trip to Cape Cod, Massachusetts, with their class. They each wrote an account of what they saw and did. Read their accounts.

Jeongsoo's Account

I had looked forward to our Cape Cod whale-watching trip all year. When we finally got on the boat, I thought, "This is it!" After a year of studying everything about whales, we were finally going to see them. Being on the boat was great. It was sunny and windy, the waves were enormous, and it wasn't long before we noticed our first whale, a huge finback that spouted water up through its blowhole just a few feet from the boat. We saw 12 whales altogether, including minke whales, humpbacks, and the endangered right whale. And I videotaped them all! They were the most amazing creatures I'd ever seen.

Samuel's Account

All year our class had studied whales, and I worked really hard learning about them and about the ocean. I could hardly wait to see the whales in their own habitat, and I was excited when we finally got to the boat. The waves were huge, though, and when the boat started moving, I began to feel weird. Then I got nauseated—really, really nauseated. I spent the whole day miserable with seasickness, curled up in a chair in the boat's cabin. I heard everyone shouting as the whales breached and spouted, but I missed it all. Luckily, Jeongsoo videotaped the whales, so I got to see his video. The whales really were awesome.

SKILL PRACTICE Read the item. Write your response.

1. Name two similarities between Jeongsoo's and Samuel's accounts.

2. What did Jeongsoo do that ended up helping Samuel?

3. Why was Jeongsoo's experience more enjoyable than Samuel's?

STRATEGY PRACTICE Are the accounts organized by cause and effect, sequence, or main idea and details? How does the organization help you compare and contrast the accounts?

READ THE PASSAGE Use clues from the passage to make inferences about microfinance.

A Little Can Go a Long Way

In a village in Uganda, a woman named Fatima Serwona ran a small store. She sold food and other useful items. However, she had trouble making enough money to keep the shelves stocked. To stay in business, Fatima got a microfinance loan—a small sum of money from a person in another country. It was just enough for her to buy a cellphone. She let villagers make calls using her phone and charged them a small fee for each call. This helped her make enough money to keep her shelves stocked with items. Fatima then used the money to send her children to school and improve their lives, as well as her own.

Microfinance is the practice of giving small loans to people in need. Most microfinance loans are for less than two hundred dollars. The loans are used to start or expand a small business, such as catching fish, raising chickens, weaving, or selling produce. Lenders are willing to make these loans because most of the people who receive them are very likely to repay the loans.

Microfinance loans are important for several reasons. The businesses that these loans support often provide needed services or goods to their communities. Also, many of the people who receive microfinance loans cannot get money any other way. And although they have to pay a high rate of interest on the money they borrow, the rate is lower than if they borrowed from a local moneylender.

It doesn't seem like such a small amount of money could make a big difference, but microfinance loans have been shown to help improve individual lives and revitalize whole communities like Fatima's.

SKILL PRACTICE Read the item. Write your response.

1. Why did Fatima Serwona buy a cellphone?

____

____

2. Why do so many microfinance borrowers repay their loans?

____

____

3. Why do the microfinance loans come from outside Uganda?

____

____

STRATEGY PRACTICE If you were given a microfinance loan, what would you do with the money?

____

____

READ THE PASSAGE Use what you know about ecosystems and food webs to help you understand the passage.

The Return of the Wolf

Wolves once prospered in Yellowstone National Park, but by 1926, humans had hunted them to extinction there. The absence of wolves affected many parts of the Yellowstone ecosystem. Most significantly, the disappearance of wolves led to a huge increase in the number of elk. This in turn had negative effects on plants and animals in the park.

Park authorities tried to keep the elk population under control by hunting, but in the late 1960s and 1970s, the U.S. government and the park managers began considering a new policy. They wanted to return to natural processes for regulating the balance of wildlife in the park. In 1995, Congress authorized reintroducing the gray wolf to Yellowstone. The first wolves were brought in from Canada a year later.

Almost immediately, authorities noticed differences in the park. As a result of the reintroduction of wolves, the number of elk declined. This led to an unexpected change. The number of willow trees and aspen, which elk eat, increased. Beavers, which feed on willows, in turn grew more numerous. In addition, the populations of some songbird species and small mammals that live in aspen stands have since grown. Other animals and people have benefited, too. Scavengers, or animals that eat dead animals, have increased in number. And visitors to Yellowstone are able to see and hear wolves in the park again.

SKILL PRACTICE Read the item. Write your response.

1. Why were there too many elk in Yellowstone National Park in the early 1990s?

____

____

2. Without wolves in the park, how and why was the vegetation at Yellowstone affected?

____

____

3. Why has the number of scavengers risen since the reintroduction of wolves?

____

____

STRATEGY PRACTICE Is the passage organized by compare and contrast, cause and effect, or problem and solution? Explain.

____

____

READ THE PASSAGE Look for the details that describe how Maria and Ellen are similar and different.

My Scientist Hero

My name is Maria Ochoa. I'm in sixth grade. For as long as I can remember, I have been interested in space. I sleep under a ceiling of glow-in-the-dark stars. I have a poster of the solar system across from my mirror. When I grow up, I want to be an astronaut, just like Ellen Ochoa.

I first heard about Ellen Ochoa in school. How cool that the first Hispanic woman in space has the same last name as mine! We have other things in common as well. We were both born in Los Angeles, raised by one parent, and have four siblings. We even both play the flute and volleyball!

Ellen studied physics and electrical engineering in college. A few years later, she was chosen to be trained as an astronaut, but only the best become astronauts. They are taught more math, science, and technology, as well as how to live in space. For example, they learn about wearing a space suit and how to float in space when they are weightless. Ellen became an astronaut in 1991, when she had to get even more training! She had to learn things such as how to do experiments in space and go on spacewalks.

In 1993, Ellen flew to space for the first time on the shuttle *Discovery*. She told reporters that she could only imagine the pride her grandparents would feel, knowing that their granddaughter grew up to travel in space. The crew collected lots of data on how the sun affects Earth's ozone layer, which absorbs the sun's ultraviolet light. The ozone layer keeps Earth warm enough to live on; holes in the ozone are dangerous.

I want to be an astronaut scientist, too. I won't be the first Hispanic woman to leave Earth, but I hope to be the first one to land on Mars!

SKILL PRACTICE Read the item. Write your response.

1. How are both Maria and Ellen similar?

____

____

2. Why do you think astronaut scientists need so much extra training?

____

____

3. Name two adjectives that describe Ellen Ochoa. Explain your choices.

____

STRATEGY PRACTICE Think about what you might want to do later in life. Who is a good role model? How can that person help you work toward your goal?

____

____

WEEK 10

Character and Setting

Students practice analyzing character and setting by looking at the traits and motivations of a character and where and when a passage's events take place.

Theme

Students practice identifying the theme by looking for the central message or lesson in a passage.

DAY 1

Introduce the *Character and Setting* skill to students. Say: **The characters are who or what a passage is mostly about. Good readers study a character's traits. This means they know what the character looks like or what the character says, does, and believes. The setting is where and when a passage takes place.** Tell students they are going to read a biography about a man who opened schools in Pakistan and Afghanistan. Say: **Studying the character and setting of a biography helps us better understand why the author thinks this person is important to write about.** Then remind students of the *Monitor Comprehension* strategy (Week 1). Say: **As you read, notice if your focus drifts from the passage. If that happens, pause for a moment and think about what you can do to refocus. Then begin reading again.** Have students read the instructions at the top of the page and the passage. When students have finished, direct them to complete the skill and strategy practice activities. Review the answers together.

DAY 2

Remind students of the *Character and Setting* skill. Then tell students they are going to read a first-person account of someone's trip to an unusual place. Say: **Because this is written in the first person, the main character is also the writer. As you read, pay attention to what the writer says and does to better understand his character.** Then remind students of the *Visualization* strategy (Week 3). Say: **As you read, make a mental image of the important details.** Have students read the passage. When students have finished, direct them to complete the skill and strategy practice activities. Review the answers together.

DAY 3

Introduce the *Theme* skill to students. Say: **A theme is a lesson or view about life that the author wants to share. Most of the time, the theme is not stated directly in a passage or story. You must look at what happens or study the main ideas in a passage or story to understand the theme.** Tell students they are going to read a folk tale. Say: **A folk tale usually has a moral or lesson about life. As you read, think about the lesson that the author is trying to teach.** Then remind students of the *Monitor Comprehension* strategy. Say: **A good way to make sure you understand the theme is to reread the story after you think you know what the theme is. Then you can check to see if your theme makes sense in the story.** After students finish reading, direct them to complete the skill and strategy practice activities. Review the answers together.

DAY 4

Remind students of the *Theme* skill. Say: **Nonfiction passage themes are usually views about the world that an author has. When you look for the theme of a nonfiction passage, ask yourself, *Would the author agree with this statement about the world?*** Then remind students of the *Visualization* strategy. Say: **If you visualize what is happening in the passage, you may find it easier to understand what the author's theme is.** Have students read the passage. When students have finished, direct them to complete the skill and strategy practice activities. Review the answers together.

DAY 5

Tell students they will practice both the *Character and Setting* and *Theme* skills by reading about a child musician. Encourage students to pay attention to who the main character is and what kind of theme his story has. Then remind students of the *Monitor Comprehension* strategy. Say: **After you read each paragraph, pause to think about the main idea.** Have students read the passage. When students have finished, direct them to complete the skill and strategy practice activities. Review the answers together.

Name: ____________________

READ THE PASSAGE Think about whom the passage is about and where the events in it take place.

One School at a Time

Greg Mortenson is an adventurer who once loved to climb mountains. Born in 1957, he grew up on the slopes of Mt. Kilimanjaro in Tanzania, Africa. After his sister Christa died in 1992, he decided to try climbing Pakistan's K2, the second-highest mountain in the world, in her memory. Although Mt. Everest in the Himalaya Mountains is higher, K2 is considered more difficult and treacherous to climb. During an attempt to climb the mountain in 1993, snow, ice, and bad weather forced Mortenson to turn back.

Mortenson recovered from frostbite and exhaustion in the rural Pakistani village of Korphe. There he saw a group of children writing in the dirt with sticks. He learned that they had no pens or pencils, no books—not even a school or a teacher. Mortenson promised to build them a school, even though he had no idea how he would accomplish it.

It took years to raise the money to build the school. Some of the contributions to Mortenson's cause came as pennies donated by American schoolchildren. Mortenson even sold his own belongings to raise cash. The Korphe School was finished in 1996.

Since then, Mortenson has established more than 75 schools in rural Pakistan, Afghanistan, and Tajikistan. His schools educate both boys and girls in an area where schooling for girls is very rare. Mortenson's aim is to use education to promote peace in this often dangerous and violent area, one school at a time.

SKILL PRACTICE Read the item. Write your response.

1. How did the time Mortenson spent in Korphe change his life?

____

____

2. How did Mortenson's goal change between the beginning of the text and the end?

____

____

3. Name two nouns that apply to Greg Mortenson. Explain your choices.

____

____

STRATEGY PRACTICE How do you think Mortenson changed between 1993 and the time described at the end of the passage? How do you think the setting contributed to the change in his character?

____

____

READ THE PASSAGE Think about how the character describes his actions and the place he visited.

The Blue Lagoon

I have always loved going to unique, out-of-the-way places, but the strangest place I've ever visited was the Blue Lagoon in Iceland. The seawater of the Blue Lagoon is heated far beneath Earth's surface. Although most lagoons are natural, this one is man-made. A nearby power plant pumps the hot water up from a mile (1.6 km) below the surface, through a lava formation. The water that's not used to make heat and electricity at the power plant is sent into the huge lagoon cut out of solid black rock formed from lava. The water is very warm—about 104°F (40°C). It's also full of minerals that make it appear a bright, shockingly blue color.

When I visited, I walked along a pathway carved through rock, toward a bathhouse. There, I changed into a swimsuit and ran outside. The air was freezing, so I plunged into the lagoon, shivering. In a minute I was warm—except for the top of my head, which was out of the water. Clouds of steam rose into the chilly air above the water so thickly that I could hardly see the dozens of other people bathing. The water felt silky, and I slathered an unusual mud on my face from wooden tubs around the lagoon. I rinsed the mud off under a hot waterfall. By the time I left, I was sure I would never experience anything stranger or more wonderful than the Blue Lagoon.

SKILL PRACTICE Read the item. Write your response.

1. What is the setting for this text? Include as much detail as possible in your response.

____

____

2. Why was the narrator warm despite the freezing air temperature?

____

____

3. Did the narrator enjoy spending time at the Blue Lagoon? Cite text evidence in your response.

____

____

STRATEGY PRACTICE Write the words or phrases from the passage that helped you visualize the Blue Lagoon.

____

____

READ THE PASSAGE Think about the moral, or lesson, of the passage.

The Most Powerful Thing in the World

Long ago, there lived a man who worked as a humble stonecutter. He was not happy with his job or his position in life. As he struggled at his work, chipping away at stone, he saw a wealthy merchant pass by and thought, "How I wish I were as powerful and influential as that merchant!" Suddenly, the stonecutter was transformed into a wealthy and powerful merchant. Others now envied him.

One hot day, as the wealthy man walked around the town observing all that he owned, he became annoyed by the strength of the sun's rays. "How I wish I were as powerful as the sun!" he thought, and suddenly he became the sun, scorching others with his heat and brilliance.

Then one day a dark cloud crossed beneath him. Rain poured down and the wind blew, limiting the sun's power over others. "How I wish I were as powerful as the storm!" he thought, and he became a storm with rain and wind. People feared his great force, but when he blew against a huge rock, the rock did not move. "How I wish I were as powerful as that rock!" he thought, and in a moment he became the rock.

Not long afterward, he heard a hammering sound and felt a part of himself change. "What could be more powerful than me, the rock?" he wondered. He looked down and saw, much to his surprise and disappointment, that a humble stonecutter was chipping away at him.

SKILL PRACTICE Read the item. Write your response.

1. What is the theme of this text?

____

____

2. Why is the stonecutter eventually unhappy with each of his transformations?

____

____

3. What will probably happen next? Explain your reasoning.

____

____

STRATEGY PRACTICE If the stonecutter had stopped making wishes after he became a merchant, how would it have affected the passage's theme?

____

____

____

Name: ____________________

READ THE PASSAGE Think about how the author feels about animals and people working together.

Helping Horses

Many people with visual impairment use guide dogs to help them get safely from place to place and to alert them to danger. But what can blind people do if they are allergic to dogs or just don't like them? For some people, the answer is provided by the Guide Horse Foundation.

Janet and Don Burleson founded the nonprofit organization in 1999. They began training miniature horses to help guide visually impaired people. Miniature horses look just like regular horses, only much smaller. They are generally less than 34 inches (86 cm) tall.

Cuddles was the foundation's first guide horse in full service. She became 45-year-old Dan Shaw's helper. Shaw has an eye disease that caused his sight to deteriorate. One night, while filling out an application to get a guide dog, Shaw heard a news story on TV about people training horses to guide the blind. Shaw loves horses and wanted a guide animal that would live a long time. He applied, and a year later, Cuddles and Shaw began training as a team.

On a trip to New York, Cuddles helped Shaw safely navigate Times Square, a very busy part of the city at night. The next day, Cuddles calmly rode the elevator with Shaw to the crowded top of the Empire State Building, a famous skyscraper. Cuddles even guided Shaw on the ferry ride to the Statue of Liberty, rode the escalator in a store, and traveled on the subway system.

Shaw says that he feels truly blessed to have Cuddles. He believes that Cuddles has changed his life for the better by giving him more independence and self-reliance.

SKILL PRACTICE Read the item. Write your response.

1. How are guide horses and guide dogs similar?

____

____

2. Describe two qualities that are important in a guide horse. Explain why each quality is essential.

____

____

3. How did people probably react when they saw Shaw and Cuddles in New York City?

____

____

STRATEGY PRACTICE Describe how you visualized Cuddles and Dan Shaw on the city streets.

____

____

READ THE PASSAGE Think about whom the passage is about and what the theme of the story is.

A Musical Prodigy

Imagine knowing at age two what you want to do for the rest of your life. Jay Greenberg, nicknamed "Bluejay" because these birds make a lot of noise for their size, did just that. He has been called the greatest musical talent to come along in 200 years. And all of this praise was said about a teenager!

When Greenberg was just two years old, he started drawing pictures of musical instruments and wrote the word *cello*. His parents got him a cello, and by age three, he was composing music. In 2001, at age ten, he began attending the Juilliard School, one of the world's best music conservatories, in New York City. Within two years, he had composed five symphonies. And by 2009, he had written more than 70 musical compositions for such groups as the New Haven Symphony and the London Symphony Orchestra.

Greenberg is a musical prodigy, or extremely gifted young person. Unlike most kids, he doesn't download music from the Internet; he downloads it from his own mind! When he composes works, he hears them in his head complete, as if an orchestra were playing them. His hero is Beethoven, and for fun, he fools around with classical music compositions, changing and rewriting them. He is completely devoted to his calling, once telling his mother that he would die if he could not compose music.

SKILL PRACTICE Read the item. Write your response.

1. What is the theme of this text?

____

____

2. Name two achievements that made it clear that Greenberg was a musical prodigy.

____

____

3. When do you think Greenberg's parents first realized that he was extremely talented?

____

____

STRATEGY PRACTICE What information in the passage helps you understand why Jay Greenberg is called a prodigy?

____

____

WEEK 11

Author's Purpose

Students identify the author's reason for writing about a subject.

Prediction

Students practice using clues from a passage to predict what will happen next.

DAY 1

Introduce the *Author's Purpose* skill to students. Say: **Authors write for a variety of reasons, including to entertain us with a story, to inform us about a topic, to teach us how to do something, and to persuade us to take action or think a certain way. By understanding the author's purpose, we can better understand the main ideas that the author is trying to convey.** Tell students they are going to read a passage about arts programs in schools. Then remind students of the *Ask Questions* strategy (Week 6). Say: **As you read, ask yourself questions about what you have read, especially if there is anything you don't understand.** Then have students read the instructions at the top of the page and the passage. When students have finished, direct them to complete the skill and strategy practice activities. Review the answers together.

DAY 2

Remind students of the *Author's Purpose* skill, and review the common reasons authors write (to entertain, to inform, to teach, and to persuade). Tell students they are going to read about a way of harvesting rain to deal with drought. Then remind students of the *Make Connections* strategy (Week 2). Say: **As you read, think about what else you have heard or read about water conservation. This will help you better understand what the author is telling you.** Have students read the passage. When students have finished, direct them to complete the skill and strategy practice activities. Review the answers together.

DAY 3

Introduce the *Prediction* skill to students. Say: **When we make a prediction, we use clues from the text and our background knowledge to predict what will likely happen next.** Invite volunteers to share experiences when they were able to successfully predict what would happen. (e.g., A student saw two people walking without looking where they were going and predicted they would run into each other.) Tell students to think about the clues they noticed and the background knowledge they used to make their predictions. Then remind students of the *Ask Questions* strategy. Say: **Asking questions about what you have read is a good way to check that you understood everything in the passage.** Have students read the passage. When students have finished, direct them to complete the skill practice activity. Review the answers together. For the strategy practice activity, pair students or complete it as a group.

DAY 4

Review the *Prediction* skill with students. Then tell students they are going to read about a critically endangered animal. Remind students how to use the *Make Connections* strategy. Say: **As you read, think about what else you have heard or read about other endangered animals.** Then have students read the instructions at the top of the page and the passage. When students have finished reading, direct them to complete the skill and strategy practice activities. Review the answers together.

DAY 5

Tell students that they will practice both the *Author's Purpose* and *Prediction* skills by reading a passage about two boys searching for a special bird. Then remind students of the *Ask Questions* strategy. Say: **Check your comprehension by asking questions as you read. When you think of a good question, write it in the space provided for the strategy practice activity.** Then have students read the passage. When students have finished, direct them to complete the skill and strategy practice activities. Review the answers together, and invite volunteers to share their questions to see if other students can answer them.

Name: ______________________

READ THE PASSAGE Think about why the author wrote the passage.

Don't Cut the Arts

Has the number of art classes at your school been reduced? Did your school cancel next year's play? Have band classes been eliminated? When school budgets are under pressure, the arts always seem to be the first programs that are cut. Classes in painting, drama, dance, and music—as well as after-school arts activities—are often the first to go.

Some people believe that arts funding should be cut. They claim that school performance is measured by standardized test scores, not by a successful arts program. So why shouldn't schools cut arts programs when money is tight?

According to the National Governors' Association (NGA), there are many reasons to preserve the arts in schools. Students exposed to the arts have higher academic achievement and are better at planning and working toward goals. Students who study the arts are:

- four times more likely to get academic awards or win a writing award;
- four times more likely to take part in a math or science fair; and
- more likely to score higher in creative thinking, fluency, and originality.

In their report "The Impact of Arts Education on Workforce Preparation," the governors also observe that schools with strong arts programs have:

- significantly fewer discipline problems;
- less absenteeism; and
- lower dropout rates.

Should we cut the arts in times of economic difficulty? This author says "No!"

SKILL PRACTICE Read the item. Write your response.

1. What is the author's purpose for writing this text?

____

____

2. Why did the author use bulleted lists?

____

____

3. Why did the author quote the National Governors' Association in this text?

____

STRATEGY PRACTICE Write one question you had while reading the passage. If you found the answer, write it, too.

____

____

Name: ____________________

READ THE PASSAGE Think about why the author wrote the passage and what it is mostly about.

Harvesting Rain the Easy Way

As people in the American Southwest become concerned about long periods of drought, many are rediscovering water-harvesting techniques from ancient times. Water harvesting is the capturing, moving, and storing of rainwater for later use, often in landscaping. Rain barrels attached to a roof's downspouts are one low-tech way of harvesting rainwater, but an even simpler and cheaper method is to build *swales* and *berms*.

What are swales? Swales are simply depressions, or low areas, in the ground. They allow rainwater to stay put for a while so that it can soak into the soil. This enables fruit trees, vegetable gardens, and landscape plants to use it as needed. And berms? Berms are raised areas that direct water into swales.

One simple way to create berms and swales is to dig a hole in the soil about a foot deep and pile up that same dirt to create a berm around it. The dirt is then pounded down to form a sturdy wall around the swale. Doing this over and over can create a whole network of berms and swales. Boomerang-shaped berms can direct water toward trees or other plants. Repeating serpentine-shaped berms can provide the water needed to turn a barren slope into a beautiful garden. And it's easier than you think. Once again, a low-tech approach works just fine! Just gather your friends, provide plenty of lemonade and music, and have a swale-stomping dance party in your yard.

SKILL PRACTICE Read the item. Write your response.

1. What is the author's purpose for writing this text?

2. Does the author think that berms and swales are useful for irrigation? Cite text evidence in your response.

3. What possible problem can you foresee with the use of swales?

STRATEGY PRACTICE Explain why some people, according to the author, are concerned about conserving fresh water. Is this a concern where you live?

READ THE PASSAGE Look for clues in the passage that help you figure out what will happen next.

The Dog Hoser

The United States has been the birthplace of thousands of important inventions, from the incandescent light bulb to the computer mouse. However, the U.S. has also seen the birth of thousands of wacky and even ridiculous inventions. One example of an odd invention is the dog hoser.

Grooming a dog at home can be difficult. Many dog owners don't have the tools or knowledge needed to properly cut an animal's fur. For these reasons, some dog owners take their animals to professional groomers for haircuts. After groomers cut a dog's fur, they often use a vacuum cleaner to remove the cut fur from the pet's coat. This is where the real trouble starts. Many dogs are terrified of the strange machine and its scary noise.

To solve the problem, one creative inventor designed a vacuum cleaner dogs might actually like. The dog hoser is a vacuum cleaner that looks just like a dog.

Dog-shaped, with a vacuum cleaner hidden in its belly, the dog hoser looks like a furry pal. Its sound is muffled, and the hose is disguised as the dog's tail. It may look like a new friend, but what do you think happens when the groomer pulls out the dog hoser's tail and starts sweeping it across the dog's body?

After trying one in his shop, one dog groomer said, "My client's expensive poodle cowered in fear when I used it." A month later, the client reported that her dog was still afraid of interacting with other dogs.

SKILL PRACTICE Read the item. Write your response.

1. Does the dog hoser cut into professional dog groomers' business? Defend your stance.

____

____

2. What do you predict will happen with the dog hoser invention?

____

____

3. Why did the author include a quote from a dog groomer?

____

____

STRATEGY PRACTICE Write a question about information from the passage. Then ask a partner to answer it.

____

____

Name: ______________________

READ THE PASSAGE Use clues from the passage to predict what will likely happen next to the California condor.

Back from the Brink of Extinction

The California condor is not a handsome bird. Its featherless scalp is a shocking pink-orange. Its feeding habits—feasting on the flesh of dead animals—should not be mentioned at the dinner table. So why do naturalists at Arizona's Grand Canyon want to protect this bird?

These huge vultures were once found across North America from Mexico to Canada. But by 1982, only 22 existed in the world and the species faced extinction. By 1985, only nine California condors remained.

Because the loss of one species can affect a whole ecosystem, naturalists sprang into action. They decided to capture the remaining condors to begin a captive breeding program. As females produced eggs, some eggs were removed and raised by people, using a hand puppet that looked like a condor head. This was done to keep chicks from imprinting on humans, or thinking humans were their parents. Naturalists wanted the chicks to feel safe with other condors, not with humans.

The captive population increased dramatically. Then, beginning in 1992, newly bred chicks were released into the wild. In 1996, two males and four females were released 30 miles north of the Grand Canyon. In 2004, the first condor that had been hatched and raised in Arizona in more than a century took flight. Although it died in 2006, others have since hatched and taken flight. Today, around 80 California condors soar majestically above northern Arizona's canyon country.

SKILL PRACTICE Read the item. Write your response.

1. What would probably have happened to the condors without the captive breeding program?

____

____

2. What might occur if a condor chick imprinted on a human?

____

____

3. Predict what is likely to happen to the California condor in the future.

____

____

STRATEGY PRACTICE What other animals do the California condors remind you of? Why?

____

____

READ THE PASSAGE Think about why the author wrote the passage, and use the clues in the passage to predict what will likely happen next.

A Wild Flamingo Chase

Rodney read the headline in the local paper: "Flamingo Flocks to Fern Fields." An exotic bird had found its way to his small California town. It was a flamingo, the report said, a real one—not like the faded plastic version planted in Rodney's neighbor's yard. The town didn't even have a zoo, so this news was really exciting. But where was the bird? Rodney thought it would stick out like a sore thumb.

Only one man in town claimed to have seen the wild bird, in a wetland park on the outskirts of town. He described the flamingo's pink feathers and said it stood approximately 3 feet (0.9 m) tall. He also said the flamingo did not seem sick or hurt.

Rodney thought the story sounded suspicious, though, so he decided to go on a flamingo-finding expedition. He also decided to take his best friend, Paul, with him. "If we find it," Rodney said, "we can write a report on protecting wild species." The boys assembled their gear—tall rubber boots, binoculars, and a camera. They packed some peanut butter sandwiches, too. Then they set out for the wetlands.

With boots up to their thighs, Rodney and Paul trudged through muck and mud for what seemed like an eternity, but they never spotted the flamingo. Finally the sun began to set, and a cold wind cut through the boys' jackets. Rodney and Paul decided to head home.

As they turned onto Paul's dark street, they saw Paul's mom waiting on the porch. Paul dragged his feet up the driveway. His mother put her arm on his shoulder, and the two went inside.

Rodney continued down the street toward his house, past his neighbor's yard and that ridiculous plastic pink flamingo. "Great," Rodney thought, "now they have a pair." Out of the corner of his eye, Rodney saw something move.

SKILL PRACTICE Read the item. Write your response.

1. What is the author's purpose for writing this text?

____

____

2. What will Paul probably tell his mother?

____

____

3. What is apt to happen next? How do you know?

____

STRATEGY PRACTICE Write a question you thought of while you read the passage.

____

WEEK 12

Nonfiction Text Features

Students practice identifying and comprehending common features of nonfiction text.

Visual Information

Students examine and evaluate information that is depicted visually.

DAY 1

To introduce the *Nonfiction Text Features* skill to students, point out the title and boldfaced glossary entries on the student page. Say: **Nonfiction writing often includes text features that are not part of the main body of text but still contain important information about the topic. Good readers know how to use these features to help them understand what they read.** Tell students they are going to read pages from a glossary about African instruments. Then remind students of the *Determine Important Information* strategy (Week 5). Say: **As you read, look for the features that make a glossary different from other nonfiction texts.** Then have students read the instructions at the top of the page and the passage. When students have finished, direct them to complete the skill and strategy practice activities. Review the answers together.

DAY 2

Remind students how paying attention to nonfiction text features can aid comprehension. Have students identify some of the features of a table of contents. (title, chapter titles, page numbers, etc.) Ask: **What does a table of contents tell us?** (the type of information that can be found in a book and the page numbers where chapters start) Tell students they will read the table of contents for a book on video games. Then remind students of the *Organization* strategy (Week 4). Say: **As you read, notice how the chapters in the book are organized.** When students have finished reading the table of contents, direct them to complete the skill and strategy practice activities. Review the answers together.

DAY 3

Introduce the *Visual Information* skill to students. Say: **Not all information is delivered in the form of words. Pictures, graphs, and other visual media can present information, as well.** Point out the population pyramid graph on the student page and say: **Graphs are a good way to show information about numbers in a visual way.** Tell students they are going to read about a type of visual information called a population pyramid. Then remind students of the *Determine Important Information* strategy. Say: **As you study the population pyramid graph, pay attention to the labels, numbers, and text to the left of the graph. This will help you better understand what you are looking at and what is most important.** When students have finished reading the passage and studying the graph, direct them to complete the skill and strategy practice activities. Review the answers together.

DAY 4

Review the *Visual Information* skill with students. Say: **Information can be shown and understood with pictures, graphs, diagrams, and other visual media. Knowing how to interpret and understand visual information is an important part of being a good reader.** Tell students they are going to read a passage and study a graph about languages spoken around the world. Then remind students of the *Organization* strategy. Say: **As you study the graph, pay attention to how the information is organized.** Have students read the passage and study the graph. When students have finished, direct them to complete the skill and strategy practice activities.

DAY 5

Tell students they will read a passage and study a diagram about the eye in order to practice both the *Nonfiction Text Features* and *Visual Information* skills. Remind students of the *Determine Important Information* strategy. Say: **Pay attention to words with special treatment. Think about why these words look different from the other words around them and why they might be important.** When students have finished reading, direct them to complete the skill and strategy practice activities. Review the answers together.

Name: ______________________________

READ THE GLOSSARY Pay attention to the important features on the page.

African Instrument Glossary

Mbila: (m-BIL-uh) A wooden xylophone played by striking planks with a rubber mallet. Shells mounted under the wooden boards amplify the sounds. These instruments can be several feet long and can be played by two or more musicians at one time. (Origin: Mozambique)

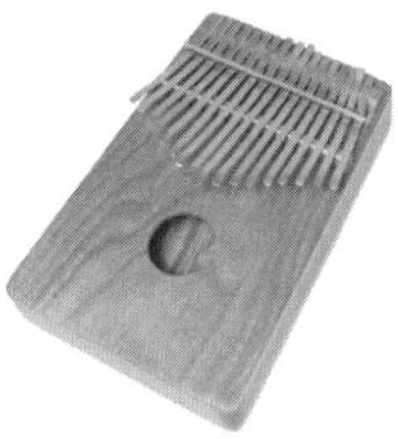

Mbira: (m-BIR-uh) A hand-held piano with 22 to 28 metal keys attached to a wooden board that amplifies the sounds made by plucking the keys with the thumbs. Modern mbiras often use recycled materials for the keys, such as furniture springs or bicycle spokes. Bottle caps, shells, or other objects are attached to the wooden board. They create a buzz that adds depth to the sound and increases volume. (Origin: Eastern and Southern Africa)

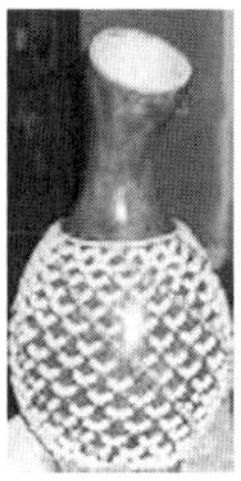

Shekere: (shay-KUH-ray) A percussion instrument made out of a dried gourd covered with a beaded net. Most shekeres are held in two hands. Players shake, twist, drop, or slap the instrument to create rhythmic sounds. (Origin: Nigeria)

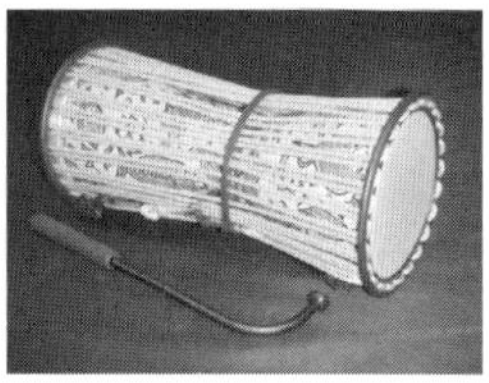

Talking Drum: A two-headed drum that is shaped like an hourglass and can produce a wide variety of pitches. The drum's heads are made of goat, lizard, or fish skin that is stretched over wooden hoops. The two heads are connected by leather cords. Holding the drum under one arm, the player squeezes the cords to change the drum's pitch. Notes are played by striking the heads with a special stick. The instrument is called a talking drum because it can be used to reproduce the sounds of spoken language. (Origin: Nigeria and Ghana)

SKILL PRACTICE Read the item. Write your response.

1. In what ways are the mbila and mbira similar?

____

____

2. Describe how a musician holds a talking drum.

____

____

3. Which instrument's name is pronounced with two long vowel sounds? How can you tell?

____

STRATEGY PRACTICE How is the first sentence in each glossary entry important?

____

____

Name: ______________________________

READ THE TABLE OF CONTENTS Pay attention to how the table of contents is organized.

A Beginner's Guide to Video Game Design

TABLE OF CONTENTS

SKILL PRACTICE Read the item. Write your response.

1. In which chapter would you look to find the definition of role-playing games?

____

2. If you were writing a report about how physics influences video games, to which page would turn? How do you know?

____

____

3. Explain the reasoning behind the Part Four section title.

____

____

STRATEGY PRACTICE Why do you think this book is divided into four parts?

____

____

Name: ______________________________

READ THE PASSAGE Look at the information presented in the graph.

Population Pyramids

How can you see an entire population at once? More than a quarter billion people live in the United States. That's a large number to understand, but statistics can give an overall view of the population's characteristics. A population pyramid is a graph used to show how an area's population is divided into ages and genders. Each bar in a population pyramid represents the percentage of the male or female U.S. population in a specific age range.

The shape of a population pyramid gives information about a population, too. For example, a pyramid that is wider on top than it is on the bottom means that there are more older people than young people. Reasons for this pattern might include a low birth rate, a high death rate among young people due to wars or disease, or the increase in the nation's young people moving to other countries. Similarly, a pyramid that is heavier on the bottom means there are more young people than old.

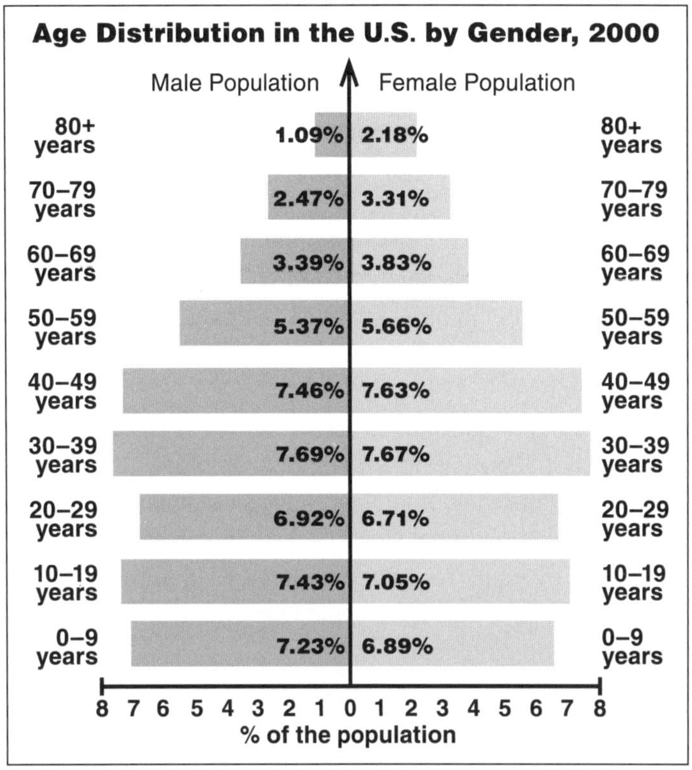

SKILL PRACTICE Read the item. Write your response.

1. *There are more females than males in their thirties.* Use the graph to prove this statement true or false.

____

____

2. Draw a conclusion based on your comparison of the 10–19 age group with the 40–49 age group.

____

____

3. In which age group are there twice as many females as males? What are the actual percentages?

____

____

STRATEGY PRACTICE According to the passage, why is the shape of a population pyramid significant?

____

____

Name: ______________________________

READ THE PASSAGE Think about what the information tells you.

Top Five Languages Spoken Worldwide

There are over 6,800 distinct languages spoken on Earth. But which languages are spoken by the most people? And which language is spoken in the most countries?

According to people who study language, Mandarin is spoken by more people than any other language. It is the most common language spoken in China, which is the country with the largest population.

Although Mandarin is spoken by the greatest number of people, English is spoken in more countries than any other language. The United States has the largest English-speaking population, followed by India, Nigeria, the United Kingdom, and Germany. This includes people who speak English as a second language.

Other languages with many speakers include Hindi and Urdu, which are forms of the same language, Hindustani. They are official languages in India, Pakistan, and Fiji. Spanish is the official language in most of Latin America and South America. Arabic, which is spoken in most Middle Eastern and North African countries, is the fifth most common language. It is an official language in 16 countries.

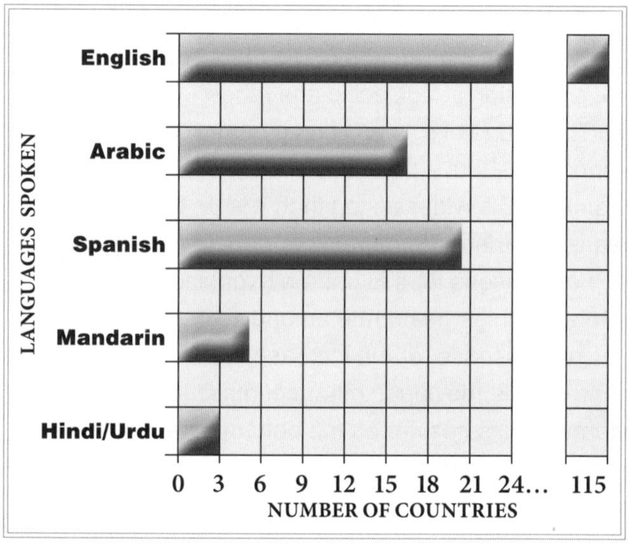

SKILL PRACTICE Read the item. Write your response.

1. Which language in this graph is spoken in the fewest number of countries?

____

2. According to the text, which country has the second-largest English-speaking population?

____

____

3. Draw a conclusion about why Mandarin is spoken by more people than English when English is spoken in 115 countries.

____

STRATEGY PRACTICE Describe how the information in the graph is organized.

____

____

Name: ______________________

READ THE PASSAGE Study the passage and the diagram.

The Way We See

Light rays enter the eye through the transparent **cornea**. The rays then pass through the **pupil,** which changes size to adjust to different light levels. The pupil dilates, or becomes bigger, in dark rooms and will contract, or become smaller, in brightly lit places.

The **iris** is the colored part of the eye, and it controls the opening and closing of the pupil. Irises can be blue, green, brown, gray, or hazel.

The **lens** focuses the light rays on the retina. The **retina** is tissue at the back of the eye that is sensitive to light. Nerves in the retina convert light energy into electrical energy, which is sent along the **optic nerve** to the brain. The brain interprets the electrical energy as an image.

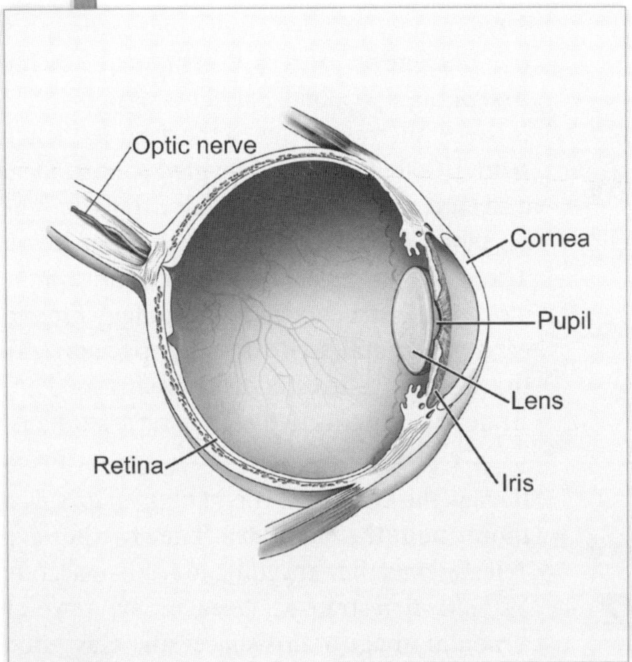

SKILL PRACTICE Read the item. Write your response.

1. What do the diagram labels identify?

____

____

2. Why are there boldfaced words in the text?

____

____

3. Which parts of the human eye are located behind the lens?

____

STRATEGY PRACTICE List two important facts about the pupil.

____

____

WEEK 13

Main Idea and Details

Students look for the central idea or message of a passage or story. They also find details that best support the main idea.

Sequence

Students look for the order of events or steps in a process.

DAY 1

Review the *Main Idea and Details* skill with students. Say: **Writers do not always state the main idea of a passage or paragraph explicitly. You have to infer what the main idea is.** Model by reading the first paragraph aloud. Say: **This paragraph is introducing the sea wasp.** On the board, write: "The sea wasp of Australia is one of the deadliest jellyfish in the world." Say: **I took the most important details from the sentences and formed a main idea statement. To help you monitor your comprehension and find the main idea, pause after you read each paragraph and ask yourself, *What is this paragraph mostly about?* Check to see if your main idea matches the details in the paragraphs.** Then remind students of the *Monitor Comprehension* strategy (Week 1). Ask for a volunteer to read aloud the instructions for the strategy practice activity. Then say: **As you think of the main idea for each paragraph, write it in the space provided for the strategy practice activity.** Have students read the passage. When students have finished, invite volunteers to share the sentences they wrote for the strategy practice activity. Then have students complete the skill practice activity.

DAY 2

Review the concept of the *Main Idea and Details* skill with students by saying: **Good details tell us more about the main idea. They further explain what the author wants you to know about a topic.** Tell students they are going to read an account of an unusual spacewalk. Then remind students of the *Visualization* strategy (Week 3). Say: **As you look for good details, notice which ones help you make a mental image of this spacewalk.** Have students read the passage. When students have finished, direct them to complete the skill and strategy practice activities. Review the answers together.

DAY 3

Remind students of the importance of paying attention to sequence in a passage. Say: **By understanding sequence, we can understand nonfiction texts that tell the history of someone or something. As you read this passage about a sport called *skeleton,* pay attention to the dates mentioned in the passage. Dates usually indicate when something important happened.** Then remind students of the *Monitor Comprehension* strategy. Read aloud the instructions for the strategy practice activity. Say: **Taking good notes to monitor your comprehension includes summarizing main ideas or significant events from a passage.** Tell students to write notes in the space provided for the strategy practice activity as they read the passage. Have students read the passage. When students have finished, direct them to complete the skill practice activity. Review the answers together, and invite volunteers to share the notes they took while reading.

DAY 4

Review the *Sequence* skill with students. Say: **The plot in a work of fiction is usually told sequentially. By understanding sequence, you can better understand what happens in a story and when it happens.** Tell students they are going to read a folk tale. Then remind students of the *Visualization* strategy. Say: **As you read, look for vivid verbs and adjectives that help you picture what is happening.** Have students read the passage. When students have finished, direct them to complete the skill and strategy practice activities. Review the answers together.

DAY 5

Tell students they will practice both the *Main Idea and Details* and *Sequence* skills. Remind students of the *Monitor Comprehension* strategy. Say: **Rereading is a good way to monitor your comprehension and make sure you understood the main ideas and sequence of a passage. After you finish reading this passage, read it again to make sure you did not miss anything important.** Have students read the passage. When students have finished, direct them to complete the skill and strategy practice activities. Review the answers together.

Name: ____________________

READ THE PASSAGE Think about the main idea of each paragraph.

Deadly in the Water

Jellyfish can be beautiful to look at as they float gracefully in the sea. But most jellyfish have a painful sting, and one variety of jellyfish is considered the most dangerous living creature in the world. This creature, the sea wasp of Australia, can kill a large fish or even a human in minutes.

Sea wasps aren't the biggest jellyfish, but they can grow as large as a basketball. They have up to 60 long tentacles. The tentacles can dangle 15 feet (4.6 m) down into the water and are loaded with thousands of stinging cells. When the sea wasp's tentacles brush up against an animal, chemicals on the animal's skin trigger the release of the sea wasp's venom. The venom affects the nerves and heart of the prey. Usually the sea wasp uses its venom on fish, which it then eats. But sometimes humans are unlucky enough to come into contact with a sea wasp's tentacles. These victims can suffer excruciating pain, nausea, breathing problems, and occasionally even death.

Australians have developed an antivenom to treat the sea wasp's stings. Like the antivenom used for poisonous snake bites, it counteracts the poison from the sting. But there is an easier, although very unusual way to avoid stings in the first place. Australian lifeguards and surfers often wear women's pantyhose on their arms and legs! This thin layer of nylon prevents sea wasps from touching people's skin, which keeps the tentacles from releasing their venom.

SKILL PRACTICE Read the item. Write your response.

1. How do sea wasps attack their prey?

____

____

2. Why does the author include the definition of *antivenom* in the text?

____

____

3. What do Australian lifeguards do to protect themselves from the sea wasps?

____

____

STRATEGY PRACTICE In your own words, write a sentence that tells the main idea of each paragraph.

____

____

____

READ THE PASSAGE Look for good details that help you picture events from the passage.

Rain in Space?

One of the most thrilling and dangerous jobs of an astronaut is the spacewalk—leaving a spacecraft and floating in space while connected to the craft by a tether. One astronaut, Alexander Kaleri, took a spacewalk that was even more exciting and perilous than he had planned. On February 26, 2004, Kaleri and Commander Mike Foale were at the International Space Station in orbit around Earth. They planned to leave the space station to perform a list of repairs and experiments. It was the 52nd spacewalk at the space station.

At 4:17 PM, the hatch of the docking module opened, and the men began their spacewalk. The astronauts had five hours to complete their work.

Everything proceeded normally until 7:23 PM. At that time, Kaleri reported to Mission Control that there was water inside his spacesuit, saying, "I have rain inside the helmet. I have water inside the visor." He also reported that the water was "quite some amount, a significant amount. It felt like rain."

Immediately, officials on the ground grew worried. They found that a cooling device in the suit was not working correctly. They ordered the astronauts to return quickly to the space station, and by 8:12, the two men were back inside. It was the first spacesuit malfunction on a spacewalk—but it ended happily, with both astronauts safe and unhurt.

SKILL PRACTICE Read the item. Write your response.

1. What would be a better title for this text?

____

____

2. About how long did the February 26, 2004, spacewalk last? Explain how you know.

____

____

3. What went wrong with Kaleri's spacesuit?

____

____

STRATEGY PRACTICE Write details from the passage that were easy to visualize.

____

____

____

READ THE PASSAGE Pay attention to dates and important events described in the passage.

Skeleton on the Ice

Zooming downhill on a sled can be incredibly thrilling. But what if you were going 80 mph (129 kph)? That's how fast the world's best competitors go in the sport of skeleton.

Skeleton competitors wear tight, stretchy uniforms that help lower wind resistance. They also wear helmets and goggles for protection. They need this special equipment for speed and safety while zipping down an icy track with hairpin turns.

Each skeleton sled holds one person. To take off, the athlete sprints as fast as possible, pushing the sled. Then the slider dives headfirst onto the sled, lying on his or her stomach. There is no steering or brakes on a skeleton. The slider steers the skeleton by shifting his or her body weight.

Skeleton began in 1892 in St. Moritz, Switzerland. Toboggans, which are long wooden sleds, were already popular, but the early skeleton sled was made mostly of metal. It looked like a skeleton, which may be how the sport got its name. The first skeleton race occurred in 1905. In 1928, when the Olympics were held in St. Moritz, skeleton became an Olympic sport. An American, Jennison Heaton, won the gold medal. The Olympics included skeleton again in 1948.

In 2000, the sport underwent another change when women began competing at the World Championships. The sport was part of the Olympics once again at the 2002 Games in Salt Lake City, Utah, when it became a permanent part of the winter Olympics. This dangerous sport with the spooky name is now practiced on a competitive level by men and women in 30 countries.

SKILL PRACTICE Read the item. Write your response.

1. How does an athlete start his or her skeleton run?

____

____

2. What happened to the sport of skeleton in 2002?

____

____

3. *The sport of skeleton was invented in 1905.* Prove this statement true or false using information from the text.

____

____

STRATEGY PRACTICE As you read, write down notes that tell you about the history of the sport of skeleton.

____

____

Name: ________________________

Sequence **WEEK 13 DAY 4**

READ THE PASSAGE Pay attention to what happens in the passage and when it happens.

The Greedy Tiger and the Big Wind

Long ago, the rains did not fall, and there was a terrible drought. It was hard to find food, and the animals became hungry and thirsty. Only one tree had fruit. It was a big, beautiful pear tree that grew in the middle of a field. Its roots reached deep into the earth, where they drank from an underground spring. Its pears were plump and juicy. The tree, however, was guarded by a cruel and greedy tiger. Although he couldn't possibly eat all the fruit that the tree provided, Tiger wouldn't let any of the other animals touch the pears.

The desperate animals went to Rabbit and asked for help. Rabbit helped them form a plan. Then he went to Tiger and said, "Tiger, a great wind is coming. It will be so strong that it will blow everyone off the earth!" While Rabbit talked to Tiger, the birds, which were hidden in the forest, began to flap their wings wildly, creating a strong breeze. Next, other animals beat on the ground and swung through the trees, causing the trees to sway and shake. Tiger believed that the great wind had come, and he was terrified.

"I will tie you down with rope so the wind cannot blow you away," Rabbit offered. Tiger agreed, and Rabbit tied him tightly to a tree. Finally, Rabbit called the other animals, who came out of the forest and ate every delicious pear on the tree, laughing at the selfish tiger who watched helplessly.

SKILL PRACTICE Read the item. Write your response.

1. Why do the other animals probably agree to participate in Rabbit's plan?

____

____

2. Why did it take all of the animals working together to trick Tiger?

____

____

3. What is the moral of this folk tale?

____

____

STRATEGY PRACTICE List the words or phrases from the passage that helped you visualize the details.

____

____

____

READ THE PASSAGE Look for good details that support the main idea. Also, look at the order of important events mentioned in the passage.

Dinosaur Buddies

Triceratops, the plant-eating dinosaur with three horns on its head, was long considered a solitary animal. Fossils for more than fifty adult triceratops have been found, and each triceratops was found with no other triceratops nearby.

Scientists revised their theory of the lone triceratops in 2005, though. In southeastern Montana, they discovered a site that contained triceratops fossils embedded in rocks that were 66 million years old. The person who found the site named it the Homer site, after Homer Simpson from the television show *The Simpsons,* because the plodding dinosaurs reminded the scientist of the cartoon character.

At the Homer site, paleontologists, or scientists who study fossils, found a group of three young triceratops fossils. It was evident to the paleontologists that the fossils were not found together by chance. The scientists deduced that the bodies of the juvenile dinosaurs had been deposited by a flood and that they were part of a herd of young triceratops that lived together.

Paleontologists admit they don't know how much time the young triceratops spent together, or even why they were in a group. The scientists believe the animals might have banded together for protection. The young of other similar dinosaurs have been proven to have lived in herds. Based on this finding, the scientists concluded that young triceratops probably lived in herds as well. They expect to find still more fossils of young triceratops at the Homer site.

SKILL PRACTICE Read the item. Write your response.

1. Why do paleontologists believe that young triceratops may have lived in herds?

____

____

2. How did paleontologists develop their original theory about triceratops? Cite text evidence in your response.

____

____

3. What killed the triceratops whose fossils were found in 2005?

____

____

STRATEGY PRACTICE Write two details that support paleontologists' theory about young triceratops.

____

____

WEEK
14

Cause and Effect

Students practice identifying cause-and-effect relationships by looking for what happens (the effect) and why it happens (the cause).

Evaluate Evidence

Students practice evaluating evidence by identifying the author's main idea and examining the evidence the author uses to support that idea.

DAY 1

Review the *Cause and Effect* skill with students. Say: **An effect is something that happens. The cause is why the effect happened. Some causes can have multiple effects, and some effects come from multiple causes.** Tell students they will read about what causes smells and how they affect people differently. Then remind students of the *Determine Important Information* strategy (Week 5). Say: **As you read, look for the important information that helps you understand the cause-and-effect relationships.** Then have students read the instructions at the top of the page and the passage. When students have finished reading, direct them to complete the skill and strategy practice activities. Review the answers together.

DAY 2

Review the *Cause and Effect* skill with students. Tell them they are going to read an excerpt of a girl's cooking journal. Say: **Sometimes you might read only the cause or effect of something and have to infer the rest of the cause-and-effect relationship. You have to think actively about what is happening and why it happens.** Then remind students of the *Ask Questions* strategy (Week 6). Say: **As you read, think of questions you have about Carole or her experiences in the Cooking Club.** Have students read the passage. When students have finished, direct them to complete the skill and strategy practice activities. Review the answers together.

DAY 3

Review the *Evaluate Evidence* skill with students. Say: **Writers include details, sometimes called *evidence,* to support their main ideas, sometimes called *claims.*** Model by saying: **If I made the statement that lemons and limes contain vitamin C, that would be a claim. If I told you how scientists know what is inside fruits and vegetables, that would be part of the evidence to support my claim.** Tell students they are going to read about identical twins. Then remind students of the *Determine Important Information* strategy. Say: **As you read, look for important information that provides evidence in support of each main idea, or claim.** When students have finished reading, direct them to complete the skill and strategy practice activities. Review the answers together.

DAY 4

Tell students that sometimes the people we are reading about make claims and support those claims with evidence. Then tell students they will read about a science topic that has been investigated for many years. Review the *Ask Questions* strategy. Say: **By asking questions as we read, we remember our purpose for reading, which can help us stay focused and interested. Think about what you know and want to know about conducting science experiments. As you read, write a question in the space provided for the strategy activity. As you continue reading, look for the answer to the question.** Then direct students to read the passage and complete the skill and strategy practice activities. Review the answers together, and allow volunteers to share the questions they wrote.

DAY 5

Tell students they will practice the *Cause and Effect* skill with the *Evaluate Evidence* skill as they read a passage about mosquitoes. Say: **As you read, look for causes and effects, and evaluate the evidence that the writer gives to support her claims.** Then remind students of the *Determine Important Information* strategy. Say: **Look for the information that you think offers the strongest evidence to support the writer's claims.** Have students read the passage. When students have finished, direct them to complete the skill and strategy practice activities. Review the answers together.

READ THE PASSAGE Look for causes and effects that explain our ability to smell things.

Get a Whiff of This

A fresh rose, a puddle of gasoline, or a trash bin of rotting garbage—you know it when you smell it! But where do smells come from? Odors are chemicals found in tiny molecules that float in the air. Anything with a smell, whether it is minty toothpaste or a moldy bathmat, sends off a mixture of these tiny molecules. When they reach your nose, you inhale and some of the chemicals reach nerve cells in your nasal cavity. Nerves send the message to your brain: "Something smells in here!"

Not everyone reacts to smells in the same way. Some people are very sensitive to specific smells, and others can hardly smell anything at all. Researchers have discovered that our ability to detect odors is genetic, which means that it is passed on from parents to their children. Every person recognizes smells differently.

Strong smells linger because the chemicals do not change easily. One of the most pungent aromas known is that of a skunk's spray. Getting rid of the smell on a person or dog that has been sprayed can be quite difficult. Some traditional methods, such as bathing in tomato juice, only mask the odor. Other mixtures, such as a mixture of hydrogen peroxide and baking soda, work better because they actually change the chemical composition of the odor molecules. But they can't neutralize the smell completely. Wetness can bring out a smell that you thought you had gotten rid of. So, a dog might smell OK when its fur has dried after a bath, but when it starts to rain, you might need to hold your nose again!

SKILL PRACTICE Read the item. Write your response.

1. What causes odors?

____

____

2. Why do different people react differently to the same odor?

____

____

3. What is the only way to actually neutralize an odor?

____

____

STRATEGY PRACTICE Explain which information in the passage is most important to understand for knowing how to deal with skunk spray.

____

____

READ THE JOURNAL Think about the causes for the effects you read about.

Carole's Cooking Journal

Monday, April 6
This month, we had to choose an optional activity to do during last period. Should it really be called "optional" if you have to do it? Unfortunately, I waited until the last minute to sign up. Many of the activities were already full, but I decided to join the Cooking Club because at least that way I would get a snack to eat.

Tuesday, April 7
Like many of my ideas, joining the Cooking Club made sense at first but is turning out to be a disaster. Most people have been in the club for more than a year, so they already know what they're doing. And since they all know each other, they aren't exactly interested in a newcomer.

Thursday, April 9
How was I supposed to know that if a recipe says to beat cookie batter, you're not supposed to do it with your fists? I thought the other kids would never stop laughing. And it's not easy to get cookie batter off your clothes.

Friday, April 10
More fun in Cooking Club. Now I know that chocolate mousse is a dessert and it isn't spelled m-o-o-s-e. "Mousse" and "moose" sound exactly the same. So I don't think my question about whether vegetarians can eat chocolate mousse was really that silly.

Monday, April 13
One of my bright ideas worked out for a change! Everyone laughed when I handed out the chocolate "moose" cookies that I made yesterday, but this time I was laughing, too. The peanut butter antlers were a huge hit. We're even planning to make another batch for the bake sale next week.

SKILL PRACTICE Read the item. Write your response.

1. Why did Carole join the cooking group?

____

____

2. What idea did Carole have that proved to be a "hit" with the other members of the club?

____

____

3. Why did Carole beat the cookie batter with her fists?

____

STRATEGY PRACTICE Write one question about Carole that you thought of while reading the journal.

____

Name: ________________________________

READ THE PASSAGE Look for evidence that supports the author's main ideas, or claims.

How Identical Is Identical?

Everyone knows that identical twins look alike, right? Not quite. Although it may be very hard to tell identical twins apart, no two people are exactly the same—even identical twins.

Identical twins develop from the same fertilized egg, so they share the same genes. Genes contain the information that determines people's physical traits. While most people have their own unique set of genetic instructions, identical twins are unusual because they both have the same set. But researchers have discovered that those instructions do not tell the entire story. The environment in which each twin grows and develops also affects many aspects of their physical appearance and personality. Even small differences can have considerable effects.

Fingerprints are a good example. One might assume that identical twins have the same fingerprints. But detectives have known for many years that this is not the case. Like snowflakes, no two fingerprints are alike. Unique patterns on the tips of the fingers appear as the child develops in the womb. While genetic instructions are the primary influence on fingerprint patterns, researchers have discovered other factors that also have an impact. The rate of bone growth, or environmental factors such as pressure in the mother's womb and contact with fluid, can also affect the developing twins' fingerprint patterns. So even though two twins grow next to each other in the womb, they experience slightly different environments. As a result, they develop slightly different fingerprints.

SKILL PRACTICE Read the item. Write your response.

1. Cite text evidence that proves that before identical twins are born, they can develop differences.

____

____

2. Name what identical twins share in common. Be specific.

____

____

3. *The amount of noise a fetus is subjected to can affect his or her fingerprints.* Prove this statement true or false.

____

____

STRATEGY PRACTICE In paragraph 3, the author says that fingerprints are a "good example." What are they a good example of? Why?

____

____

Name: ______________________________

Evaluate Evidence

READ THE PASSAGE Look for the reasons the author gives to prove the claims he makes.

Mixing Ice Cream and Science

Erasto Mpemba took a cooking class at a high school in Tanzania in 1963. The class was making ice cream by boiling milk and sugar together and then freezing the mixture. Erasto put his mixture in the freezer right away; the other students waited until the mixture cooled. To his surprise, his hot ice cream froze faster than his classmates' cool mixtures! A teacher told him he must be confused. But then the teacher tried it and got the same result. Scientists call this strange phenomenon the Mpemba Effect.

In 2008, Olivia Mangino tried to demonstrate Erasto's result for a science fair at her school in New Zealand. However, she didn't have any details about what he had done. How much milk and sugar? What kind of pot? What size freezer? She had so many questions! She mixed the milk and sugar and poured it into two labeled bowls. She heated the Hot bowl in the microwave oven and left the Cool bowl as it was. She put both in the freezer and checked the temperature of each mixture every hour. Neither one froze. She tried again, using a different beater to mix the ingredients and a different freezer. This time, the cooler mixture froze, but the hot mixture did not. She concluded that many factors might affect freezing time.

Later, Olivia read about other people's experiments. In one, a metal container froze the mixture faster than a plastic container. In another, the hot mixture was still close to the boiling point and the cool mixture was close to the freezing point. Olivia's temperatures had been much closer together.

Scientists have proven that it is possible for water-based liquids to freeze faster when they start hotter. But they still don't know why. There are many factors that affect the result. They are probably having a delicious time trying to figure out the right combination!

SKILL PRACTICE Read the item. Write your response.

1. What evidence made the teacher believe Erasto's claim?

____

____

2. Why did the teacher probably have more success with the experiment than Olivia did?

____

____

3. What evidence led Olivia to her conclusion?

____

STRATEGY PRACTICE Write another question that Olivia might have wondered about as she set up her experiments.

____

____

READ THE PASSAGE Look for cause-and-effect relationships that the author describes. Think about the evidence that the author gives to support her claims.

What Mosquitoes Like About You

Do you ever feel like mosquitoes single you out in a crowd? Do you think your blood must be extra tasty because you're the one who always gets bitten when no one else does? It turns out that mosquitoes do have preferences, but it isn't tasty blood that attracts them to their target. It's all about how easy a person is to find. Mosquito expert Susan Paskewitz explains that "the main things are how you smell and how warm you are."

Two scents that are particularly attractive to mosquitoes are carbon dioxide and lactic acid. Both of these chemicals are produced when you breathe or sweat. So, when you exercise, mosquitoes may zoom after you. That's because exercising causes your muscles to build up lactic acid. Also, your sweat emits carbon dioxide, and your body temperature increases. But not everyone produces carbon dioxide and lactic acid at the same rate. Some people produce higher levels, so they are more likely to attract mosquitoes.

Even your sense of style can affect whether or not you get bitten. Mosquitoes use color to decide where to land, and they prefer dark colors. Wearing a black or dark blue T-shirt is a good way to turn yourself into a giant target for mosquitoes. Wear white, and they might fly right by.

SKILL PRACTICE Read the item. Write your response.

1. Why are mosquitoes especially drawn to people who are exercising?

____

____

2. Why did the author quote Susan Paskewitz?

____

____

3. Name two things you can do to help prevent being bitten by mosquitoes.

____

____

STRATEGY PRACTICE What information does the author give as evidence of which senses mosquitoes use to find their prey?

____

____

WEEK 15

Compare and Contrast

Students practice comparing and contrasting by looking at the similarities and differences between two or more people or things.

Make Inferences

Students practice making inferences by using clues in a passage to understand what is being implied or inferred.

DAY 1

Review the *Compare and Contrast* skill with students. Say: **When we compare and contrast, we look at how two or more things are alike and different.** Tell students they are going to read about two superheroes. Then remind students of the *Make Connections* strategy (Week 2). Say: **As you read this passage, think about other superheroes you know about. Think of how those superheroes are similar to and different from the superheroes in this passage.** Then have students read the instructions at the top of the page before they read the passage. When students have finished reading, direct them to complete the skill and strategy practice activities. Review the answers together.

DAY 2

Remind students of the *Compare and Contrast* skill. Then tell students they are going to read about different types of volcanoes. Say: **Scientists classify volcanoes based on the differences between how they form and how they erupt. Pay attention to these differences as you read.** Then remind students of the *Monitor Comprehension* strategy (Week 1). Say: **A good way to monitor your comprehension is to annotate, or mark up, the passage. As you read, underline three ideas that you think are important to remember.** When students have finished reading, direct them to complete the skill practice activity. Review the answers together. For the second part of the strategy practice activity, pair students or complete it as a group.

DAY 3

Review the *Make Inferences* skill with students. Say: **When we make an inference, we use clues from the passage and our background knowledge to figure out information that is not directly stated in the passage.** Tell students they are going to read a passage about two men who discovered a cave. Then remind students of the *Make Connections* strategy. Say: **In order to make good inferences, you have to connect what you are reading to what you already know. As you read, use your background knowledge about caves, explorers, and protecting the environment to help you infer.** When students have finished reading, direct them to complete the skill and strategy practice activities. Review the answers together.

DAY 4

Remind students of the *Make Inferences* skill. Then tell students they are going to read about an ancient library. Say: **This library is unlike the libraries you may have visited. However, you can still use your background knowledge about libraries to help you make inferences as you read.** Then remind students of the *Monitor Comprehension* strategy. Say: **A good reader will often reread a passage to make sure he or she understands the writer's main ideas about a topic. After you read the passage, read it again to make sure you did not miss any important information.** When students have finished reading, direct them to complete the skill and strategy practice activities. Review the answers together.

DAY 5

Tell students they will practice both the *Compare and Contrast* and *Make Inferences* skills as they read a story about living on a new planet. Say: **When writers make up new worlds or write about things that do not exist, they still have to make these things understandable to readers. I could invent an alien language, but if I wrote a story only in that language, you could not understand it. Good writers invent settings, characters, and situations that their readers can compare to people, places, and events in the real world. As you read, you can also use clues to make inferences. This will help you better understand the unusual things you read about.** Direct students to read the passage and complete the skill and strategy practice activities.

Name: ______________________________

READ THE PASSAGE Think about how the heroes are alike and different.

Two New Superheroes Make Their Debut

Have you ever created your own superhero? I have! My superheroes are named Clockwork and Chrysalis. Like most comic book heroes, my superheroes fight for truth and justice. They deliver criminals to the police and have secret identities.

Clockwork spends his days as Henry Kadosh, a geeky, mild-mannered science teacher who frequently ruins his experiments in class. No one suspects he's really a brilliant scientist who has discovered how to travel through time. The youngest of eight children, Henry has always idolized his oldest brother Raul, also a scientific genius. After Raul was hurt in a lab accident, Henry helped his brother by taking over Raul's work. Eventually, Henry discovered the secret to making time travel possible. Now, as Clockwork, he serves humanity by traveling back in time and stopping crimes before they happen.

Chrysalis was born a Cherokee in 1833. She and her tribe lived off of the land and had a deep respect for nature. One day as she gathered food, she was simultaneously stung by a scorpion and bitten by a rattlesnake. The combination of the venoms gave her the ability to change into different animals and use their powers. For instance, she can temporarily blind enemies by becoming an octopus and shooting ink in their eyes. Or she can stun her enemies the way an electric eel does. She can also see as well as a hawk does. Chrysalis channels her power into fighting crimes against the environment. Once, after shape-shifting into an arctic clam to eavesdrop on whale hunters, she gained the clam's ability to live for centuries. Chrysalis has countless secret identities.

SKILL PRACTICE Read the item. Write your response.

1. How are Clockwork and Chrysalis like all other superheroes?

____

____

2. Describe the common thread in the events that led to Clockwork and Chrysalis becoming superheroes.

____

____

3. Do you consider Clockwork or Chrysalis more interesting? Defend your stance.

____

____

STRATEGY PRACTICE Describe a superhero you know about and how Clockwork or Chrysalis is like that character.

____

____

READ THE PASSAGE Think about how the different kinds of volcanoes form and erupt.

Cinder Cones and Stratovolcanoes

What do you think of when you hear the word *volcano*? Most likely, you get a picture in your mind of a stratovolcano. Shaped like a cone with a crater at the top, stratovolcanoes are characterized by violent, explosive eruptions. Huge quantities of hot gases, ash, and rocks explode into the air. Lava rushes down the volcano's sides. These eruptions come from one or more vents, or "chimneys," inside the volcano. Stratovolcanoes are sometimes called composite volcanoes because they are built up, layer on layer, by repeated eruptions of ash and lava over hundreds of years. They can rise more than 8,000 feet (2,438 m) from their base. Some of the world's most spectacular mountains are actually stratovolcanoes.

Another kind of volcano is the cinder cone. Like stratovolcanoes, cinder cones are cone-shaped. They often have a crater at the top. Cinder cones, however, are tiny compared to stratovolcanoes. According to the U.S. Geological Survey, they are "built from particles and blobs of congealed lava ejected from a single vent." As the gas-charged lava shoots into the air, it breaks into small pieces. These small pieces quickly become solid and fall to the ground as cinders. As more cinders erupt from the vent, they fall on top of one another. Gradually, the cone-shaped mound of volcanic rocks grows taller. Once all the gases have escaped and eruptions cease, lava may continue to flow out of the vent and down the sides of the cone. Cinder cones usually build up over a period of several months to a few years. But they seldom grow to more than 1,000 feet (305 m) tall.

SKILL PRACTICE Read the item. Write your response.

1. Name two ways in which cinder cones and stratovolcanoes are similar.

____

____

2. Name two differences between cinder cones and stratovolcanoes.

____

____

3. You live near a cone-shaped extinct volcano that is 850 feet (259 m) tall. Explain which type of volcano it is and how you know.

____

____

STRATEGY PRACTICE Underline three ideas in the passage that you think are important to remember. Show a partner the ideas you underlined and explain why you chose them.

READ THE PASSAGE Use clues from the passage and your own experiences to make inferences as you read.

Secrecy at Kartchner Caverns

On a cool November day in 1974, two young men made the discovery of a lifetime. Randy Tufts and Gary Tenen had been searching for caverns in the limestone mountains of southern Arizona. Limestone dissolves when water seeps through it, often forming underground cavities and deposits of a mineral called calcite. As a geology student and someone who liked to explore caves, Tufts hoped to find caverns in the area. But what they discovered was remarkable! What Tufts and Tenen had found was a "living" cave—a cave with calcite formations that are still growing—and it was untouched by humans.

Tufts and Tenen knew immediately that the caverns had to be protected. If word got out, curious visitors would come and disturb the cave. They would leave behind footprints and litter. The resulting microbes would begin destroying the delicate formations and ecosystem of the cave.

The two men shared their secret with just enough friends to limit the explorers' impact on the caverns' environment. For a year, they explored in their socks, touching as little as possible. The moist, humid cave was 2½ miles (4.0 km) long with two huge rooms and 26 smaller ones. Nearly all the rooms contained formations such as icicle-shaped stalactites, as well as more unusual deposits called soda straws, draperies, and cave bacon.

Eventually, Tufts and Tenen told others what they had found. First they notified the owners of the land, and then they told Arizona officials. A secret for just over two decades, the caverns became a state park. Rangers now protect the caves with elaborate procedures. Visitors enter through airtight chambers designed to keep dry air out of the caverns. Because of this and other precautions, geologists hope Kartchner Caverns will remain a living cave for many years.

SKILL PRACTICE Read the item. Write your response.

1. Why did Tufts and Tenen keep their discovery a secret for so long?

____

____

2. Cave bacon is comprised of which mineral? How do you know?

____

____

3. Why do you think these caverns became a state park?

____

STRATEGY PRACTICE Describe a place you know of that is worth protecting.

____

____

Name: ______________________

READ THE PASSAGE Use clues from the passage to infer information about the ancient library.

Ashurbanipal's Library

Many of us have to pay fines when we return overdue library materials. Even worse, if we lose the materials, we may have to pay to replace them. While we may dislike these penalties, we should consider ourselves lucky. At least one early library threatened people with much harsher punishments.

The world's first known library with a system of organization and cataloged materials was in the ancient city of Nineveh, Assyria, near what is now Mosel, Iraq.

Unlike Egyptians, who wrote on a paper called papyrus, Assyrians wrote manuscripts on clay tablets. In the 1800s, archaeologists discovered vast numbers of these manuscripts in Nineveh's ruins. Scholars were able to read them and found notes at the bottom of each tablet that told who had owned them. They were part of the private library of King Ashurbanipal (AH-shoor-BAHN-ih-pahl), who ruled Assyria from 668 BC to 627 BC. Unlike many kings of that time, Ashurbanipal was able to read and write.

Scholars believe that Ashurbanipal's library contained more than 1,200 titles on thousands of tablets. Many had been taken from defeated enemies during wartime—a common practice at the time. Others had been copied from earlier tablets. The library contained dictionaries as well as tablets on religion, science, magic, and history. It also contained literature, such as the *Epic of Gilgamesh,* a famous story from the region. Materials were even organized into different rooms, much like today's libraries.

Although this was a private library, other people could use it. However, unlike today's library books, materials from Ashurbanipal's library contained curses threatening the wrath of the gods against anyone stealing or writing on the manuscripts. Maybe today's library fines really aren't so bad.

SKILL PRACTICE Read the item. Write your response.

1. Why does the author start and end the text by mentioning today's library fines?

____

____

2. Draw two conclusions about King Ashurbanipal.

____

____

3. Why did Assyrian manuscripts survive better than ancient Egyptian ones?

____

____

STRATEGY PRACTICE Describe something in the passage that you understood better after rereading it.

____

____

READ THE PASSAGE Use your background knowledge and information from the passage to compare Siara 5 to Earth and to make inferences about life in the future.

Transfer to Siara 5

Aray Singer and his father gazed down on the fields of grain below as their sky taxi flew from the spaceport orbiting Siara 5, their new home. Many things on this planet were already familiar to Aray. Flying taxis, hearing implants that translated languages, and clothing that adjusted to the weather were common on Earth. Aray had been surprised, though, by how many activities were handled by machines on Siara 5. It seemed like the machines did everything. Unlike on Earth, visitors to Siara 5 transferred from spacecraft to sky taxi without the help of shuttle drivers or immigration officials.

As Aray looked more closely at the fields below him, he realized things weren't as automated as he had first thought. The land was clearly worked not by machine, but by hand—or rather, paw. Apes and monkeys were the workers that plowed fields, planted seedlings, and even harvested grain. As he and his father flew over orchards, Aray saw spider monkeys handpicking bizarre fruits, while orangutans packed the fruits into crates.

Aray and his father got out of the shuttle at a high-rise building and were greeted graciously by a staff member who offered to take them up to Mr. Singer's new office. The staff member was a gorilla! "Your meeting is already in progress," the gorilla said. Auto-translators made communication easy, even among different species.

Emerging from the elevator, Aray scanned the office: baboons, gorillas, chimpanzees, gibbons, and other kinds of apes and monkeys sat around a massive wooden table. "I hope you don't mind if my son sits in on the meeting," said Mr. Singer. "We haven't had time to go to our new apartment."

SKILL PRACTICE Read the item. Write your response.

1. How does the futuristic technology on Earth differ from our current technology?

____

2. How do you think Aray feels when he sees the apes and monkeys working on Siara 5?

____

____

3. What is the genre of this text, and when did you first identify it?

____

____

STRATEGY PRACTICE Describe how the passage is like another science fiction story or movie you know.

____

____

WEEK 16

Character and Setting

Students practice analyzing character and setting by looking at the traits and motivations of a character and where and when a passage's events take place.

Theme

Students practice identifying the theme by looking for the central message or lesson in a passage.

DAY 1

Review the elements of characters and the setting with students. Say: **Stories can have many characters, although usually just one is the main character. The setting is where and when the events in a passage take place.** Tell students they will read about a girl named Shakira. Then review the *Monitor Comprehension* strategy (Week 1). Say: **Taking notes is a good way to make sure you are understanding the characters and settings in a story. As you read this passage, take notes about Shakira and Mattie and what you think these characters are like. Write your notes in the space provided for the strategy practice activity.** Have students read the instructions at the top of the page and the passage. When students have finished, direct them to complete the skill practice activity. Review the answers together, and invite volunteers to share the notes they took.

DAY 2

Review the *Character and Setting* skill with students. Say: **Like fiction passages, nonfiction passages can also have characters and settings. It is important to know how to find the character and setting of biographies, for example, to best understand the life and times of a famous or important person.** Tell students they are going to read a passage about Julius Caesar, a famous Roman leader. Build background by explaining that "the ides" refers to the 15th of March, May, July, and October, and the 13th of the other months. Remind students of the *Visualization* strategy (Week 3). Say: **As you read, look for words and phrases that help you create a picture in your mind.** When students have finished reading, direct them to complete the skill and strategy practice activities.

DAY 3

Review the definition of *theme* with students. Say: **A theme is a lesson or a view about life. Often a passage's theme will not be directly stated. Instead, you have to infer whether the theme is based on what happens in the passage or based on opinions that the writer expresses.** Tell students they are going to read a passage about elephant tusk trading. Then remind students of the *Monitor Comprehension* strategy. Say: **Taking notes is a good way to remember important events, thoughts, or ideas you come across in a passage. As you read, make notes about the topic that help you understand the theme. Write your notes in the space provided for the strategy practice activity.** Have students read the passage. When students have finished, direct them to complete the skill practice activity. Review the answers together, and invite volunteers to share the notes they took for the strategy practice activity.

DAY 4

Review the *Theme* skill with students. Say: **When you are trying to understand the theme of a nonfiction passage, look for value words that the author uses. For example, if I used the word *disgusting* to describe fast-food hamburgers and fries, would you think my view about these things is positive or negative?** (negative) **If I have a negative view of fast food, would you expect to see a theme of my writing to be how eating unhealthy food is a good thing?** (no) Tell students they are going to read about a special fish called the anglerfish. Then review the *Visualization* strategy, and tell students to make a mental picture of what they read. Have students read the passage. When students have finished, direct them to complete the skill and strategy practice activities.

DAY 5

Tell students they will practice both the *Character and Setting* and *Theme* skills as they read about two students who are competing in a poster contest. Then remind students of the *Monitor Comprehension* strategy. Say: **As you read, stop after each paragraph and tell yourself what it was mostly about.** Have students read the passage. When students have finished, direct them to complete the skill and strategy practice activities. Review the answers together.

READ THE PASSAGE Pay attention to how each girl behaves and where the passage takes place.

On the Outs

Shakira could feel the difference from the first minute she stepped into the classroom on Monday morning. Eva and Willa didn't smile at her, and the other kids didn't even look at her. "Why did I ever want to be Eva's friend?" she asked herself. Shakira hadn't even had that much fun being part of their group, although at the time she had thought popularity was more important than having fun. She had abandoned her old friends and her favorite activities, and now she had no one. After a while, though, Shakira had become invisible to Eva's group. Shakira should have known that they would discard her the way they had so many other people.

Shakira took her seat, her cheeks burning. "I didn't do anything wrong!" she told herself, but it didn't make her feel any better. Then she noticed Mattie, who sat to her right, motioning to her with a kind smile. Mattie and Shakira had been friends back in fourth grade, but Mattie had never gotten into Eva and Willa's group, and she didn't care. She just played her guitar, ran track, and did what she wanted to do without worrying about what anyone else thought.

"Do you want to sit with me at lunchtime?" Mattie whispered. Shakira nodded gratefully, knowing that she had never been invisible to Mattie.

SKILL PRACTICE Read the item. Write your response.

1. How is the setting important to the events in the text?

____

____

2. Describe how Shakira is feeling in the second paragraph.

____

____

3. How does Shakira feel about Mattie at the end of the story? Why?

____

____

STRATEGY PRACTICE As you read the passage, make notes about Shakira and Mattie to help you understand their character traits.

____

____

____

Name: ______________________________

READ THE PASSAGE Pay attention to what happens to Julius Caesar and when it happens.

Beware the Ides of March

"Beware the ides of March!" According to ancient legend, that's just what a fortune teller told Julius Caesar, dictator of Rome, warning him to be careful on March 15. In 44 BCE, the Roman Republic was at the height of power. With his army, Caesar had conquered what is now Spain, Greece, Egypt, and France. He had brought social reform to Rome, improving the lives of average citizens.

Although Caesar refused to be called "king," he appointed himself dictator for life. Many Roman senators resented Caesar's great power, though. They wanted Rome to remain a republic governed by a group of senators, as it had been for hundreds of years.

More than 60 people plotted against Caesar, led by Marcus Junius Brutus. Brutus was Caesar's friend, but Brutus also wanted to restore the republic. On March 15, the ides of March, the plotters put their plan into motion and killed Julius Caesar.

The republic was not restored, though. Generations of emperors followed Caesar, ruling until Rome fell hundreds of years later.

SKILL PRACTICE Read the item. Write your response.

1. What did you conclude about Caesar when he appointed himself dictator?

____

____

2. When did the plotters' plan take place?

____

____

3. What was Brutus's motivation for helping to kill his friend?

____

____

STRATEGY PRACTICE Describe what you visualized happening as you read the first paragraph.

____

____

____

Name: ____________________

READ THE PASSAGE Think about the author's view of the world.

Trading Tusks

You may have seen elephants at a zoo and admired their long white tusks. But did you know that those ivory tusks are worth a lot of money? In the 1980s, the elephant population in Africa dwindled from 1.2 million to 600,000. Poachers, people who kill animals illegally, slaughtered more than half a million elephants just for their tusks.

Iain Douglas-Hamilton, a British authority on African elephants, brought this fact to the world's attention. Because of his efforts, the United Nations (UN) banned ivory trading in 1989. Poaching declined, and the elephant population rebounded. In 1993, Douglas-Hamilton founded an organization called Save the Elephants. It works to track and report on elephants, poaching, and ivory sales.

In 2002, the UN relaxed the ban on ivory trading. It allowed some countries to sell ivory that had been collected and stockpiled. These countries claimed that the ivory came from elephants that had died naturally. However, once the ban was eased, poachers once again began killing up to 20,000 elephants per year. Save the Elephants worked hard to inform organizations and governments of the effects of lifting the ban. The organization argued that the ivory trade should be outlawed again.

In June 2007, the UN once more approved a ban on international ivory trading. Douglas-Hamilton and Save the Elephants hope that the ban will help elephant populations increase to healthier levels.

SKILL PRACTICE Read the item. Write your response.

1. What is the theme of this text?

____

____

2. Use information from the text to explain what the verb *to poach* means.

____

____

3. Do you think the United Nations will remove its ivory ban again? Explain.

____

____

STRATEGY PRACTICE As you read, write notes about information in the passage that helped you understand the theme.

____

____

READ THE PASSAGE Look for value words that express the writer's views of animal adaptations.

Lights in the Depths

Deep in the darkest reaches of the ocean, an anglerfish swims. A tentacle-like stalk extends from its head, and on the end of the stalk dangles a greenish-blue light, hanging like a lantern in front of the fish. The fish uses its glowing lure to attract a smaller fish. Snap! The smaller fish has become the anglerfish's dinner.

The remarkable bioluminescent light is created by chemicals produced in the anglerfish. It is a fascinating adaptation that helps the anglerfish survive in a difficult environment.

The anglerfish swims past a flashlight fish. This fish flashes its bioluminescent light to communicate with other flashlight fish. Then the anglerfish passes a squid, which rises to the surface, its glow helping it blend in with the moonlight. Swimming below the anglerfish is a loosejaw fish, which gives off a red light. Most fish can't see red light, so this helps the loosejaw find its prey without the prey being aware of the loosejaw's presence. But the anglerfish senses danger and swims quickly away from the loosejaw. As the anglerfish moves on, the light of an ostropod blinks behind it, trying to attract a mate. Like the neon signs on the streets of New York's Times Square, the ocean waters flash with bioluminescence. The deep-sea organisms are using their unique adaptations to survive in a variety of ways.

SKILL PRACTICE Read the item. Write your response.

1. What is the theme of this text?

____

____

2. What two words in the text indicate the author's opinion about bioluminescence?

____

____

3. How are flashlight fish and ostropods alike?

____

____

STRATEGY PRACTICE Describe how you visualized the anglerfish as it swims around the ocean depths.

____

____

____

READ THE PASSAGE Think about the lesson that Shawn and Neela learn.

The Poster Contest

Shawn had been working on his entry for the school's poster contest for weeks. The topic of the contest was recycling, and the winner would receive the honor of having his or her poster displayed all around the school. Shawn was sure his was the best in the class—certainly better than Neela's! Shawn and Neela competed in everything, and their test scores and grades were just about equal. They almost never spoke to each other, but everyone in the class knew they were rivals. One thing Shawn excelled at, though, was art. His poster, which showed a garbage heap threatening to crush the school, looked really good. The only problem was the slogan, which was a little boring. It read, "Recycle."

Mr. Wu evaluated all the posters carefully and said, "These are all excellent, but there are two entries that really stand out." Shawn grinned as Mr. Wu held up his poster and the class clapped. But then Mr. Wu held up Neela's poster, too. The artwork wasn't great, Shawn saw, but the words written across the top were powerful. They read, "It's Your Planet—Recycle It!" Even Shawn had to admit it was a good slogan.

Then Shawn had an idea. "Mr. Wu," he proposed, "if Neela agrees, maybe we could work together. We could combine my art and Neela's words to make a really great poster."

Neela smiled at Shawn for the first time all year. "I think that sounds like a winning idea!" she said.

SKILL PRACTICE Read the item. Write your response.

1. What is the theme of this text?

____

____

2. Name two adjectives that describe Shawn.

____

____

3. Why does Neela agree to work with Shawn?

____

____

STRATEGY PRACTICE Explain how Shawn's words and actions reveal the passage's theme.

____

____

____

WEEK 17

Author's Purpose

Students identify the author's reason for writing about a subject.

Prediction

Students practice using clues from a passage to predict what will happen next.

DAY 1

Review the *Author's Purpose* skill with students. Say: **When we study the author's purpose, we think about why an author wrote a passage. For example, the author's purpose might be to entertain, to inform, to teach, or to persuade. Sometimes an author may have more than one purpose.** Tell students they are going to read a passage about how music affects people's moods. Then remind students of the *Ask Questions* strategy (Week 6). Read the passage title aloud and say: **Think of a question you have after hearing that title. Write the question in the space provided for the strategy practice activity. Asking questions before we read helps us set a purpose for reading. As you read, look for the answer to your question. If you find it, write it down.** Have students read the passage. When students have finished, ask: **What is the purpose of the first paragraph?** (to inform) Then direct students to complete the skill practice activity. Review the answers together.

DAY 2

Remind students of the *Author's Purpose* skill, and review the common purposes for writing (to persuade, to entertain, to inform, and to instruct). Tell students they are going to read about climate change during prehistoric times. Then remind students of the *Make Connections* strategy (Week 2). Say: **When you read about a topic that may be unfamiliar, you can improve your comprehension by connecting that topic to topics you are more familiar with. As you read this passage, think about what you know about climate change today.** Have students read the passage. When students have finished, direct them to complete the skill and strategy practice activities.

DAY 3

Review the *Prediction* skill with students. Say: **When we make a prediction, we use clues from the passage and our own background knowledge to figure out what will happen next.** Tell students they will read a passage about King Tutankhamen (King Tut). Then remind students of the *Ask Questions* strategy. Say: **Asking questions after we read is a good way to check that we understood the main points of a passage. When you finish reading, think of a question that can be answered by information from the passage. Write it in the space provided for the strategy practice activity.** Direct students to read the passage and complete the skill practice activity. Review the answers together. For the strategy practice activity, pair students or complete it as a group.

DAY 4

Tell students they are going to make predictions as they read a story about a spelling bee. Then have students recall the *Make Connections* strategy. Ask: **What do you know about spelling bees?** (e.g., Contestants spell words that become more difficult as the bee goes on. Contestants are eliminated after they misspell a word.) Say: **Use what you know about spelling bees to look for clues in the passage that will help you make predictions.** When students have finished reading, direct them to complete the skill and strategy practice activities. Review the answers together.

DAY 5

Tell students they will practice both the *Author's Purpose* and *Prediction* skills in connection with the *Ask Questions* strategy. Remind students: **Asking questions while you read is a good way to monitor how well you understand the text. After you finish each paragraph, ask yourself a question about what you just read. When you finish reading, pick the question you asked that helped you understand the passage or clarify your thinking the most. Write it in the space provided for the strategy practice activity.** Have students read the passage. When students have finished, direct them to complete the skill practice activity. Review the answers together.

Name: ______________________________

READ THE PASSAGE Think about why the author wrote the passage.

Feeling Blue? Play Some Music

Everyone experiences bad moods now and then, some more than others. But help may be on the way. In recent studies, scientists have found that music can improve people's moods. One study conducted by the University of Maryland showed that listening to a type of classical music called *baroque* helped improve the moods of medical workers who study images of people's organs and bones. It also helped the medical workers feel greater satisfaction with their work.

But not only classical music helps people feel better. In fact, a Penn State University study of college students showed that any kind of music the students listened to helped produce more positive emotions, such as joy, affection, and calm.

How can you help *yourself* with music? Try a music-listening diary, as did the students in the Penn State study. Before you listen to music, record how you are feeling. Then get your cellphone, CD player, or radio and turn on your favorite kind of music. The college students most often listened to rock music, but you can choose any kind. Next, do whatever activity you would normally do while listening to music. For example, the college participants studied, exercised, and socialized. After listening to the music, write down how long you listened and how you feel now. Keep the diary for a couple of weeks, and find out if music really does make a difference.

SKILL PRACTICE Read the item. Write your response.

1. Why does the author describe the University of Maryland study?

____

____

2. Why does the author describe the Penn State study?

____

____

3. What is the author's purpose in the third paragraph?

____

____

STRATEGY PRACTICE Write a question you thought of before you read the passage. If you found the answer, write it, too.

____

____

READ THE PASSAGE Think about the author's purpose for writing the passage.

Weather in the Prehistoric American Southwest

Today the American Southwest is a hot, dry place. In this region—which includes Nevada, Arizona, Utah, and parts of California—water is scarce. Yet fossils indicate that this was not always the case. Fossils of camelops (relatives of camels), American horses, and smilodons (commonly called saber-toothed tigers) have been found. Scientists believe these animals would not survive in the Southwest today. So how did they survive back then? Apparently, water was not as hard to find as it is today.

Scientists believe that more than one ice age has taken place on Earth. The most recent ice age ended about 10,000 years ago. Scientists call the period since then the Holocene period. During the Holocene period, animals had to try to adapt to a changing environment. Earlier, the Southwest had many forests and lakes, and temperatures were cooler. After the last ice age, however, many lakes dried up. New predators, including human beings, came to the Southwest, putting stress on the large animals that lived in the area. Because so many large mammals and plants became extinct during this period, scientists have named it the Holocene Extinction Event. Scientists have also detected further climate changes within the Holocene period. During the Middle Holocene period, for example, the Southwest was both warmer and wetter than it is today.

SKILL PRACTICE Read the item. Write your response.

1. Why does the author include facts about animals that used to live in the American Southwest?

____

____

2. Why does the author include information about the new predators that came into that area?

____

____

3. Why does the author include the last two sentences of the text?

____

____

STRATEGY PRACTICE Explain how using what you know about climate change helped you better understand the passage.

____

____

Could Rice Be a Dwindling Staple?

More than half of the world's population depends on rice as a food staple. Up to 90% of the world's rice is grown in Asia. In Southeast Asia, rice farming dates back as far as 5000 B.C.E. Rice thrives in hot and moist climates, which is the type of climate that much of Asia has had for centuries. Now, however, this may be changing.

Rainfall and temperature have an effect on how well rice grows. The parts of Asia where rice is grown, such as parts of China, India, and Southeast Asia, typically have a yearly rainfall of at least 40 inches (100 cm) and an average temperature of 70 degrees F (21 degrees C) during the growing season. These conditions are perfect for growing rice. Much of the land in Asia used for rice crops is flat or has gentle slopes, which is good for rice because the fields, or paddies, can retain water.

In fact, farmers build little ledges of dirt, called levees, to keep stagnant water in their paddies. Growing rice in standing water helps prevent unwanted weeds. The water also keeps destructive pests, such as plant-eating insects and rodents, away. If the water gets too deep, however, the rice plants can drown.

Some rice crops grown in the tropical and sub-tropical parts of Asia, however, are suffering due to climate change. Excessive rainfall or flooding in the last few decades has at times resulted in drowned or ruined crops. Similarly, less than usual rainfall has caused crops to fail. Another aspect of climate change that has affected the production of rice is rising temperatures. For example, daytime and nighttime temperatures throughout much of Asia have risen in recent years, and heat waves are more common. Unfortunately, rice is susceptible to heat stress. If it gets too hot during the flowering stage, for example, the plants may become sterile, resulting in no or low yield of rice. Because of changing temperatures, some rice farmers have to manage their crops differently. For example, they may have to adjust planting dates, switch up crop rotations, and even use plant varieties that mature faster in order to avoid the hottest periods of the year.

Rice has been a staple food in Asia for centuries for good reasons. The climate has been perfect for the moisture-loving, heat-loving plants. However, climate changes could have possible effects on this. Hopefully, the adjustments farmers are making to have good rice harvests will help keep rice a staple food for many more centuries.

Nonfiction
Cause and Effect
3

Name ___________________________

Could Rice Be a Dwindling Staple?

A text with a **cause-and-effect** structure states the reason that something happens. When a **cause** happens, it leads to an **effect**. You can analyze the details in a text to determine causes and effects.

An event can cause multiple effects. Similarly, an effect may have multiple causes.

Answer the items about the text you read.

1. Write one sentence to explain a cause-and-effect relationship discussed in the text.

2. What is the result of growing rice plants in standing water.

3. Explain how climate change can cause rice plants to suffer from heat stress. Then describe the effects of heat stress on rice plants and rice yields.

4. Why would a farmer choose to manage different crops differently?

5. What is a possible outcome for people if Asia stops growing rice entirely? Explain why you think so.

Name ____________________________________

Answer the items.

1. What does a text with a cause-and-effect structure explain?

____

____

2. Explain why it's important to be able to identify causes and effects in nonfiction texts.

____

____

3. How can cause-and-effect signal words and phrases help you to identify and understand cause-and-effect relationships being discussed in a text?

____

____

____

Read the paragraph. Then answer the questions.

Some people stretch their bodies before and after a workout. There are a few reasons to stretch before a workout. It can loosen your muscles, which can in turn help you to prevent a muscle injury. Stretching before a workout may also lead to better physical performance during the workout and less soreness after the workout. Stretching after a workout can also help reduce soreness. Another effect of stretching after a workout is muscle relaxation. Some experts debate whether dynamic stretching (a slow stretch combined with constant movement) is better or worse than static stretching (a stretch in which the person stays still). However, many experts agree that both types of stretching can be beneficial.

4. What are the benefits of stretching before a workout?

____

____

5. What could happen to you if you forget to stretch before and after a workout?

____

Name ______________________________

An author may use a **compare-and-contrast** text structure to write an informational text. The text explains the similarities and differences between two or more things. Sometimes an author uses signal words in the text. Look for compare-and-contrast signal words as you read.

compare:	**alike**	**too**	**also**	**both**	**similar**
contrast:	**different**	**yet**	**but**	**while**	**rather**

Photos and pictures in a text can help show similarities and differences.

Read the paragraph. Then answer the items.

Most of the similarities among the various kinds of snakes are obvious. All snakes are long and covered in scales. Also, they all shed their skin as they grow, and none of them have eyelids. The way snakes bear their young, however, marks some big differences. Most snakes are oviparous, meaning they lay eggs. Just about all oviparous snakes lay their eggs somewhere warm, such as in a nest of leaves or a hole in the ground, and leave their eggs to hatch. Yet a few kinds of oviparous snakes, such as pythons and king cobras, coil up on their eggs until the eggs hatch. While most snakes are oviparous, not all snakes lay eggs. Some are viviparous, meaning they give birth to live young. Among viviparous snakes are Anacondas, most vipers, and many sea snakes.

1. Write three compare-and-contrast signal words or phrases from the text.

   ____________________ ____________________ ____________________

2. In your own words, explain the difference between oviparous and viviparous snakes.

   ____

   ____

3. Contrast how Anacondas and king cobras give birth to their young.

   ____

   ____

   ____

Name ______________________________

A text with a **compare-and-contrast** text structure explains the similarities and differences between two or more things. Sometimes an author uses comparative and superlative adjectives to compare and contrast.

These are examples of comparative and superlative adjectives:
uglier, ugliest, more nutritious, most nutritious, less eager, least eager

Read the paragraph. Then answer the items.

Both running and swimming are great ways to get an aerobic workout. Neither requires special equipment; however, running is more convenient for people who do not live near a pool. With running, you can get up and go anywhere. You are not limited to a pool, a lake, or an ocean. Although, running is harder on your joints than swimming is. When you run, you pound your bones and joints on the pavement. Swimming is a more gentle exercise for people who may have knee or back problems, because the water provides a cushion around their limbs. Swimming also works just about every major muscle group in the body. Running does as well.

1. Explain the reasons why a person may choose to run instead of swim for exercise.

____

____

2. Explain the reasons why a person may choose to swim instead of run for exercise.

____

____

3. Compare the benefits of swimming and running.

____

____

Read the sentence. Then write **compare** or **contrast** to tell what the sentence does.

4. You sweat when swimming, just as you do when running. ____________

5. Shoes affect performance in running but not in swimming. ____________

Name ____________________________________

Electric Cars vs. Gasoline Cars

recharging electric car

refueling gasoline car

Cars powered by gasoline were sold for many years before hybrid vehicles that use gasoline, electricity, and solar energy. Car companies are now making cars that are fully powered by electricity only. How do these electric cars measure up to traditional gasoline cars?

For the most part, electric vehicles and gasoline vehicles look alike on the outside. Both come in multiple colors and have standard features such as steering wheels. Once you look under the hood of an electric car, though, you will find very different parts than inside a gas-powered car. In fact, you will find fewer parts as well. Electric cars have one main moving part: the motor. Yet gas cars literally have hundreds of parts, requiring frequent maintenance. Having fewer parts makes the electric car cheaper to maintain and less likely to have mechanical problems.

Electric vehicles are cheaper to take care of than gas-powered vehicles. That's because electric vehicles are more energy efficient. It costs an electric car approximately $1.00 to travel 43 miles, which is a stark contrast to a gas car, which costs about $1.25 to go 18 miles. Basically, an electric car can go twice as far as a gas car for the same price.

Electric vehicles do not have tailpipe emissions, making them more friendly to the environment than gasoline cars. The typical gasoline-powered car emits 4.7 tons of carbon dioxide per year.

While some details make electric cars seem attractive, other details aren't as favorable. For example, most electric cars can only travel between 60 to 120 miles on a full charge. A 15-gallon gas car can drive over 500 miles.

This means the electric car has to stop more often to get recharged. Therefore, a gasoline car would be a better option for a cross-country road trip or if you have far to drive. And electric cars aren't as convenient to power up as gas cars are. Gas stations are abundant, but charging stations for electric cars are not. Then, once an electric car reaches a charging station, it can take up to six hours to charge.

There are certainly benefits to both electric cars and gasoline cars. For some people who don't do a lot of driving, an electric car is ideal. And, it's better for the environment. It's good to know that electric cars are an option.

Name ______________________________

Electric Cars vs. Gasoline Cars

A text with a **compare-and-contrast** text structure explains the similarities and differences between two or more things.

Consider the features of the two things being discussed in the text. Visual information may provide additional details that can help you to compare and contrast.

Answer the items about the text you read.

1. Write two benefits of electric cars that gasoline cars don't have.

____

____

2. Write two benefits of gasoline cars that electric cars don't have.

____

____

3. Why does the author state that gasoline cars are "traditional"?

____

____

4. Explain the reasons why electric cars are cheaper to care for than gas cars.

____

____

5. Write one similarity or difference between gas and electric cars that you can determine from the photographs.

____

____

Name ______________________________

Answer the items.

1. Write two comparison signal words.

   ______________ ______________

2. Write two contrast signal words.

   ______________ ______________

3. Explain why it's necessary to analyze details in a text in order to compare and contrast details from the text.

   ____
   ____
   ____

4. Explain how visual information can help you compare and contrast things you read about.

   ____
   ____
   ____

Read the paragraph. Then answer the question.

5. Seals and sea lions may have some similarities in appearance, but they are different animals with entirely different behaviors. Sea lions have small floppy ears while seals merely have holes in their heads. Sea lions have skin-covered front flippers, but seals have furry front feet. Typically, sea lions are louder and noisier than seals. Furthermore, seals tend to be less social than sea lions. Finally, seals are more adapted to living in water than on land, so they don't move as well as sea lions do on land.

   Is the main idea of the paragraph comparing or contrasting two things? Explain how you know.

   ____
   ____

Name ____________________

An author may use a **sequence** text structure to write an informational text. In a sequence text, the author describes details in the order they happen. The details may be events, steps in a process, or stages in a cycle.

Look for these signal words and phrases to identify the order of details:

before **after** **next** **then** **finally** **last** **first** **second** **at last**

Read the paragraph. Then answer the items.

Doctor William Key, also known as Doc, showed the world that animals need patience and respect. He was born into slavery in 1833. As a young boy, he clearly had a special way with animals, especially horses. After the Civil War, Doc became free from slavery, and in the late 1800s, he became a renowned veterinarian and businessman. In 1889, Doc's beloved horse died after giving birth to a weak foal. Doc expected the foal to die but lovingly took good care of it and named it Jim. Doc even let Jim sleep with him! To Doc's surprise, Jim started to get stronger and followed doc everywhere. Doc noticed that Jim was extremely intelligent, so he decided to try an experiment. First, he taught Jim the letters of the alphabet. When Jim chose the right letter, Doc rewarded him with sugar or apples. Then he used the same method to teach Jim to recognize colors. Jim eventually learned how to make change from a cash register! Finally, Doc decided to share the success of his experiment with others. He and Jim performed all over the country, showing millions that treating animals with love and respect can do wonders. In no time, Doc and Jim became very famous.

1. Explain how you can determine that this text has a sequence text structure.

____

____

2. Write three events from the text in your own words. Write them in the order they happened.

____

____

____

Name ______________________________

How to Make a Mini Hovercraft

Did you know that you can make your own fun, homemade hovercraft? Hovercrafts, sometimes called air-cushion vehicles or hovercraft boats, are vehicles that float on a layer of pressurized air that comes into contact with the surface it travels upon. The pressurized air reduces friction, allowing the hovercraft to move over many surfaces such as mud, sand, concrete, ice, and water.

hovercraft driving on a frozen river

If you want to see a hovercraft in action, you can easily make one at home with simple materials. Making a homemade hovercraft is a great way to practice your engineering skills, and it can be a fun project. You won't be able to ride it, but you can get an idea of how it works. Before you begin the project, you must gather the materials you'll need, which are the following:

- an old or unwanted CD
- duct tape
- a pop-up lid and nozzle from a sports drink, water bottle, or dish soap bottle
- a balloon

After you've gathered the necessary materials, the first thing you should do is remove the nozzle from the bottle, and make sure it's clean and in the closed position. Discard the bottle. Next, place the plastic nozzle over the hole in the CD. Create an air-tight connection by taping duct tape around the nozzle and the CD. Then, place the balloon over the nozzle. After you do this, blow through the hole, thereby blowing up the balloon. Be sure to keep the balloon inflated by pinching the opening with your fingers. Finally, put the hovercraft in position, with the CD on the bottom. Let go of the balloon, and watch it go! It should shoot across the surface as the air is forced out of the balloon through the hole in the CD. Follow these steps, and enjoy your new mini hovercraft!

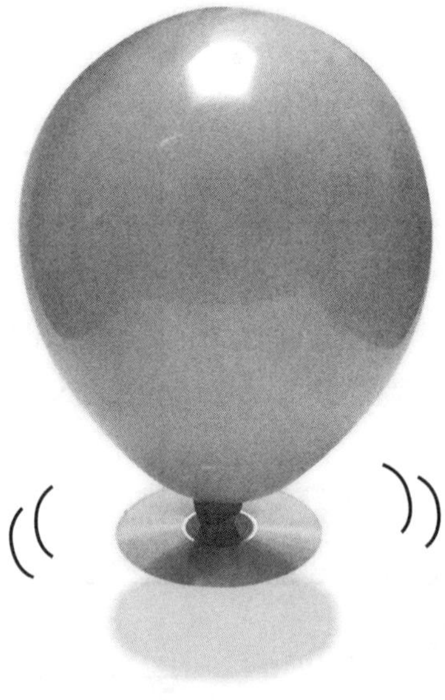

Name ____________________

How to Make a Mini Hovercraft

An author may use a **sequence** text structure to write an informational text. In a sequence text, the author describes details in the order they happen. The details may be events, steps in a process, or stages in a cycle.

Look for signal words that tell the order of details in the text.

Answer the items about the text you read.

1. Explain how you can tell that this text has a sequence text structure.

   ____

   ____

2. What would happen if you were to blow through the hole in the CD before attaching the balloon to the plastic nozzle? Explain why you think so.

   ____

   ____

   ____

   ____

3. Why does the author suggest that you duct tape the nozzle to the CD before you blow air into the balloon?

   ____

   ____

4. Why do you need to put the hovercraft into a certain position before you use it?

   ____

   ____

   ____

Name ____

Answer the items.

1. Why would an author choose to write a text with a sequence text structure?

____

____

____

2. Write three sequence signal words.

______________ ______________ ______________

3. Why do you think it's important to follow steps in the order they're given when you're reading a how-to text, or a text that details a process?

____

____

Read the paragraph. Then answer the question.

4. Did you know that a monkey once sued a man in court? Well... that is kind of true. In 2011, a British photographer named David Slater traveled to Indonesia and took some selfies on his camera with a macaque. Interestingly, the macaque actually pressed the shutter on the camera, which is a piece that can block the lens and move to allow pictures to be taken. Because the macaque did this, some people believe that the macaque (not David) was the creator of the photos. Years later, David tried to sue some websites for using the photos without paying him, but the sites refused to stop using the photos, claiming that they belonged to the macaque. The story got even more complicated when, the following year, the People for the Ethical Treatment of Animals, or PETA, sued David Slater on behalf of the monkey. They claimed that the macaque owned the copyright to the photos. In 2017, the court case was settled.

What events happened before PETA sued David on behalf of the macaque monkey?

____

____

____

____

Name ______________________________

An author may use a **problem-and-solution** text structure to write an informational text. In a problem-and-solution text, the author describes a problem in detail. Then the author describes solutions or ideas to solve the problem.

Read the paragraphs. Then answer the items.

The Great Pacific Garbage Patch is a soupy collection of floating litter in the North Pacific Ocean. Although there are some large objects in the patch, such as plastic bottles, shoes, and fishing gear, most of the patch consists of tiny pieces of plastic called microplastics. This plastic has been broken down into tiny pieces and is harmful to marine wildlife. For example, albatross think the minute bits of plastic are eggs and feed them to their chicks, ultimately killing them. Bigger pieces of plastic are harmful too. Many marine animals, such a turtles and seals, ingest plastic and die because their bodies cannot process it. The garbage patch also affects the growth of plankton and algae, which disturbs the entire marine food chain.

One would think cleaning up the patch would be an easy solution; however, it's too large, and most of the plastic pieces are too small to remove without killing important sea organisms in the process. Most scientists agree that our best solution is to eliminate the use of disposable plastics. Local and national organizations work to make people aware of the impact that plastics in the sea have so people can make wiser choices and use biodegradable or reusable items instead. For example, a zoo in Washington has launched an exhibit of huge sea creature sculptures made entirely out of plastic items found along the Oregon coast to raise awareness. Some organizations work with companies to transition from plastic to reusable materials.

1. In your own words, describe the problem in the text.

____

____

2. Explain why raising awareness of this problem is a solution to the problem.

____

____

____

Name ____________________

Where Have All the Bees Gone?

Bees are often overlooked, but they are an extremely important part of our daily lives. That's why it's concerning that bee populations are decreasing, with entire colonies disappearing at times. It's crucial that we address this problem before all the bees vanish.

Without bees, we wouldn't have produce to nourish us. We need bees to pollinate our crops, particularly fruits and vegetables. Bees are also needed to pollinate flowers.

Despite their importance, honeybee colonies have been decreasing since the 1940s, when there were about 5 million. Today, there are approximately 2.5 million—that means that about 50% of the colonies have vanished. A U.S. Department of Agriculture survey shows that from 2014 to 2015, 42% of honey bee colonies cultivated by beekeepers died off. In Hawaii, sixty yellow-faced bee species are now threatened. Seven of those species were the first species of U.S. bees to be officially declared endangered in 2017, and a mainland U.S. bumblebee, the Bombus, has also been declared endangered. Wild bees in Europe are rapidly disappearing, too.

But why are the bees disappearing? Studies show that there are many factors. One factor is habitat loss due to urbanization and a lack of a variety of crops. With fewer planted areas, and areas where only one crop is grown, bees don't get the diversity they need to forage and nest. Another cause of this problem is pesticides. Pesticides kill off harmful pests, but they kill bees, too. The decline of bees is also partly due to parasitic mites that weaken the immune systems of honeybees. These mites introduce dangerous bacteria and viruses that can spread within a bee colony and cause an entire colony to collapse. They can even spread to other colonies.

Some scientists are developing pesticides that won't harm bees. They're also trying to develop a pesticide called miticides, that will destroy only parasitic mites. Federal and independent organizations are trying to increase the bee populations. For example, the Obama administration designated bee-friendly land for conservation programs that will help bring honeybee numbers back up. Everyone can help to solve this problem by planting pesticide-free gardens around their communities.

Bees like bright flowers, and they need places to nest. You can also contribute to the solution by supporting local beekeepers and buying their products, such as honey.

Name ____________________________________

Where Have All the Bees Gone?

An author may use a **problem-and-solution** text structure to write an informational text. In a problem-and-solution text, the author describes a problem. Then the author describes solutions or possible solutions to the problem.

Sometimes the author provides background information about the problem to get readers to consider why the problem is relevant and why they should care about finding a solution.

Answer the items about the text you read.

1. Why is it a concern that bee populations are decreasing?

____

____

2. Why does the author use facts and percentages to help illustrate the problem?

____

____

3. The text states that this problem is prevalent in Europe, Hawaii, and the U.S. mainland. Why is this significant?

____

____

4. State two examples the author provides to show that actions are being taken to solve this problem.

____

____

____

5. Explain how the problem discussed in the text is relevant to you personally.

____

Name ______________________________

Answer the questions.

1. What is the purpose of a text with a problem-and-solution structure?

____

____

2. How can facts and percentages from scientific studies help show how serious a problem actually is?

____

____

3. How does an author get a reader to care about solving a problem?

____

____

Read the text. Then answer the item.

4. Technology and the Internet can be great resources to help you get information. But some online sources are unreliable. Some sites appear to provide news or educational information, but they deliberately impart information that is inaccurate. Some people refer to the information on these sites as "fake news." Fake news sites are a problem, particularly when you are trying to do research or become well informed about a particular issue. The good news is that there are many reliable sources of information on the Internet. If you have a difficult time distinguishing reliable sources from the unreliable ones, here are some solutions to your problem.

Visit multiple sites to fact-check the original facts you read. If the same facts are repeated on several sites, this could suggest that the facts are accurate.

Keep a list of sites you know to be reliable. You can visit these sites more frequently than unfamiliar ones.

Analyze each site. If a site is missing key information, don't rely on the site. You can also see if a website cites reliable sources from which it gets its own information.

Explain how you can tell that this text has a problem-and-solution structure.

____

____

Name ______________________________

When you read, you may come across unfamiliar **vocabulary**. Clues in a text can help you figure out a word's meaning. Do the following things to find clues in a text:

Look at the surrounding words. Think about what would make sense in the sentence.

Think about what you already know about the topic.

Read the sentences before the word. Read the sentences after the word.

Read the paragraph. Then answer the items.

Many arts and dance critics say that Martha Graham was the most influential dancer and choreographer of the twentieth century. She has a repertoire of over seventy years of dance pieces she choreographed in her inimitable style, known as the Graham Technique. This unique style was a radical change from the usual type of dance in the late 1920's. Instead of flowing, lyrical movement, Graham's style was angular, sometimes harsh, and deeply emotional. Graham developed her unique style by experimenting with the human form engaging in contraction and release. Graham died in 1991, but the Martha Graham Dance Company still performs and is a source of inspiration for dancers and visual artists.

1. Mark the meaning of the word *repertoire*.
   Ⓐ a range of skills and accomplishments
   Ⓑ a group of people who form a dance company

2. Explain why you chose the answer you did for number 1.

____

____

____

3. What do you think *inimitable* means? Explain why you think so.

____

____

____

Name ______________________________

When you read, you may come across unfamiliar **vocabulary**. You can use information in the text to help you figure out a word's meaning. Check to see if the author provided a clue by providing the following:

a definition in the sentence before or after the word

a synonym, or a word that has the same meaning

an antonym, or a word that has the opposite meaning

Read the paragraph. Then answer the items.

Have you ever thought about what traveling would be like if the world were devoid of bridges to take us across rivers, straits, lakes, and valleys? Without bridges, transcontinental travel would be more challenging and time consuming. Bridges help us go over obstacles instead of having to go through them or around them. Engineers have been constructing bridges since ancient times. One ancient bridge is the beam bridge, in which a large beam rests on piers or big blocks below. Arch bridges made out of stone were also common in ancient times. Ancient bridge technology has been useful for centuries, but an unprecedented technology was used to create the suspension bridge in the 15th Century. This technology was new and creative for its time. The first simple suspension bridges were conceived by Thangtong Gyalpo in Tibet. He used ropes and chains to hold up the weight of the bridge. Today, suspension bridges like the Golden Gate Bridge use cables and towers.

1. What do you think *devoid* means? Explain why you think so.

____

____

2. Mark the meaning of the word *unprecedented*.

Ⓐ traditional, being from ancient times

Ⓑ having never been done or used before

3. Explain why you chose the answer you did for number 2.

____

____

Name ____

Government in Ancient Greece

Modern civilization and society are indebted to the Ancient Greeks for the invention of many concepts, such as Greek-inspired architecture, city planning, and rhetoric—the art of speaking and writing persuasively. The concepts of democracy and trial-by-jury also originated in Ancient Greece.

In 508 B.C.E., a new ruler, Cleisthenes, came into power in Athens. He instigated a new kind of assembly government called democracy. The word democracy derives from two Greek words —*demos*, meaning people, and *kratos*, meaning rule. In Cleisthenes' assembly, every male citizen could speak and vote, but women, people who were enslaved, and men born outside the city were barred from voting. Also, there had to be at least 6,000 citizens present for an assembly meeting to commence. Until 6,000 people arrived, everyone at the assembly would have to wait.

Assembly meetings took place every 9 or 10 days on a hill called the Pnyx, where the members debated proposals, such as whether or not to declare war on another nation. Another kind of proposal that may have been debated was how to spend Athens' money. The proposals were created by the Council. The Council was comprised of 500 citizens—50 elected from each of the ten tribes in Athens. The paramount members of the Council were 10 military commanders called strategoi, who were elected every year to lead the Council.

ruins from the city of Pnyx

The Athenians of Ancient Greece also developed the first trial-by-jury system. For male citizens over the age of 30, serving on the jury was not a choice but an obligation. All male citizens over the age of 30 were required to serve on a jury. Juries always consisted of an odd number, from 201 to 2001 citizens, so there was not an even split in the vote. A jury would be presented with the circumstances and facts of a crime and then vote to decide whether the person on trial was innocent or guilty. Each juror had two small bronze tokens called ballots. A ballot with a solid axle in the center meant not guilty, and a ballot with a hollow axle meant guilty. The ballots were put in an urn and counted in secret before being reported aloud, and the court gave a sentence.

The Athenian concepts of democracy and trial-by-jury are only two of the many remarkable achievements of Ancient Greece that are still valued today.

Name ______________________________

Government in Ancient Greece

When you read, you may come across unfamiliar **vocabulary**. You can use context clues in the text to help you figure out the meaning of **academic vocabulary** and **content-specific vocabulary**.

The term **academic vocabulary** refers to words used in texts about various topics and subject areas.

The term **content-specific vocabulary** refers to words used in texts about a specific topic or subject area.

Answer the items about the text you read.

1. What do you think *originated* means? Explain why you think so.

____

____

____

2. What do you think *instigate* means? Explain why you think so.

____

____

3. What do you think a *proposal* is, as it is used in the text? Explain why you think so.

____

____

4. Mark the meaning of the word *obligation*.

Ⓐ something that is an option

Ⓑ something that is required

5. Write a definition for the word *ballot*. Explain how you know the meaning.

____

____

Name ____________________________________

Answer the items.

1. Explain why it is important to try to figure out the meaning of unfamiliar words in a text.

2. Write two things you can do if you come across an unfamiliar word.

3. Explain the difference between academic vocabulary and content-specific vocabulary.

4. Explain how background knowledge can help you figure out the meaning of unfamiliar words.

Read the paragraph. Then write a definition for the underlined word.

5. Seismologists study earthquakes and try to develop ways to predict when and where they will happen. Unfortunately, this is impossible at the present time, and the best we can do is predict whether or not an earthquake will get worse after it's already started. It is also currently impossible to prevent earthquakes. It is <u>inevitable</u> that Earth will experience more earthquakes in the future, but there is one upside to this. More earthquakes means seismologists will have more opportunities to study them. Even though they can't predict earthquakes now, it is <u>inevitable</u> that earthquakes will keep happening. So, perhaps one day, all of the research may lead us to a point where we can predict them.

Name ____

When you **summarize** a text, you use your own words to state its most important details. You should not include your personal opinions in a summary.
Do the following when you summarize:

Write the main idea of each paragraph in a single sentence.

Provide as many of the following details as possible:
who, **what**, **where**, **when**, **why**, and **how**

Read the paragraph. Then complete the chart with details from the paragraph.

The Ringling Bros. and Barnum & Bailey Circus was a traveling circus that started in 1919. For decades, huge crowds anxiously waited for the circus, known as "The Greatest Show on Earth," to come to their town or city. The show featured wild animals doing tricks. Tigers would leap through hoops of fire and elephants would stand on their back feet. There were also displays of human strength, such as acrobats building human pyramids, riding bikes on high wires, or flying through the air from one swinging trapeze to another. In the last three decades or so, however, popularity for the circus has dwindled. Some experts say that may be because other forms of human entertainment, like video games and television, have taken the circus' place. But the biggest cause for the circus' demise is the publics' awareness of cruelty toward animals. Many believe the animals were mistreated and abused. In May 2017, the Ringling Bros. and Barnum & Bailey Circus performed for the last time.

Who or what is the topic?	
When?	
What happened?	
Why or how?	

Name ____________________________

When you **summarize** a text, you use your own words to state its most important details. The purpose of a summary is to provide a short version of the text. Do the following when you summarize:

Write the main idea of each paragraph in a single sentence.

Provide as many of the following details as possible: **who**, **what**, **where**, **when**, **why**, and **how**

Read the paragraph. Then answer the questions.

Marc Chagall was a famous artist known for his dream-like, colorful paintings. He was born in 1887 in Belarus, a country west of Russia. He became interested in art at an early age and began his formal training in painting at the age of 19. He quickly began developing his own emotional and poetic style that was a departure from the popular art of the time. After a move to Paris in 1911, Chagall settled in an artist's colony outside of Paris, where he lived and worked with other influential artists of the time. Despite the fact that his work was unusual, Chagall enjoyed some success and showed his work in public venues. He moved around a lot, at one point spending seven years in the U.S. before returning to France. Chagall's remaining years in France were amazing. He painted and worked with ceramics, sculpture, and stained glass. Commissions for his work took him all over the world. By the time of his death at the age of 97 in 1985, Marc Chagall had received many honors. He and his legacy of work are still celebrated today.

1. What is the main idea of the text?

____

____

____

2. What details support the author's statement that Chagall's remaining years in France were amazing?

____

____

____

Education in Colonial America

Education for children in colonial America was similar to education today in some ways. Back then, a child's education heavily depended on the parents' decisions and where the family lived. Still, there were key differences from school today.

In the earliest days of colonial America, when schools did not exist, most parents taught their children at home if they wanted their children to get an education. Some parents, however, chose not to educate their children at all.

Similarly to today, education in the colonies greatly depended on where people lived. In the middle and southern colonies, very few children received formal education because the colonies were sparsely populated, so they couldn't support the development of schools. In the northern colonies, though, formal education was more common. These colonies were settled by Puritans from England. They taught their small children at home. When the Puritan children got a little older, some of them attended one-room schools.

Education in the colonies usually focused on basic reading and writing. Sometimes, children learned math as well. Instead of practicing skills with books, paper, and pencils, students had hornbooks. These were not actually books at all, but wooden boards. Each hornbook had a sheet of paper with the alphabet mounted onto it. The paper was covered with a thin, transparent piece of cow horn to protect the paper.

hornbook

Formal education ended for most children as they reached their teenage years. Many boys would then learn a trade from their families or pursue an apprenticeship, such as working with a blacksmith. Girls generally learned household skills, such as cooking and sewing, from their mothers. Rather than learning a trade, some students attended college or studied the arts, including playing music, painting, and speaking a foreign language.

Over time, education in colonial America became more regulated. For example, in 1642, Massachusetts passed a law that required parents to teach their children to read. In 1647, another law passed stating that towns with 50 or more families had to have a schoolteacher whose salary was paid by the town's inhabitants. Gradually, with the passing of time, school regulations were added and changed, which is how the education system of the colonial times transformed into the system we have today.

Name ______________________________

Education in Colonial America

When you **summarize** a text, you use your own words to state its most important details. You should not include your personal opinions in a summary.
Do the following when you summarize:

Write the main idea of each paragraph in a single sentence.

Provide as many of the following details as possible:
who, **what**, **where**, **when**, **why**, and **how**

Answer the items about the text you read.

1. In your own words, state the main idea of the text.

____

____

2. Summarize the text. For each paragraph in the text, write one sentence that tells the most important details.

____

____

____

____

____

____

____

____

3. Write two ways that education in the colonies was different from education today.

____

____

Name ______________________________

Answer the items.

1. Explain how to summarize a text.

____

____

2. Write the six one-word details that you should try to include in a summary, if possible.

__________ __________ __________

__________ __________ __________

3. Why is it best to leave your personal opinions out of a summary?

____

____

4. A summary is always shorter than the original text it summarizes. Explain why.

____

____

Read the paragraph. Then answer the item.

5. Did you know that a cat can be a hero? In 2015, a cat named Major Tom saved his owner's life. Major Tom and his owner, Grant MacDonald, were aboard a yacht called the *Osprey*, about 40 miles (64 km) off the coast of Australia, when the boat started to flood. It was the middle of the night, and MacDonald was fast asleep. Major Tom was aware of the flooding and did everything he could to wake up MacDonald. Major Tom head-butted MacDonald and made continuous noise until he finally woke up and realized that he had to abandon the yacht using the life raft. Major Tom saved his owner's life!

Write one sentence to summarize the text.

____

____

____

Name ______________________________

When you **predict**, you think of what will probably happen next. You can make a prediction about something that hasn't happened yet. Or, you can make a prediction about details in the text that will be revealed later.

As you read farther in the text, your prediction will often be correct. But it may also be incorrect. That's okay. Sometimes an author wants to surprise you.

What is important is that you think about the text and consider what is likely to happen.

Read the text. Then answer the items.

Cheetah and Dog Buddies

When animals get stressed out, zoo caretakers worry about them. For years, zoos have been pairing cheetahs with dogs to help cheetahs relieve stress. This is almost always done when the cheetah is a cub and the dog is a puppy. The relationship is usually symbiotic, meaning that both the cheetah and the dog benefit from spending time together. The best part is that the cheetah and dog usually become fast friends, growing up together, playing, and being inseparable. Some people are critical of pairing cheetahs and dogs because they think this relationship would never happen in nature. However, both cheetahs and dogs are intelligent and capable of forming lasting bonds, so zoos feel that these relationships do more good than harm to the animals.

1. How did the title help you predict what the text would be about?

____

____

2. Predict what will happen if a new cheetah is born at a zoo and shows signs of stress.

____

____

3. Predict what would happen if an adult cheetah were to see an adult dog in the wild.

____

____

Name ______________________________

Tiny Houses

Since 1970, the size of a new home, on average, grew larger, even as the size of the American family grew smaller. As often happens with trends, the large-home trend experienced a reversal, with some people preferring smaller spaces. Enter the tiny house movement. While there is no set definition for a tiny house, it generally refers to a dwelling that is between 100 and 400 square feet (smaller than an average small apartment). It can be portable, or it can be permanently located. The exact number of tiny homes is unknown, but in 2015, about 30 tiny house communities were scattered across the U.S., with several others planned.

Affordability

One appeal to living in a tiny house is affordability. In May 2017, the median sale price of a traditional new house was $324,300. In contrast, the median cost of a tiny house is $57,500. Many people who do purchase a traditional house must work hard to afford them. They often spend their spare time on maintenance: mowing, cleaning, painting, and gardening. With a tiny house, there is less to maintain.

The price of a tiny house can range anywhere from $10,000 for a build-it-yourself model, to $100,000 for a custom built home. Even the most expensive tiny house is less expensive than a traditional house.

Buyers of Tiny Houses

Tiny houses appeal to many different people. Some people want to downsize and live in a smaller space. They want fewer rooms to clean and fewer repairs to make due to living in a smaller building. Some people want to move frequently, and some tiny houses are built on wheels or can be moved easily due to their size, which suits these people's needs. And, of course, some people find that living in a tiny house requires you to live with fewer possessions, which some people enjoy.

Interest in Tiny Houses

Studies have shown that an increasing number of people are becoming interested in tiny houses. The number of people searching for information on the Internet and the number of sources that offer information about tiny houses has been rising.

Some people think tiny homes are just a fad. Others believe that tiny homes will grow in popularity and eventually become common. Tiny houses may not be for everybody, but they are a good option for some people.

Name ___________________________

Nonfiction

Predict

2

Tiny Houses

When you **predict**, you think of what will happen next. You can predict as you read. Use what you read and your own background information to predict what will happen later. A prediction is always about what will happen later.

Ask these questions to help you make predictions:

What are all the possible things that can happen?

What information tells me what will likely happen?

Answer the items about the text you read.

1. Do you predict that the number of people who are interested in tiny houses will increase or decrease in the future? Explain your answer.

____

____

2. If the price of tiny houses rises to the price of other houses, how will this affect the number of people buying tiny houses? Explain why you think so.

____

____

3. Explain how the title and headings helped you predict what you would read next.

____

____

4. Do you think the number of tiny house communities will increase or decrease in the future? Explain your answer.

____

____

____

Name ______________________________

Answer the items.

1. Explain how you can make predictions as you read a text.

____

____

2. Explain the difference between a prediction and a guess.

____

____

Read the paragraph. Then answer the item.

3. Desalinization is the process of turning salty seawater into drinkable water by removing the salt. It is predicted that desalinization may happen on a large scale by the 2030s. Currently, it is estimated that about 10% of the world's population does not have access to clean drinking water. This is a serious problem. Worse still, this percentage could rise as climate changes lead to more water vapor forming, leaving less actual water.

   Predict the effect that large-scale desalinization will have on the world's population.

____

____

4. Indigenous populations in South America have declined significantly in the last few centuries. Brazil is home to a number of "uncontacted tribes," or tribes that have not been impacted greatly by other cultures. In 1988, Brazil arranged in its constitution for large areas of forest to be safely reserved for indigenous people. About 12.5% of Brazil's total land was designated for about 450,000 indigenous people, which has helped them to increase their population. Of the entire indigenous population in Brazil, 60% live in the Amazon. The areas where they live are protected, so most farmers, landowners, and land developers do not frequent these parts of the Amazon.

   Predict what would happen to Brazil's indigenous population if Brazil's constitution were to no longer protect certain areas of the Amazon.

____

____

Name ____________________

Some nonfiction texts contain both **facts** and **opinions**.

A fact is information that can be proven true. Research findings and data help us determine facts that are true.

An opinion is what a person thinks, feels, or believes about something. An opinion is a person's judgment. People can have different opinions about a single topic.

Read the paragraph. Then answer the items.

Research has shown that dark chocolate, which is made from the seed of the cacao tree, has nutrients that are beneficial to your health. Consumed in moderation, dark chocolate can help lower the risk of heart disease. Dark chocolate has also been proven to help lower high blood pressure. Dark chocolate has half the sugar and four times the fiber of milk chocolate. Dark chocolate also has fewer calories. Milk chocolate contains less of the cacao bean than dark chocolate, and milk chocolate also contains milk, sugar, and cream. That's what makes it so creamy and delicious. There is no denying that dark chocolate is better for you than milk chocolate, but dark chocolate has a bitter and unappealing taste. Dark chocolate simply doesn't taste as good as milk chocolate.

1. Write one sentence from the text that states an opinion. Use quotation marks.

____

____

2. Write one sentence from the text that appears to state a fact. Use quotation marks.

____

3. The author mentions research. Do the facts in the text support what the research shows? Explain your answer.

____

____

____

Name ____________________

Bizarre Deep-Sea Creatures

The deep sea, where sunlight does not reach, is a dark, cold, spooky place. With the aid of remote-controlled cameras and submersible robots, scientists have been able to explore the mysterious depths of the ocean. During their research, scientists have come upon the most bizarre creatures ever seen, some of which scientists were not expecting and had not yet seen or identified.

The northern stargazer is a type of fish that was found off the eastern coast of the United States. It grows to around 20 inches (50 cm) in length. It has a black-brown body and a striped tail. The markings of the fish are certainly unusual, but the most striking feature of this fish is the location of its eyes and mouth. They are situated at the top of its head!

The red handfish, found in the waters of Australia, is another strange-looking fish. Instead of the flat fins that characterize other fish, this creature has fins that look like tiny human hands. Rather than swimming, the handfish uses these hand-like fins to grip the ocean floor and move about.

Dumbo octopus

The Dumbo octopus is another odd creature that lives on the floor of every ocean in the world. It's a cute creature. It grows to about 8 inches (20 cm) in length. The Dumbo octopus has eight arms like a regular octopus, but it also has a pair of ear-like fins that make it look like Disney's Dumbo the Flying Elephant.

The bioluminescent octopus was found deep in the Gulf of Maine. This octopus got its name because it emits its own light, as a firefly does. The light lures prey into swimming right into the mouth of the octopus.

yeti crab

The odd looking yeti crab was discovered in Antarctica. It was named after the Abominable Snowman, which is also called Yeti. This white, hairy-chested crab is so odd that scientists had to designate a new species of crab. It ranges from under half an inch (0.5 cm) to six inches (15 cm) in length. The Antarctic yeti crabs cluster together, one on top of another, to survive in the cold water. The hair on their bodies is called setae, and it attracts bacteria, which the crabs eat.

These are just a few of the bizarre creatures that lurk in the deep dark sea.

Name ________________________________

Bizarre Deep-Sea Creatures

Authors can include both **facts** and **opinions** in a nonfiction text. A fact is information that can be proven true. You can find a fact in multiple sources. An opinion is what someone thinks, feels, or believes. A person can disagree with another person's opinion.

Fact: Humans are mammals.

Opinion: Humans are better than animals.

Answer the items about the text you read.

1. Explain how the title tells you the author's opinion about deep-sea creatures.

____

____

2. Write three details from the text that tell the author's opinion.

____

____

____

3. Write three details from the text that appear to be facts.

____

____

____

____

4. Do the photos make you agree with the author's opinion that these deep-sea creatures are bizarre and strange-looking? Explain your opinion.

____

____

Name ______________________________

Answer the items.

1. Explain the difference between facts and opinions.

____

____

____

2. How do you identify whether a statement shares a fact or an opinion?

____

____

____

Read the paragraph. Then answer the items.

We all know that teachers assign students grades. Should students also be able to grade their teachers? Some people think so. Schools around the U.S. are already involved in programs that help assess a teacher's performance. In some schools, students complete questionnaires that ask them to evaluate their teachers. The questions are not only about academics. Some questions are about communication skills. For example, some questions ask how well the students feel that their teacher is connecting with them and how comfortable the students feel approaching their teacher with questions. One concern that some educators have about asking students to grade a teacher is whether or not students will be fair and honest about their teacher's performance.

3. Does this text include both opinions and facts? Explain your answer.

____

____

4. Write a statement that shares your opinion about this topic.

____

____

Name ________________________________

You can **make inferences** as you read a text to better understand it. When you make an inference, you use background knowledge and clues in the text to figure out something that is not directly stated.

Even though you don't read an inference directly, it is a detail that you believe is true based on the information you have.

Read the paragraph. Then answer the questions.

People who live in areas with mountain lions have to make certain considerations that other people do not have to make. For example, pet owners living in such areas may want to consider keeping their dogs and cats indoors. Additionally, people may want to consider doing activities such as bike riding and jogging in areas that don't have mountain lions. Mountain lions are known for pouncing on moving objects. Mountain lions attack prey and anything that they think is invading their territory. Still, it's important to remember that it is not in a mountain lion's nature to attack a human, which is why attacks on humans happen so rarely. Mountain lions typically prey on smaller animals.

1. Why should some pet owners consider keeping their domestic dogs and cats indoors?

____

2. How would we know if it were in a mountain lion's nature to prey on humans?

____

Read the paragraph. Then answer the item.

3. Ticks are organisms that live on the outside of animals, including dogs and cats. When they bite, ticks irritate an animal's skin. Ticks can get carried into houses by pets, posing a threat to humans in addition to animals. Shampoo your pets with medicated ingredients provided by a veterinarian, and give your pets oral medications regularly.

   Explain what the medications mentioned in the text probably do. Then explain how giving your pets these medications would benefit you.

____

____

Name ______________________________

You can **make inferences** when you read a text. Making inferences will help you to understand it better. Inferring is figuring out something that the author didn't tell you. It is "reading between the lines" in order to find out why something happens.

Read the paragraph. Then answer the items.

Many people are affected by a condition that causes them to sneeze uncontrollably when they are suddenly exposed to bright sunlight, such as when leaving a dark movie theater. This genetic condition is known as the photic sneeze reflex. Although an episode of uncontrolled sneezing might prove embarrassing, it is generally harmless. There are situations in which it can be dangerous, however. Imagine a pilot in flight experiencing such an episode and losing control, even for a few seconds.

1. Why does the author suggest that a pilot in flight experiencing a photic sneezing episode could cause a dangerous situation? Explain how this is possible.

____

____

2. Write two scenarios or situations that could bring about a photic sneezing episode.

____

____

Read the paragraph. Then answer the question.

3. Many people suffer with hay fever, an allergic disorder. People with hay fever may have a runny nose, itchy throat, and watery eyes, and they may cough and sneeze often. Pollen and other plant substances can cause hay fever to flare up. There are two types of hay fever: seasonal (flaring up at a certain time of the year) and perennial (flaring up all year round).

   How would you know if you have seasonal or perennial hay fever?

   ____

   ____

Name ____________________

Trademarks

You and your family are on the highway, on a road trip, when you spot a restaurant just off the road. Even though you've never been to this place before, you know for certain that it's a restaurant because you've seen its colors and designs before. Your little sister, who can't even read yet, knows very well what those colors and designs represent, too. Lunch!

The large recognizable figures you see from the highway are trademarks. Fast food restaurants, grocery stores, websites, and other kinds of businesses use trademarks. A trademark is a recognizable word, symbol, or graphic, or a combination of these. A trademark identifies a brand name, product, or service. Shapes, sounds, and colors can also be trademarked. For example, the yellow color of *Yellow Pages* (a phone book that was popularly used to get phone numbers for decades) is trademarked. No other phone book could have that specific shade of yellow.

A successful trademark is one that you recognize right away. Customers see the trademark and immediately know what product, service, or company it represents. Say you have a terrific product, and you want to trademark it so no one else can copy it. Before you register a trademark to represent your product, you need to do a search to find out if the trademark is available. That is, it should not be in use by someone else. Next, you should make sure your trademark is strong. You do this by making the design distinctive, original, and unique. For instance, a generic term, such as *apple*, cannot be trademarked if it refers to a fruit. However, Apple™, when it refers to computers, can be trademarked. In this case, the word *apple* has nothing to do with the product it represents. It's a unique, creative name for a brand of technology products.

Trademarks vary in strength. The government is more likely to register your trademark and protect it if you have a strong trademark. There are five trademark categories, which are listed here from weakest to strongest:

- Generic—This is very general. An example is a word such as *paper* to describe actual paper.
- Descriptive—This describes a geographic location or part of the product or service.
- Suggestive—This is a word related to the product or service, such as Rent-a-Bike™.
- Arbitrary—This is a common word unrelated to the product, such as Amazon™.
- Fanciful—This is an invented word that has no meaning apart from the company, product, or service it represents, such as Xerox™.

Next time you're on the highway and you notice a trademark image, think about how strong it is!

Name ____________________

Trademarks

You can **make inferences** as you read a text to better understand it. When you make an inference, you use knowledge and clues in the text to figure out something that is not directly stated in the text.

Even though you don't read an inference directly, it is a detail that you believe is likely to be true based on the information you do have.

Answer the items about the text you read.

1. The author states that before you register a trademark, you need to do a search to find out if it is available. What does the author most likely mean by the phrase "do a search"?

   Ⓐ Drive on the highway.

   Ⓒ Do research online.

   Ⓒ Look in an encyclopedia.

   Ⓓ Watch television.

2. A company with the trademark name "Koco-berreez" sells chocolate covered fruits. Which category would its trademark fall into? Explain how you know.

   ____

   ____

3. Which category of strength would the trademark name "Bank of Oregon" fall into? Explain how you know.

   ____

   ____

4. Describe the features of an unsuccessful trademark. Explain why you think a trademark like this would be unsuccessful.

   ____

   ____

   ____

Name ______________________________

Review

Answer the items.

1. Explain how to make inferences as you read a text.

____

____

____

2. Explain how making an inference is different from guessing as you read a text.

____

____

____

3. Why do you think that making inferences is an important skill?

____

____

Read the paragraph. Then make an inference to answer the question.

4. Hot chocolate is a favorite treat for many people. If you're worried about burning your tongue when you drink it, pour some milk straight from the refrigerator into your hot chocolate mug.

   What effect would the author's suggestion have on the hot chocolate?

____

5. Instead of munching on chips, try snacking on nuts or sunflower seeds, which are also crunchy. Replace sugary candy with dried fruit or fruit yogurt, which can be naturally sweet. You can also add vegetables to meals that are already your favorites.

   What is the purpose of the text that this paragraph is from?

____

____

Name ____________________

Authors always have a **purpose** for writing a text.
These are reasons authors write:

to inform, or tell facts

to entertain, or tell an interesting story

to persuade, or give opinions

to teach, or give instructions about how to do something

Read the paragraph. Then answer the question.

1. The State Hermitage Museum in Saint Petersburg, Russia, is one of the world's oldest and largest museums. It is a sprawling complex of interconnected buildings that house a vast collection of paintings and artwork, which in the 18th century belonged to Catherine the Great. At that time, cats guarded the artwork against rats and mice. Dozens of cats still live in the museum's basement, serving the same purpose.

   What is the author's purpose for writing this paragraph? Explain how you know.

   ____

   ____

Read the paragraph. Then answer the questions.

The cats at the Hermitage Museum live a charmed life, nesting in baskets and blankets placed in the basement. Still, things need to change. Some people drop off their unwanted cats at the museum, possibly believing that the museum is a cat shelter of some kind. It's not right to abandon a pet, and people need to stop doing this. Someone should write a letter to the authorities in Saint Petersburg urging them to take action against this practice.

2. What is the author's purpose for writing this paragraph? Explain how you know.

   ____

   ____

3. How can you tell that the purpose is not to teach?

   ____

Name ______________________________

Deserts of Australia

Australia, the driest continent in the world, is known for its vast, remote areas. Collectively, these areas are famously called the Outback. Some parts of the Outback feature grasses, shrubs, and a few trees, but most of the Outback is desert. The five major Australian deserts are Great Victoria Desert, Great Sandy Desert, Tanami Desert, Gibson Desert, and Simpson Desert.

outback road in the Northern Territory of Australia

The Great Victoria Desert, at 250,000 square miles (647,000 square km), is the largest desert in Australia. It is made of small sand hills and areas of gravel. It also contains salt lakes.

The Great Sandy Desert is 150,000 square miles (400,000 square km). This desert is the second largest desert in Australia. It contains rows of red sand dunes that are hundreds of miles long.

The Tanami Desert is 71,000 square miles (184,000 square km). It is located in the Northern Territory, and it is considered one of the most isolated places on Earth. It is made up mostly of sandy plains with grasses and shrubs.

The Gibson Desert is 60,000 square miles (155,000 square km), and it consists mainly of gravel hills and dry grasses with areas of sandy dunes. The desert was named after Alfred Gibson, an explorer who died while searching for water.

The Simpson Desert is 56,000 square miles (145,000 square km). Located farthest east, this desert is dominated by red sand dunes that can be up to 100 miles (161 km) long. It is home to the largest dune, nicknamed Big Red, which is over 130 feet (40 km) high.

The Australian deserts are home to a variety of animals that have adapted to the harsh environment. Snakes thrive in the scorching heat, as do lizards such as bearded dragons, geckos, and thorny devils. The bilby, a small marsupial, is nocturnal. This means it spends the hot daytime deep underground and comes out only during the cooler nights. Other small mammals, such as the hopping mouse, also burrow to keep cool. Birds such as parrots, owls, and hawks fly long distances to find water.

Unfortunately, many desert animals are endangered or have already gone extinct. This is due to competition with nonnative animals, or animals that people have introduced into the Australian deserts. Feral cats, pigs, foxes, rabbits, and camels now compete with native animals for food.

Name ______________________________

Deserts of Australia

Authors always have a **purpose** for writing a text.
These are reasons authors write:

to inform, or tell facts

to entertain, or tell an interesting story

to persuade, or give opinions

to teach, or give instructions about how to do something

As you read, ask, "What does the author want me to think about or know?" This can help you to identify the author's purpose.

Answer the items about the text you read.

1. What is the author's purpose for writing this text? Explain how you know.

____

____

____

2. How can you tell that the purpose is not to entertain?

____

____

3. Write two details from the text that support your answer to number one.

____

____

____

4. How does the main idea of the text illustrate the author's purpose?

____

____

Name ______________________________

Answer the items.

1. Write four purposes that authors may have for writing a text.

   to ____________________ to ____________________

   to ____________________ to ____________________

2. Explain how you can identify the author's purpose when you read a text.

   ____

   ____

3. How can knowing an author's purpose help you to better understand a text?

   ____

   ____

   ____

Read the paragraph. Then answer the items.

Have you ever taken pictures on your smart phone but then wished you had them on your computer? It's easy to move pictures from your phone to your computer. One way you can do it is by following these simple steps. First, go into the gallery or storage area of your phone, where your photos are saved. Next, look for a menu. Most smart phone galleries have a menu that you can go into and see various options. Select the "share" option. At this point, you can click on as many of your saved photos as you want. Choose the photos you want to move. Somewhere on your phone's screen, you will see the word *share*—press it. Next, email yourself the photos. Finally, sign in to your email account on your computer, open the email from your smart phone, and download the photos to your computer.

4. What is the author's purpose for writing this text? Explain how you know.

   ____

   ____

5. Write one detail from the text that supports your answer to number four.

   ____

Name ____________________

The purpose of **expository nonfiction** text is to inform the reader about a topic, which may be a person, place, thing, event, or idea. Expository nonfiction informs by giving facts and providing explanations.

Expository texts state a main idea and provide facts that support it. You can find expository nonfiction in textbooks, on websites, and in other types of resources.

Read the paragraph. Then answer the items.

A heat wave is defined as record-high temperatures persisting for five or more consecutive days. A heat wave is especially dangerous in a city, where the air is stagnant. In this case, a heat wave is a mix of polluted air and extreme heat. The poor air quality can create many health problems for people. In addition, the concrete in a city retains heat during the day, gradually releasing that heat at night. These higher nighttime temperatures produce what is called the "urban heat island effect."

1. Explain how you can tell that the author's purpose for writing this text is to inform.

____

____

2. Write the text's main idea.

____

____

3. State details from the text that help you understand why a heat wave in a city is especially dangerous.

____

____

____

4. Did you know about urban heat island effect before you read this text?

____

Name ________________________________

Augusta Savage

Augusta Savage was a sculptor, educator, and activist who inspired people with her talent and determination.

Augusta was born in Green Cove Springs, Florida, on February 28, 1892. She was the seventh of fourteen children. From an early age, she displayed talent as a sculptor. She began sculpting with the natural red clay that was abundant around her neighborhood. Augusta's family was not wealthy, and her father didn't support her interest in art. Still, Augusta was determined to be a sculptor. When her family moved to a different part of Florida that did not have red clay, Augusta was able to obtain materials from a local potter. She created figures and entered them in a county fair competition. She won a special prize of $25 for her work.

As an adult, Augusta moved to New York City to study art. In 1923, she applied to an art program in France. Her application was rejected because she was black. Augusta was upset over this injustice and sent letters to newspapers. Although her story made headlines and made people angry, it did not help her gain acceptance into the art program. This loss was the beginning of Augusta's lifelong struggle for the rights of African American artists.

Augusta's art represented African American culture. One of Augusta's most famous sculptures is Gamin, based on the likeness of her nephew.

Augusta working intently on a sculpture

Augusta also sculpted a bust of the well-known African American writer W. E. B. Du Bois for the New York Public Library. One of Augusta's most breathtaking sculptures was Lift Every Voice and Sing, also known as The Harp. This 16-foot sculpture was created for the 1939 World's Fair in New York. The sculpture showed twelve black singers lined up to symbolize the strings of the harp. Augusta did not have the money to cast the sculpture in metal. It was made of plaster and, unfortunately, was destroyed after the fair, along with other art pieces. Only photographs of it remain.

In the years that followed, Augusta started the Savage Studio of Arts and Crafts, where she taught and created art. She also helped found the Harlem Artists' Guild and the Harlem Community Art Center. The goal of the guild was to create free, accessible art instruction for people of all races.

Augusta spent the last decades of her life teaching art. In 1960, she moved in with her daughter, and she passed away in 1962 in New York City.

Name ____________________________________

Augusta Savage

The purpose of **expository nonfiction** text is to inform the reader about a topic, which may be a person, place, thing, event, or idea. Expository nonfiction informs by giving facts.

When you read expository nonfiction, try to identify the main idea and supporting details to better understand the text.

Answer the items about the text you read.

1. Explain what makes this an expository text.

 ____

 ____

2. Write the text's main idea.

 ____

 ____

3. Describe what you learned from reading this text.

 ____

 ____

 ____

4. Write one sentence from the text that appears to state a fact. Use quotation marks.

 ____

 ____

5. Write two things Augusta accomplished during her lifetime.

 ____

 ____

 ____

Name ____________________

Review

Answer the items.

1. What is the purpose of expository nonfiction text? Why would you read an expository nonfiction text?

2. Write two types of resources in which you can find expository nonfiction text.

3. How do you think expository nonfiction is different from persuasive nonfiction?

Read the paragraph. Then answer the items.

Lobsters are crustaceans, which means they have an exoskeleton, or outer skeleton. Their exoskeleton is usually hard. However, their exoskeletons do not grow as their bodies grow, so lobsters shed their hard outer shell at times, exposing a soft, new exoskeleton. It takes time for the new exoskeleton to harden, so lobsters are at risk until this happens. Lobsters have ten legs, as shrimp and crabs do. Lobsters rely on feeling and touching to catch prey. Some deep-sea lobsters are blind. Lobsters have been known to eat other lobsters.

4. Explain what makes this an expository text.

5. Write a fact that you learned from the text.

Name ____

The purpose of **persuasive nonfiction** text is to convince the reader to have a particular opinion about a topic. The author states an opinion and provides facts and reasons to persuade the reader to have the same opinion.
The opinion the author states is usually the main idea of the text.

When you read persuasive nonfiction text, analyze the author's arguments and reasoning to determine whether or not you agree.

Read the paragraph. Then answer the items.

All schools should require students to wear uniforms to benefit the school as well as the students. For one thing, having a standard uniform for all students would save students time every day because they wouldn't have to figure out what to wear each morning. Also, students would not have to worry about peer pressure to follow fashion trends if everybody at their school has to wear the same thing every day. Having uniforms would benefit schools because they wouldn't have issues with students not following school dress codes. In fact, requiring uniforms may eliminate the need for schools to have any dress code at all because the outfits that the school finds appropriate would be determined by the school. And many school uniforms are cute. If your school ever conducts a vote to see how many people are in favor of requiring student uniforms, raise your hand up high and vote for that fabulous option.

1. What is the main idea of the text?

____

____

2. What details does the author provide to support the main idea?

____

____

3. Write a sentence from the text that states an opinion. Use quotation marks.

____

____

Name ____________________

Project-Based Learning

Many teachers in the United States and abroad attest that project-based learning is an effective way to learn. Students prefer project-based learning because it is not boring. All teachers should incorporate project-based learning into their curriculums.

Project-based learning, or PBL, is a teaching approach in which students work on a project with the goal of answering a real-world question or solving a meaningful problem. PBL requires students to use skills such as critical thinking, problem solving, creativity, and collaboration. Additionally, students take pride in their work because they will need to present their ideas to an audience. PBL leads to the creation of a product, such as a performance or an artifact. An important part of PBL is audience feedback and comments.

PBL can fit into any curriculum or subject area. In social studies, for example, students can research the history and culture of their community, culminating in a festival for the community, complete with traditional costumes, food, art, and music.

In math, students can create a quilt or a mosaic that contains symbols of their community's heritage. This project combines elements of geometry, art, and history. It would require math skills to measure the material used to make the quilt. The quilt could be displayed at a county fair or a school assembly.

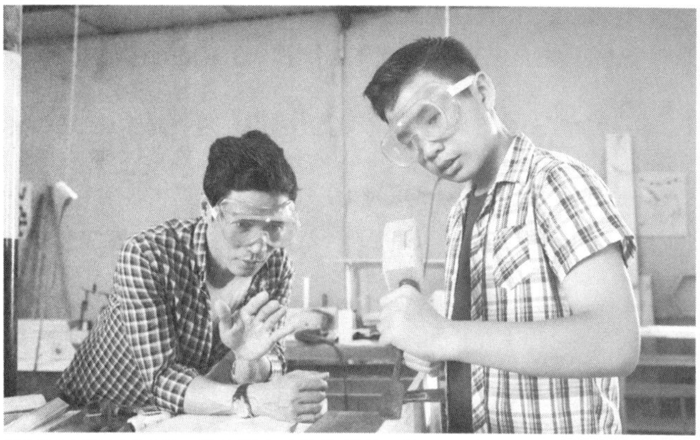

In language arts, students could team up with a school from a different culture. Initially, they could exchange information through a class website. Then they could put together a package of items that represent their school or culture. Students would write an informative description of each item and why it is relevant. Finally, the students could exchange the packages through the mail and ask follow-up questions about the items they received.

In science, students could research native and invasive plants, and they could use their findings to build a habitat in the school garden. This may include removing weeds, adding plants to attract butterflies, and building bird feeders.

An important part of PBL is that failure is understood to be an essential part of the learning process. One of the goals of PBL is to struggle productively and work through problems. All schools and educators should embrace PBL!

Name ______________________________

Project-Based Learning

The purpose of **persuasive nonfiction** text is to convince the reader to have a particular opinion about a topic. The author states a viewpoint and provides facts and reasons to get the reader to view the topic in the same way.

A persuasive text usually favors one viewpoint.

You can find persuasive nonfiction text in advertisements, pamphlets, movie reviews, blogs, and many other sources.

Answer the items about the text you read.

1. Explain what makes this text persuasive nonfiction.

____

____

____

2. What is the author's opinion statement, or the main idea? Explain how you know.

____

____

3. In your own words, write one opinion statement presented in the text.

____

____

4. Do any of the facts the author provides support the opposite viewpoint, or the concerns with PBL? Explain your answer.

____

____

5. Do you agree with the opinion the author promotes in the text? Explain why or why not.

____

Name ____________________

Review

Answer the questions.

1. What is the purpose of persuasive nonfiction text?

____

____

2. How do facts and opinions help an author convince a reader?

____

____

Read the sentence. Then write **Y** on the line if the sentence is likely to be from a persuasive nonfiction text. Write **N** on the line if the sentence is probably not from a persuasive nonfiction text.

3. Don't feed animals at the park or in your yard because you are doing more harm than good by possibly making the animals dependent on the food you give them. ______

4. Some people do cardiovascular exercise, such as running, every day of the week. ______

5. Some people think that only organic vegetables are nutritious, but you should buy and eat vegetables even if they're not organic because those are nutritious as well. ______

Read the paragraph. Then explain what makes this a persuasive nonfiction text.

6. Eleven years of age is not too young to get a smart phone. First of all, a smart phone can come in handy for doing school assignments. Students can type, email, and share assignments with a phone. Eleven years of age is a perfect time to get a cellphone because students have to do research for homework assignments and projects. Secondly, children can use a smart phone to easily communicate with relatives, such as grandparents, who live far away. Finally, there are a lot of online news sources that are meant for young audiences, so smart phones can help children to be well informed, which is important.

____

____

Name ______________________________

Narrative nonfiction tells a story about true events experienced by real people. Although narrative nonfiction has literary elements, such as setting, character, and plot, the text is nonfiction. Whenever you tell a true story about your own life or somebody else's life, it is narrative nonfiction.

A memoir is a type of narrative nonfiction. A memoir is a historical account of an event or time period, told by someone who really experienced the events in the story.

Read the memoir. Then answer the items.

When I was a young man, my parents thought it best for me to attend a boarding school in Mexico City. I agreed simply to please my dear mother, but I was not the most diligent student. Don't get me wrong. I enjoyed learning, but I did not enjoy studying. Luckily, I had an anxious roommate who would pace back and forth, studying for an exam by reading earnestly from the textbook. Meanwhile, I would lie in the top bunk, listening to him, receiving the information and capturing it in my mind, much as a voice recorder would. Sometimes, my roommate would mispronounce a word, and I would correct him. Other times, my attention would wane, and I would ask him to repeat. Invariably, on test day, I would hear my roommate's voice replaying in my mind. This is how I made top scores in class.

1. Explain what makes this narrative nonfiction.

____

____

2. What details can you infer about the person this memoir is about? Explain how you made these inferences.

____

____

3. In what ways does this nonfiction text seem similar to a fictional story?

____

____

Pup in Distress

Juan Lopez is a custodian at a community of oceanside homes in California. In August 2016, he was driving his truck through the neighborhood, making his rounds to make sure everything was in order. Suddenly, he spotted what he thought was a small dog on a bike path. It was lying motionless. Juan parked the truck and went closer to look.

When he knelt beside the animal, Juan was surprised to find himself face to face with a baby sea lion. Apparently, the pup had walked about 900 feet (274 meters) along the beach boardwalk and ended up on the narrow path that led to the homes. The pup was resting in the road after its long, harrowing journey.

Juan recently heard a report stating that high numbers of sea lion pups have been washing ashore in California in recent years. Sea lion mothers go out to sea for days to hunt for food, leaving their pups near shore. Perhaps this pup had been left by its mother for a long period of time and started to panic. Maybe that's why the pup came ashore and ended up on the path.

The pup looked up at Juan with big, sad eyes and let out a little whimper. Juan grabbed a blanket from his truck. His plan was to spread the blanket on the road, roll the baby onto it, and then carry the baby to the ocean. But when Juan unfolded the blanket and waved it out in midair, the pup let out a roar of distress and started backing away, shaking its head. Clearly, the pup would have nothing to do with Juan's plan. There had to be another way.

Juan had worked in the community for 25 years. Every night, he had made his rounds without incident. He always drove around, listening to the sounds of the crashing waves and the sea lions barking in the distance. Juan was hearing sea lions now. Maybe one of them was this poor pup's mother.

Suddenly, Juan had an idea. He repeated the bark he was hearing. As he barked, the sea lion pup calmed down. Juan kept barking and started making his way toward the boardwalk. Amazingly, the pup followed. Juan barked and walked along the boardwalk toward the ocean. The pup waddled behind. They walked and waddled until they reached the shore. Juan gave a final farewell bark, and the pup jumped into the water.

Name ______________________________

Pup in Distress

Narrative nonfiction tells a story about true events experienced by real people. Although narrative nonfiction has literary elements, it is based on facts. The story's settings, characters, and events are true.

Narrative nonfiction reads like a story, unlike many other types of nonfiction, which read like an essay or a news article.

Answer the items about the text you read.

1. Explain what makes this narrative nonfiction.

____

____

____

2. In what ways does this nonfiction text seem similar to a fictional story?

____

____

____

3. Write a fact about sea lions that you learned from the narrative nonfiction text.

____

____

4. How is this nonfiction text different from a news article or an essay?

____

____

5. If you saw a sea lion pup in distress, as Juan did, would you react in the same way? Explain your answer.

____

Name ________________________________

Review

Answer the items.

1. Explain how narrative nonfiction is different from other types of nonfiction texts.

____

____

____

2. What kinds of facts can you learn from narrative nonfiction text? Provide examples.

____

____

____

3. Do you think that a narrative nonfiction story can be just as interesting as a fiction story? Explain why or why not.

____

____

Read the sentence. Then write **Y** on the line if the sentence is likely to be from a narrative nonfiction text. Write **N** on the line if the sentence is probably not from a narrative nonfiction text.

4. As he did every day, President George Washington gathered his long hair in his hands and pulled it back firmly at the back of his head before tying it with a ribbon. ______

5. The ideal weight for a healthy domestic cat is 10 pounds. ______

6. Ramona decided to show all of her friends her superpowers, so she bent her knees and shot up straight into the air before flying away, high up in the sky. ______

7. Queen Elizabeth snapped another picture of her children with her camera and remembered her parents warmly, for they gave her the camera as a wedding gift years ago in 1947. ______

Name ______________________________

Descriptive nonfiction provides descriptive sensory details about a topic. The topic can be a person, place, thing, or event. Descriptive nonfiction explains how the main topic **looks**, **feels**, **tastes**, **smells**, or **sounds**.

When you read descriptive nonfiction, you feel as if you are experiencing what the writer is describing.

Read the paragraph. Then answer the items.

Have you ever eaten a spicy curry? Curry is one of the most diverse foods because it can be made in so many different ways. Eating a curry is a delightful experience that can excite all of your senses. If you do not particularly enjoy hot, pungent food that burns your tongue slightly, you can have a curry that is sweet, bitter, or tangy. While some curries have a creamy, velvety texture, others have a chunky, thick texture. And other curries have a crunch! There are vegetable curries, meat curries, and tofu curries. Curries can be orange, yellow, green, red, brown, or multi-colored with a variety of hues. One distinct quality of a curry is its tantalizing smell, which often includes hints of coriander, turmeric, garlic, ginger, pepper, cumin, chili, and more! When a curry is being cooked, you hear spices being ground up, onions and garlic sizzling, and bubbling as the curry simmers and thickens. Whenever a new ingredient is added to the curry pot, you hear sizzling, you see steam rise, you smell a unique aroma, and this makes your mouth water for the delicious curry.

1. Write words or phrases that appeal to your senses and help describe curry.

   looks: ______________________________

   smells: ______________________________

   tastes: ______________________________

   feels: ______________________________

   sounds: ______________________________

2. Based on the descriptive text, would you want to eat a curry? Explain your answer.

   ____

   ____

Name ____________________

A Memorable Modern Building

The Cleveland Clinic Lou Ruvo Center for Brain Health began operating in Las Vegas, Nevada, in 2010. It is a medical center dedicated to helping people with brain diseases. The important work that this clinic does makes it unique, but there is another thing that makes it memorable: the architecture of the building is modern and eye-catching.

From the outside, the building appears to be caving in on itself. At first glance, it may appear that this building is from a science fiction horror film in which a giant vacuum cleaner is sucking the building into a hole, causing it to crumple up and collapse on itself. Or, it's possible that a passerby may glance at the building and think that the builders made irreversible mistakes while measuring the building materials, which resulted in a structure that is crooked and strange.

Actually, the building was designed by a modern architect named Frank Gehry. The caving-in appearance of the building is an illustration of deconstructivism in architecture. Deconstructivism is a deliberate lack of symmetry and the appearance of being fragmented, or having pieces that do not go together. Therefore, the building's unusual appearance is intentional. Frank Gehry's goal in creating this building was to create a place that people would remember, talk about, and want to visit.

As visitors go near the building, they will notice a concrete courtyard shaded by vibrantly colored pillars. Colorful chairs and tables provide a bright atmosphere for an outdoor resting area. The building is painted with different colors, including yellow, blue, neon yellow, and red. The building appears to be a contradiction of straight, even lines that make up windows and some compartments, and crooked, jagged lines that make up other compartments, and it is this contradiction that creates the asymmetrical quality of the building's overall appearance. Inside is a rich red carpet and spotless, gleaming white walls. The soaring ceilings contain bright light fixtures and wide windows, allowing natural sunlight to pour in. Both the courtyard and the inside area of the Cleveland Clinic Lou Ruvo Center are spacious and clean. This is an exceptional modern building.

Name ____________________

A Memorable Modern Building

Descriptive nonfiction provides details about a topic. The topic can be a person, place, thing, or event. Descriptive nonfiction provides sensory details, or details about how the main topic **looks**, **feels**, **tastes**, **smells**, or **sounds**.

The purpose of descriptive nonfiction is to help the reader form a mental image of the topic.

Answer the items about the text you read.

1. Explain what the Cleveland Clinic Lou Ruvo Center is and where it is located.

   ____

   ____

2. How does the Lou Ruvo Center building illustrate deconstructivism in architecture?

   ____

   ____

3. Why did the architect make the building so unique?

   ____

   ____

4. Write six words or phrases from the text that describe the building.

   ____________________ ____________________

   ____________________ ____________________

   ____________________ ____________________

5. Write two words or phrases you would use to describe the appearance of the building, after looking at the picture yourself.

   ____

   ____

Name ____________________________

Answer the questions.

1. What is the purpose of descriptive nonfiction?

____

____

____

2. Why are sensory details an important part of descriptive nonfiction?

____

____

____

Read the paragraph. Then explain whether or not it is descriptive nonfiction.

3. There are over 260 different kinds of monkeys in the world. They are primates. They live all over the world. You can see them at the zoo. These animals are related to humans. They can use tools and play games.

____

____

____

4. Making your own pasta is fun, but it is hard work. You have to stir and roll dough out, which can make your arms feel sore after a while. You have to make sure the dough is well mixed. When you work with the dough, put dry flour on your hands and on the surface you're working on. You can smell the yummy, buttery scent of dough in the air as you make it. You flatten the dough and push it through a pasta maker. The dough looks like spaghetti that you can eat as it comes out of the machine, but you can't eat it yet because it's raw. You can boil the noodles and eat them.

____

____

____

Name ______________________________

Character is one of the most important elements of a story.
When you analyze character traits, it helps you to better understand the story.
A character with more than one trait is complex and realistic.
These are some traits that describe characters:

curious	**lethargic**	**cautious**	**fun-loving**
gullible	**vain**	**sweet**	**honest**

Read the paragraph. Then answer the items.

Maddie and her brother Doug watched a movie that took place during the Middle Ages. Maddie kept pausing the movie, though, to ask questions and closely study the props and costumes on the screen. "What kind of weapon is that knight using?" she asked Doug, who just shrugged. "Yum, what kind of food are they eating?" she wondered aloud. "I wonder if the women really wore those dresses!" she exclaimed.

"Enough, Maddie!" pleaded Doug. "I just want to watch the movie!" That's when Maddie realized that, perhaps, Doug wasn't as curious about the Middle Ages as she was, so she controlled herself and decided to wait until after the movie to find out more. Later, she went on the Internet and looked up books about medieval history.

1. On the lines, write two character traits that describe Maddie.

   ____________________ ____________________

2. Explain why you wrote the traits you did.

   ____
   ____
   ____

Read the paragraph. Then write two character traits that describe Sebastian.

3. Sebastian was the obedient servant of the queen—as far as the queen knew. For years, he polished her slippers, swept the palace, and fetched her tea. But secretly, Sebastian didn't like the queen because she wasn't very kind. So, one day, he came up with a plan to remove her from the throne and replace her with a new queen.

   ____________________ ____________________

Name ____________________________

When you analyze a **character** in a story, it helps you to better understand the story. Consider these questions as you analyze a character:

Why does the character do certain things?

Why does the character feel a certain way?

What is important to the character?

Do you agree or disagree with the character's actions?

Read the paragraph. Then answer the items.

Mason had a tough time dealing with his little sister, Jasmine, at the beach last weekend. She accidentally stepped on the sand castle he'd been building, so he got annoyed. When Jasmine asked him to help open her water bottle, Mason refused. Later, he walked across her beach towel, dripping sand and water all over it. Jasmine complained, but Mason just shrugged. He still felt angry. Finally, their mom intervened and told Mason he was being very unkind to his sister. "I know you're upset with Jasmine for stepping on your sand castle," his mom said. "But you have to remember, she's just three years old. She didn't mean to do that." Mason sighed. His mom was right, and he actually felt really bad about how he had acted. After all, he was twelve years old, and Jasmine was only three. He went over to Jasmine and asked if she'd like to help him build a new sand castle. She said yes. It was as if she had already forgotten that Mason had been upset earlier.

1. What does Mason do to cause Jasmine to complain about him?

____

____

2. Describe how Mason's feelings change during the story. Explain how and why.

____

____

____

____

Name ____________________

Ranger Wayne

When Owen discovered the park ranger's name was Ranger Wayne, he nearly fell apart laughing. "Like the bear?" Owen asked.

"No," the man said flatly.

Ranger Wayne was the name of a cartoon bear that Owen used to watch when he was younger. The bear always had a silly grin and said, "Forest safety first!" whenever there was a problem.

Owen had come to the state park with his mom to take a survival class. They were going to learn how to build a shelter in the wild, in case they were ever lost in the woods. Owen didn't really see the point of this, though—why on Earth would he ever get lost in the woods?

"If you're lost in the wild," Ranger Wayne said, "what do you need to be most concerned about?"

Some people mentioned starvation or thirst, while others thought animal attacks were the most frightening possibility. "Boredom!" Owen called out. That earned him a stern look from his mom and the ranger, though.

Ranger Wayne looked at Owen right in the eyes, which made Owen a little nervous. Ranger Wayne said, "If you're lost in the wilderness, Son, boredom is fine. It means nothing bad is happening, and that is exactly what you want." Owen shrugged as the ranger continued.

"Those were all good answers," he said, "but animal attacks are more rare than folks realize. Food and water... these are important, but you can survive for a few days without either, if you really have to. Believe it or not, the number one danger that a person faces in the wilderness is exposure. Who can tell me what that is?"

Owen raised his hand. "Does it mean you're exposed to something, like the cold, maybe?"

Ranger Wayne nodded approvingly. "Yep. Stranded in the wild, the biggest threat you face is being unprotected from environmental conditions, such as extreme temperatures. Freezing at night is a survivalist's biggest concern. So, now, you're all going to learn how to construct a warm shelter with nothing but the materials lying around in the forest."

Ranger Wayne asked Owen to help him lean a log against a tree. As Owen helped stack sticks and stuff handfuls of leaves into the shelter's structure, he realized he was having fun. When the shelter was complete, he slithered in and was amazed by how warm it was.

"It feels safe in here," Owen said.

Ranger Wayne let the tiniest of grins form on his serious face. "Forest safety first; that's what I always say."

Name ______________________________

Ranger Wayne

When you analyze a **character** in a story, it helps you to better understand the story. Consider the following as you analyze a character:

character traits	**dialogue**
characters' actions	**characters' feelings**

Answer the items about the story you read.

1. Which pair of traits best describes Ranger Wayne?
   Ⓐ courageous and cheerful
   Ⓒ angry and greedy
   Ⓒ intelligent and lonely
   Ⓓ serious and knowledgeable

2. How are Owen's character traits different from Ranger Wayne's?

   ____

   ____

3. Does Ranger Wayne have appropriate traits for his job? Explain why or why not.

   ____

   ____

4. How do the differences between Ranger Wayne and Owen create conflict in the story?

   ____

   ____

   ____

5. Explain why Ranger Wayne's last statement is funny, considering his character traits.

   ____

   ____

Name ____________________________

Review

Answer the items.

1. Explain why it is important to analyze character traits as you read a story.

____

____

2. Why would an author write about a character who has more than one trait?

____

____

3. On the lines, write three character traits that you can think of.

______________ ______________ ______________

4. How do character traits help to shape the plot of a story?

____

____

Read the paragraph. Then answer the question.

5. On Friday evening, Avery and her dad made cookie dough. Then they put it in the fridge to bake the next day. Dixie, the babysitter, came over, and Avery's dad went to work. Then Avery said, "I'm going to surprise my dad and bake the cookies tonight." Dixie wasn't sure this was such a good idea. "I'm allowed to use the oven, and I don't need help," said Avery. She knew that her dad's rule was that she couldn't use the oven on her own, but she thought he'd be okay with it once he found out that she wanted to surprise him. She heated the oven and put in the dough. After a while, she and Dixie smelled something burning, and they saw smoke. All of the cookies were burned and inedible. Still, Avery refused to throw them out. "I'll cut off the worst burned bits, and we can still eat them. It'll be fine," she said. Dixie just shook her head.

   Which trait do you think best describes Avery: thoughtful or headstrong?
   Explain your answer.

____

____

Name ______________________________

Setting is one of the most important elements of a story. When you think about the setting, it helps you to better understand the story. Think about how the setting influences the characters to do certain things.

As you read, ask these questions about setting:

What descriptive details help you form a mental image of the setting?

How do the characters feel in the setting?

What do the characters do in the setting?

Read the paragraph. Then answer the items.

Kevin and his friends had been standing in line for just a few minutes, and they were already roasting from the sun's heat. Keven could feel drips of sweat roll down his back, and his shirt was starting to stick to his body. The sidewalk in front of the Moonlight Roller Rink had a bike rack and a trash can, but no shade at all. Finally the doors opened, and people rushed in. Kevin smiled as the cool breeze from the air-conditioners hit him. The place was dimly-lit, with red walls. Bright speckles of light flashed from a disco ball that hung in the middle of the rink. As always, the music was loud, which Kevin loved. He could feel the thumping beat of the music pound against his chest and immediately felt happy. Being at the rink made him feel as though he could never run out of energy. The combination of the loud music, the exercise, and seeing all his friends made it his favorite place to go every Saturday. He found it exciting.

1. Contrast how Kevin feels outside the roller rink and inside it.

____

____

2. Write three details from the text that show why Keven finds the rink exciting.

____

____

Name ______________________________

When you analyze the **setting** of a story, it can help you to better understand the story. Think about how the setting influences the plot and conflict in the story. These are details you can analyze about a setting:

descriptive words and phrases that help you form a mental image

characters' actions, feelings, and dialogue

clues that provide additional details

Read the paragraph. Then answer the question.

1. A chill ran down Devon's spine as she entered the dark and creepy room. The floor was slanted, and she felt like she was going to fall over. Spooky sounds filled the air. As the large group of people entered a pitch-black hallway, Devon felt a hand grasp her shoulder. Whew! It was her mom. After passing through a huge room filled with cobwebs, a fake mummy suddenly popped out of a coffin with an agonizing groan. Devon shrieked and bolted out of that room. She stepped through a door and breathed a sigh of relief as she realized that she was in the sunlight. "I'm never going into a haunted house again," she exclaimed to her mom, "even if it *is* Halloween!"

   What clues tell you that the setting is a house that is actually not haunted?

   ____

   ____

Read the paragraph. Then answer the question.

2. When Augie first saw his new house, he was creeped out. Paint was peeling, windows were broken, and the roof sagged. Mom said it would be a great house after it was fixed up. Augie wasn't so sure. It reminded him of the haunted house in a movie he'd just seen. They went inside, and the first thing Augie saw was a humongous spider web on the staircase bannister. A moment later, he heard a loud creaking sound. "A ghost!" Augie cried, running back out.

   Dad laughed and said, "It's just a creaky door, Augie!"

   How does the setting help to create the plot and conflict in the story?

   ____

   ____

Name ______________________________

The Flea Market

"We have arrived," Mom sang happily as she pulled to a stop in the dusty parking lot. The lot was situated at the top of a hill, so Antwon and his older sister, Destiny, had a full view of the entire flea market. He saw colorful tents lined up as far as his eyes could see. Crowds of people were zooming around busily, kicking up clouds of dust as they walked. "This is going to be a long, hot, dusty day," Antwon thought.

Antwon groaned as he, Destiny, and Mom headed down to where the tents were. Whenever they had come to the flea market in the past, Mom would stop at as many tents as she could. She loved to walk around for hours and rummage through bins and tables and racks of everything you can think of. She always called the flea market her "wonderland of treasures." And, usually, Destiny was just as bored as Antwon at the flea market. She would drag her feet and groan as they entered each tent. She and Antwon would beg Mom to take them back home. Today, however, Destiny and Mom were on a mission to find the perfect dresser for Destiny's room. Destiny insisted on having a purple dresser, and Mom had been searching for one for months. The flea market always had unique items, so Mom insisted on checking it out.

Colorful rugs with intricate patterns hung in the first tent they went into. The place was dark and smelled of scented candles. Antwon saw that its shelves were packed with candles, bowls, and jewelry, but he wasn't interested in any of that. Mom didn't find a purple dresser, so they all wandered over to the next tent.

Antwon walked into it and found himself face-to-face with a frightening wooden mask. Other masks filled one wall. Some had horns, others had big eyes, sharp teeth, and spooky grins.

The next tent they went into had only statues, but Mom stayed in there for a long time anyway. After the family had gone to five more tents, Antwon started to feel hot, thirsty, and frustrated. He was sick of walking past crowds of hot bodies. "Mom, I think I've had enough of the flea market for today," he said in his whiniest voice. Suddenly, he realized that both Destiny and Mom were annoyed and glaring at him.

"Antwon, I'm having fun and I am not leaving this flea market without a purple dresser," said Destiny sternly. Antwon gulped. He realized that his complaining wasn't going to work today.

Name ______________________________

The Flea Market

When you analyze the **setting** of a story, it can help you to better understand the story. Think about how the setting influences the plot and conflict in the story.

As you read, ask these questions about setting:

What descriptive details help you form a mental image of the setting?

What do the characters' actions, feelings, and dialogue tell you about the setting?

How do different characters view the setting differently?

Answer the items about the story you read.

1. Contrast how Antwon and his mom view the setting.

____

____

____

2. How has Destiny's view of the flea market changed?

____

____

____

3. How does the setting help to create conflict in the story?

____

____

4. Write three descriptive words or phrases that help you form a mental image of the setting.

______________ ______________ ______________

Name ______________________________

Answer the items.

1. Write a question you can ask yourself about the setting in a story.

____

____

2. How can understanding a setting help you to better understand characters' actions?

____

____

3. How can the setting affect the plot and conflict in a story?

____

____

4. Why is it important to recognize how different characters view a setting differently?

____

____

____

Read the paragraph. Then answer the question.

5. As soon as Dale got home from football practice, he turned on the television, turned on all the lights downstairs, and turned up the heat. It seemed as though his parents were still at work. Dale had just sat on the sofa when he heard stomping on the stairs and figured it was his older sister, Rachel. "You made it way too warm in here," she said, frowning and turning the heat off as she spoke.

"It was freezing when I got home," argued Dale. "I don't understand why you can't let me be comfortable." Rachel said she was roasting. Dale rolled his eyes and quietly decided that he would turn the heat back on as soon as Rachel went back upstairs.

How does the setting help to create conflict in the story?

____

____

Name ______________________________

Plot is one of the most important elements of a story. When we talk about plot, we refer to the events in a story. These are important parts of a plot:

Exposition: The author gives information about character, setting, and conflict.

Rising action: The character tries to resolve the conflict. The conflict becomes complicated or the character fails.

Climax: This is the turning point or the most exciting part of the story.

Falling action and **Resolution:** The action is slower, and the conflict gets resolved.

Read the paragraph. Then answer the items.

Mr. Galloway looked at his overgrown lawn and sighed. As goats romped and grazed on the farm next door, long grass and weeds were taking over his own property. His lawnmower was broken. Hoping to fix it himself, he took apart the motor, but some of the parts were too badly worn to repair. Weeks went by, and the top of the grass reached the bottom of his kitchen window. He was desperate to shorten the lawn now, so he decided to bring the mower to a repair shop. As he loaded the mower into his truck, his neighbor wandered over and asked if he'd like to buy a goat. "He's a friendly goat," the neighbor said. "And, he'll take care of that grass for you in no time at all." Mr. Galloway agreed. Later that day, he relaxed on his front porch as his new pet goat grazed happily.

1. Describe the information provided in the exposition of the story.

____

____

2. What happens during the story's climax?

____

____

3. How was the conflict in the story resolved?

____

Name ______________________________

When you analyze the **plot** of a story, you gain a better understanding of the story. An author arranges the events in the story so that the story is interesting. If a story doesn't keep moving and isn't interesting, you may not want to read the entire story. These are the elements of plot that keep the story moving:

There is major conflict in the story.

Characters' actions relate to the conflict. Characters keep the story moving by trying to solve the problem.

There is a suspenseful climax or a surprising twist in the story.

Read the paragraph. Circle it if it has a complete plot.

1. Sophie's sister had a birthday coming up. Sophie couldn't think of a good gift for her sister. Sophie watched TV for three hours and then had dinner. She had ice cream for dessert. The next morning she forgot all about the birthday gift.

2. Zeke wanted to buy a book for his sister for her birthday. Unfortunately, he didn't have any money. He searched all over his house for loose change but found only a dollar. Then he noticed leaves in his neighbor's yard and offered to rake them up. He earned ten dollars by doing that job and was able to buy the book for his sister.

3. Rohi had an awesome birthday. She went camping with her family. At the campsite, she ate hot dogs and chips. Then everyone sang happy birthday to her, and she ate her favorite kind of cake: red velvet. She ended the day by sitting around a campfire with her whole family.

Read the paragraph. Then state what is missing from the plot. Explain how you know.

4. At first, Everly was excited for her birthday party, but then she became frustrated with her dad. She told him that she didn't want any grown-ups at her party. "Everly, if you want, you can just ignore me and your mom while your friends are here," her dad said, "but we are going to make sure that there is an adult in the room at all times." Everly thought her parents were being so unfair. She thought about calling off the party.

____

____

Run Free

Roxy was horrified when her dad signed her up for Run Free, the afterschool cross country running team. She immediately threw down the book she'd been reading. "I can't run! I'm like the worst athlete in the entire school!"

The one time Roxy had played a recreational sport—basketball, last winter—had been a total disaster. Quinn, the star of her team, complained every time Roxy made a mistake. There was no way Roxy was going to go out and embarrass herself in a running club. Her dad, however, persisted, and Roxy soon came to the conclusion that she had no choice in the matter.

The weekend before the club's first session, her dad took her to a running store to purchase some quality running shoes; Roxy barely made eye contact with the woman who helped her try on various pairs. Finally, Roxy found a pair that felt comfortable, but she still wasn't enthusiastic about gasping for breath and tripping over her own two feet while running on the cross country team.

Later that day, Roxy's dad suggested she go on a run on the bike trail. Roxy really didn't feel like it. "Come on," said her dad, "you can take Buster with you. That'll make it more fun, won't it?" Roxy did love taking the family dog, Buster, out for long walks sometimes. So, she put on her new running shoes, secured Buster's leash, and took him outside.

It was a really nice day. After a few minutes of walking on the trail, Roxy thought she'd give jogging a try. She saw a lamppost in the distance and decided to try to make it to that spot. To her surprise, she did it, but she felt completely out of breath by the end. Buster handled the run a little better.

When Roxy got home, she told her dad about her experience. "And it's only going to get easier," said her dad. "Pretty soon, if you run each day, you'll be running farther, and you'll be less out of breath, too." Roxy thought about what her dad said, and she went out running with Buster again the next day. This time, though, she decided to run farther than the lamppost.

Roxy did go farther, and even though she ended up out of breath again, she kind of liked challenging herself to see how far she could make it. She ran every day that week, going a little farther each time. By the end of the week, she was looking forward to the first cross country team meeting.

Name ____________________

Run Free

Plot is what happens in a story. Conflict is an important part of a story's plot. Without conflict, a story would not be very interesting. These are five kinds of conflict that are common in literature:

Person vs. Person: A character struggles with another character.

Person vs. Nature: A character struggles with environmental issues, such as the weather or a natural disaster.

Person vs. Self: A character struggles with a decision or his or her own thoughts.

Person vs. Technology: A character struggles with a machine, which has non-human traits.

Person vs. Society: A character struggles with the rules of a large group.

Answer the items about the story you read.

1. What do you find out in the story's exposition?

____

____

2. What kind of conflict does Roxy struggle with most in the story: Person vs. Person, or Person vs. Self? Explain your answer.

____

____

3. Explain how the events in the story relate to the conflict.

____

____

4. Describe the conflict's resolution.

____

____

Name ____________________

Review

Answer the items.

1. Explain why plot is an important story element.

____

____

2. What would a story be like if there were no conflict? Explain why you think so.

____

____

3. Explain what each kind of conflict is:

   Person vs. Person: ____________________

   Person vs. Self: ____________________

   Person vs. Nature: ____________________

   Person vs. Technology: ____________________

   Person vs. Society: ____________________

4. Explain what an exposition is in a story.

____

____

5. Explain what rising action is in a story.

____

6. Explain what a story's climax is.

____

7. Explain what falling action and resolution are in a story.

____

Name ________________________________

Theme is an important story element. It is a message or lesson in a story. A theme can be personal. That means that different individuals may take away different messages after reading the same story. These are some possible story themes:

A true friend is loyal.

Material things cannot make you as happy as love and kindness.

The most important possession you have is your honor.

Read the paragraph. Then answer the items.

The handlebars shook as Zinnia rocketed down the steep trail. The last time she'd raced this course, Zinnia braked too hard, missed a turn, and tumbled into a creek. Luckily, she only ended up with some scrapes, but the incident had shaken her. Worry flooded her head, but she shook it off—she must stay focused! Zinnia saw the turn approaching. Visions of crashing flashed before her eyes, and she did everything she could to push them out. It was one crash, no reason to think it would happen again. She pumped her brakes gently. Slowing down just enough, she eased through the turn and then shot down toward the finish line. Zinnia cried out, "Yes!"

1. What is a possible theme of this story?
   - Ⓐ It is always unwise to attempt things that scare you.
   - Ⓑ If you fall, you can pick yourself up and try again.
   - Ⓒ Be a good sport when you compete against others.
   - Ⓓ Allow fear to rule your life.

2. Explain why you chose the answer you did for number 1.

   ____

   ____

   ____

3. Write a detail from the story that helps to show why Zinnia is able to succeed and make it past the turn.

   ____

Name ______________________________

Theme is a message or lesson in a story. A story can have multiple themes. Themes usually relate to important topics that the author wants to explore, such as these:

chaos and order	**war**	**loyalty**
isolation	**darkness and light**	**love**

As you read, think about the message that you take away from the story. This can help you identify a theme in the story.

Read the paragraph. Then answer the items.

The sixth-grade badminton team had practice twice a week. The coach, Mr. Jackson, was also the coach of the eighth-grade girls' volleyball team and the eighth-grade boys' rugby team. At every badminton practice, Mr. Jackson let the sixth graders know that their team was his least favorite to coach. "Yeah, I got stuck with the little sixth graders again this year," he said into his cellphone one afternoon, to whomever he was speaking to. He said it loudly, while all the sixth graders were warming up, so they could clearly hear him. After the phone call, Mr. Jackson told the students that badminton practice would be over in five minutes. The students complained and asked why it was ending so early. Mr. Jackson said, "It's not a big deal. You're only in sixth grade. Nobody cares about the sixth-grade games. It's the eighth graders that everyone cares about. Their games are important." The team felt deflated after that. Some of them wanted to quit the team, but then they decided that they weren't going to let Mr. Jackson's negative attitude affect their school year.

1. What is a possible theme of this story?
   Ⓐ Words can be a powerful tool for bad or for good.
   Ⓑ Sports and clubs are more serious the older you get.
   Ⓒ Coaches should only work with students at a single grade level.
   Ⓓ Sometimes, quitting is the only choice that you have.

2. Explain why you chose the answer you did for number 1.

   ____

3. Write another possible theme for the story.

   ____

Name ____________________

An Interview with a Zazneraldernol Citizen

Me: Hello, Television Viewers! I am Aziza Bellamy, and thanks for watching. I want to especially thank you, Ms. Bertha, for agreeing to this interview on live television. It's a pleasure to meet you, the first-known trans-galactic visitor to Earth. Now, I understand that you are from a planet called Zazneraldernol?

Bertha: Just call me Miss Bertha or Bertha, please, but not "Ms."

Me: Okay, sorry about that. So, you've been on Earth for about a week now. What have been your biggest disappointments or challenges so far?

Bertha: It's not the worst planet I've ever been to. Mercury was much worse. The aliens—oops, I mean humans, have been horrid, overall. The family I'm staying with, for example, were nice at first. But now I've noticed that they roll their eyes whenever I open my mouth to say anything. They're not interested in any of my stories. And, I think they may be trying to avoid me. Worst of all, they make me wash my own dishes and bathe myself. They're so rude.

Me: Oh, um... wow. That's just...

Bertha: I am accustomed to having high standards when I choose where to stay, by the way. I have stayed with royalty and presidents on other planets. And they all adored me and begged me not to leave. But I gave this human family a chance to host me. I mean, really, they should be grateful that I selected them, of all the people on Earth, to wash my clothes and cook my meals and entertain me.

Me: Well, what you're saying is startling, Bertha. Do you think it's possible that this family just wants you to pitch in a little, to be a good guest?

Bertha: It's odd to me that you're not agreeing with me. If you were smarter, you'd agree with me. That's another thing. Everyone on Zazneraldernol is smarter than the smartest person on Earth. Earth is below me.

Me: You know what, Bertha? I'm starting to see why you're so unhappy here on Earth. You're just a boastful, spoiled alien.

Name ______________________________

An Interview with a Zazneraldernol Citizen

The **theme** is the message or lesson in a story. Sometimes, the theme is obvious. A theme can also be personal. That means that different individuals may take away different messages after reading the same story.
Ask these questions as you think about a story's theme:

What is the main conflict in the story?

Does a character in the story struggle with a particular issue?

Does a character learn a lesson in the story?

Answer the items about the story you read.

1. What is the theme of the story?
   Ⓐ People who boast a lot are better than others.
   Ⓑ There are many good reasons to be boastful.
   Ⓒ Being boastful will win you few friends.
   Ⓓ Boasting a lot is a good way to get people to like you.

2. How do people feel about Bertha? Explain why.

   ____

   ____

3. How and why does Aziza's attitude toward Bertha change during the interview?

   ____

   ____

4. Write two details from the story that help to demonstrate the theme.

   ____

   ____

   ____

5. Do you think that Aziza ended the interview appropriately? Explain your opinion.

   ____

Name ____________________

Answer the items.

1. Explain what a theme is in a story.

2. Explain how themes can be personal, or unique, for different people who read the same story.

3. Explain how you can identify themes in a story.

4. Why do you think theme is an important story element?

Read the paragraph. Then answer the items.

Amal took a bow, and the entire auditorium applauded her. She was beaming, smiling from ear-to-ear, as roses were flung onto the stage for her. She picked them up, bowed again, and left the stage. “That was a perfect piano recital, Amal,” said her Aunt Clarice. Amal thought back to four years ago, when she was eight years old and had just started taking piano lessons. She didn’t play well at all. But she practiced every single day and never gave up, even when it became harder to make time to practice. Now, she was a local celebrity. The mayor even came to one of her recitals.

5. Write a possible theme for the story.

6. Explain why you think this is a theme in the story.

Name ____

A story is written from the narrator's **point of view**. There are three major points of view: **first person**, **second person**, and **third person**.

first person: The narrator is in the story and says "I" and "me" while telling the story.

second person: The narrator speaks to the reader and says "you" while telling the story.

third person: The narrator is not in the story and tells a story about the actions of others.

An **omniscient** narrator knows what the main character and other characters think, feel, and plan to do and may know what will happen later in the story.

A **limited** narrator knows only what the main character thinks, feels, and plans to do and does not know what will happen later.

Read the paragraph. Then answer the questions.

Tara was delighted to be opening her birthday presents. "Exactly what I've been wishing for," she thought when she opened the headband-making kit from her uncle. "Yes!" she declared when she unwrapped the phone cover. "This is awesome," Tara thought about her new pen. Then she saw her Aunt Milly's gift: two tickets to a musical show. "Oh, no," she thought silently, unable to hide her disappointment.

"I don't think she likes my gift," thought Aunt Milly. A moment later, Aunt Milly had a change of heart. "Actually, Tara has never been to a musical before," she thought. "It won't hurt her to try a new experience, and she may love it." Little did Aunt Milly know, but her positive thoughts paid off. Tara used the tickets and ended up loving musicals.

1. Is the story written in the first, second, or third person point of view? Explain how you know.

____

____

2. Is the narrator omniscient or limited? Explain how you know.

____

____

Name ____________________________________

A Day in My Life

If I'd known today was going to be a bath day, I would have found a decent place to hide from Mom, and maybe she would have given up looking for me and found something more productive to do with her time. But, of course, I'm never told beforehand about baths. The day started like most days, with me and Dad going out for a run around the neighborhood. We ran our usual route, heading first to the park, down some side streets, and then along the entire length of Main Street.

While I was eating breakfast, my brother Elijah and my sister Rudy came downstairs and packed a bunch of random stuff into their backpacks.

"See you later, Freddy," they said as they tousled my hair, as they often do. Then I noticed that they were moving towards the door, so I starting whining and cried out, "Wait! Take me with you! I want to come too!" But they hurried out the door, letting the screen door bang shut behind them. I still don't know where they go every day.

I went outside and played in the yard for a while until Mom said it was time to come in, and I could sense right away that something was up. She had that look in her eye, and I was pretty sure I could hear the bath running upstairs. So I did what anyone would do: I ran as fast as I could. I could hear Mom yelling for me to come inside. Eventually, I had to go in. If I hadn't, I'd get in trouble.

At first I tried to hide behind one of the kitchen chairs. Mom's hands grabbed for me, so I bolted past her and tore down the hallway. As I rounded the corner, though, I came face to face with Mom! I don't know how she made it there so fast. Anyway, she dragged me into the bathroom and plopped me right in the tub. She covered me in bubbles and dumped water on me. It was awful. The thing that really bothers me is that she never does this to Rudy or Elijah.

After my bath, Mom gave me a snack, which made me feel better. Then she let me run around in the yard. I looked for the annoying squirrel that sometimes invades our yard and climbs up our tree, but I didn't see it.

Before I knew it, Rudy and Elijah returned home! Rudy played ball with me for a long time. I told her that I wanted a snack, and she ran in and got one for me. I told her to eat with me, but I guess she didn't want to. Then Rudy wanted me to give her a high five, so I did, and she said "Good Doggie!" What a silly sister I have, huh?

Name ______________________________

A Day in My Life

Point of view is an important element in a story. The narrator's perspective, or view, frames the story. Often, the reader knows only what the narrator knows. When you think about point of view, ask the following questions:

Is the story told in the first, second, or third person point of view?

Is the narrator omniscient or limited?

What details do I know because the narrator told me?

Do I agree with or recognize the narrator's perspective?

Answer the questions about the story you read.

1. What point of view is the story told in: first, second, or third person? Explain how you know.

____

____

2. Is the narrator omniscient or limited? Explain how you know.

____

____

3. How might the story be different if it were told from Mom's first-person point of view?

____

____

____

4. What might the title be if the story were told in the third person point of view?

____

5. Before you had read the ending of the story, were you able to tell that the story was being told from a dog's perspective? Explain why or why not.

____

Name ______________________

Answer the items.

1. Explain why point of view is an important element in a story.

2. Explain the difference between a narrator who is omniscient and a narrator who is limited.

3. Explain how a narrator's perspective can make some events in the story more of a focus than other events.

Read the paragraph. Then answer the item.

4. Uncle Vernon took me sailing last weekend. I had never been sailing before, and I was a bit nervous. I helped him raise up the sail and untie the boat. After a little while, we were on the open ocean. I noticed that the waves were rougher and more choppy the farther out we sailed, and the wind had picked up. Soon, it started to get really rough and choppy out there. The boat went up and down so violently that it felt like we were on a roller coaster at one point. I wondered if Uncle Vernon had ever sailed in weather like this before or if he was nervous. He didn't appear to be nervous. He calmly said that it was time to turn the boat around and head back to shore.

What point of view is this story written in? Include whether the narrator is omniscient or limited. Then explain how you know the point of view.

Name ______________________________

When you come across unfamiliar **vocabulary** in a story, you can use context clues to figure out the meanings of the words you don't know.

Look at the surrounding words. Think about what would make sense in the sentence.

Think about what you know about the topic.

Try replacing the word with a word you already know that may have a similar meaning.

Read the paragraph. Then answer the items.

The wall shook as monotonous dance music blasted from Erika's room. The music never changed. The beat, the tones, the pitches—it was just the same sounds over and over again. Sitting in his bedroom, Dave looked at his oboe and sighed. It was inconceivable for him to practice with that repetitive music playing, so he didn't even know why he was thinking about it. Perhaps he was still hoping to practice because he knew he had a band concert coming up in a few weeks. But Erika played the same music every single day. Dave was in a real predicament, so he was worried.

1. Mark the meaning of the word *monotonous*.

   Ⓐ unique and unusual

   Ⓑ repetitive and unchanging

2. Explain why you chose the answer you did for number 1.

   ____

   ____

3. What do you think *inconceivable* means? Explain why you think so.

   ____

   ____

4. What do you think *predicament* means? Explain why you think so.

   ____

   ____

Name ________________________________

Kitchen Champ

"Can we order out tonight?" Sam asked her dad. "I want tacos."

"Yeah," Gabe chimed in. "There's no good food in the house."

"Not tonight," Dad said, "and besides, we have plenty of food, we just need to be creative. I know we have a lot of nutritious foods in our cupboards."

As Dad rummaged through the pantry, a smile spread across Mom's face. "Let's have a cooking competition—we can determine who in our family has the best culinary skills! And the winner will not have to help do dishes tonight!"

"Cool!" Sam said. "Just like on TV!"

Soon a plethora of ingredients crowded the counter-top—rice, apple cider vinegar, cinnamon, eggs, red bell peppers, an eggplant, and several other foods. Mom and Dad were positive that a nutritious meal could be devised using these ingredients, but Sam and Gabe were dubious—they doubted these food items could produce a decent meal.

Mom suggested each family member would have one hour to devise his or her own meal. Sam wanted to know if she could look up some recipes on the Internet, but that was out of the question, as far as Dad was concerned. "You'll just have to improvise," he said. "The whole point of this competition is to think on your feet and to make creative decisions without planning ahead."

"Let's start cooking!" Mom said. In a sizzling hot pan, she seared a salmon steak so it appeared charred and slightly burned on the surface.

Sam chopped tomatoes, mushrooms, and cashews on a chopping board. Dad kneaded a thick orange dough on the counter. Gabe boiled some eggs. Everyone was off to a great start, chopping, grating, peeling, stirring, and baking. They stayed busy and focused for the entire hour, which passed quickly.

Finally, Mom declared that the competition was over. "Now it's time to taste everything and vote on what tastes best," she said. Dad made a pizza with a sweet potato crust. Sam made spicy vegetarian lettuce wraps. Mom made seared salmon, which she served with lemon wedges. Gabe made boiled egg whites stuffed with salsa. All four of the meals were so delicious that the family had a serious problem: they could not decide who'd be excused from helping with dishes!

Name ____________________________

Kitchen Champ

When you come across unfamiliar **vocabulary** in a story, you can use context clues to figure out the meanings of the words you don't know.

Look at the surrounding words, and think about what would make sense in the sentence.

Think about what you know about the topic.

Try replacing the word with a word you already know that may have a similar meaning.

Pictures can help you figure out what a word means.

Answer the items about the story you read.

1. Mark the definition of the word *culinary*.
   Ⓐ related to household management
   Ⓑ related to the kitchen and cooking
2. What do you think *sear* means? Explain how the picture helped you know.

   ____

   ____
3. What do you think *dubious* means? Explain why you think so.

   ____

   ____
4. What do you think *improvise* means? Explain why you think so.

   ____

   ____
5. What do you think *devise* means? Explain why you think so.

   ____

   ____

Name ________________________________

Answer the items.

1. Explain how you can use context clues to figure out a word's meaning.

____

____

____

2. Explain how pictures can help you figure out a word's meaning.

____

____

Read the paragraph. Then answer the item.

3. My older brother, Hugh, is 22 years old. He has a job and lives at home with Mom, Dad, and me. Last summer, he went on a three-week-long trip to Florida with his friends. He asked me to take care of his plant, which he keeps in his room, while he is away. He loves that plant, and he takes really good care of it so it stays green, strong, and healthy. "Make sure you water it every other day," Hugh told me. "The soil can't become dry because it's not good for the plant." I promised Hugh that I'd take care of it. The three weeks that Hugh was gone went by quickly. I went with Mom and Dad to pick him up from the airport. Hugh greeted us with a big smile and gave us each a tight hug. "I missed you guys," he said. In the car, he was all smiles and chatty. "How's my plant doing?" he finally asked me. I froze. Oh. My. Goodness. I had completely forgotten about Hugh's plant. I never went into his room during the three weeks that he was gone. I gulped. I stuttered. I felt my face becoming red. I finally told Hugh that I hadn't watered the plant at all. His countenance immediately changed. Whereas before he was smiley, now he frowned and looked half angry and half sad.

What do you think a person's *countenance* is? Explain why you think so.

____

____

____

Name ____________________

In a story, details that **foreshadow** are clues about what might happen later in the story. Foreshadowing can help you make predictions about the story as you read.

Example:

> If the main character sees a crow several times in the story, and something bad always happens right after the main character sees a crow, this is an example of foreshadowing. The next time the character sees a crow, you can predict that something bad is likely to happen.

Read the paragraph. Then answer the item.

1. Clara loved traveling the world by herself, hiking and sightseeing. Now she was in Mongolia. She'd heard about a scenic trail leading up a mountain to a plateau. From there, she would have a breathtaking view of the green plains below. One day, she decided to travel by camelback to search for the trail. It was a beautiful sunny day. Her camel was a mild-natured creature, gentle and calm. Clara heard birds tweet and saw happy, lazy yaks grazing as she traveled. In the distance, though, she saw a mountain peak that was enveloped in gray, evil-looking clouds. Abruptly, Clara came upon a wide trail. "This must be the trail I'm looking for," she thought. She observed that it led to the misty, dark mountain. She followed the trail for a while. Then she came upon an old woman walking along the trail. She had a walking stick, which a raven sat upon. Suddenly, the old woman turned to Clara and said, "I would not travel up that mountain alone, if I were you." As Clara rode on, the clouds grew darker. The more Clara stared at them, the more they looked like a skull, with hollow eyes. As Clara got closer to the mountain, her camel suddenly dug its heels into the ground. It refused to go any farther, grunting and spitting, protesting in any way it could. Clara decided to turn around and abandon her plan.

   Write three details from the story that foreshadow that the mountain may be dangerous.

   ____

   ____

   ____

   ____

Name ____________________________________

In a story, details that **foreshadow** are clues about what might happen later in the story. Foreshadowing can help you make predictions about the story as you read. Authors use foreshadowing to help readers make predictions and to build suspense in the story.

These are some questions to ask as you read and think about foreshadowing:

Do the words or pictures suggest something good or bad might happen?

Is a character wishful for something or nervous about something in particular?

Do the characters see or experience something that they have seen or experienced earlier in the story?

Read the paragraph. Then answer the question.

1. Miguel's best friend, Ashanti, said on the telephone that she was bringing over a humongous piece of cake, left over from her mom's party. But when Miguel saw the cake, it was only a teeny piece. He wasn't surprised at all. Ever since Miguel knew Ashanti, she would exaggerate about pretty much everything. She once convinced him to watch a movie, which she described as a short movie. Was it short? No! It was a three-and-a-half-hour-long movie. When they went bowling, Ashanti selected a bowling ball for Miguel while he was in the restroom. "It's really light. It's the perfect size for you," said Ashanti. Miguel immediately discovered that it was 16-pound ball, and it was too heavy for him to even lift. Miguel had been getting excited for his birthday, which was fast-approaching. Ashanti told him not to plan anything. "I know just what you'll want to do, the perfect activity for you," she said. "I'll plan a huge celebration. I'm your best friend, after all. It'll be the most fun birthday bash you've ever had." Miguel thought it was nice of Ashanti to offer. He really did want a huge birthday bash. When his birthday finally arrived, he went to Ashanti's house, where the party was supposed to be, but he was so disappointed. The only thing Ashanti had planned was to make some popcorn and play video games. To be fair, she did choose video games Miguel likes.

   What details in the story foreshadow that Ashanti is going to disappoint Miguel with her plan for his birthday?

   ____

   ____

   ____

Mischief at the Museum

"Here are your tickets," the woman behind the counter said. "Enjoy the museum. Oh, and if the Neanderthal guy says anything to you, just be polite." Ireeni and her dad chuckled as they walked into the natural history museum.

After spending nearly two hours in the dinosaur exhibit, Ireeni wandered over to a water fountain for a drink. She happened to glance down and noticed a faint but large footprint. Whoever made it had been barefoot—who would walk around the museum without shoes?

In the North American mammal exhibit, a small crowd had formed in front of one of the dioramas. Inside, a man was standing a fake antelope back up on its feet. Apparently, it had fallen over. Ireeni gasped when her eye caught something on the ground near the antelope—another footprint, exactly like the one she'd seen earlier! The man caught Ireeni's eye and must have realized she was staring at something because he immediately covered up the footprint. "Weird," Ireeni thought.

"The Hall of Human Origins," Dad said, reading aloud the sign over the next exhibit they walked into.

Ireeni and her dad were finally face to face with the Neanderthal the woman at the front desk had mentioned. Wearing a fur hide and barefoot, he stood stone-still over a fake fire. In his hand was a big piece of meat on a bone, which he was presumably cooking over the fire, in the diorama scene. "That's so strange," Ireeni said. "His eyes seem to follow me as I walk around the room."

Ireeni moved along, examining other parts of the exhibit. She studied a case filled with stone tools. When she moved toward another case, she caught some movement in the corner of her eye. She knew it was impossible, but the Neanderthal seemed to be holding the meat up a bit higher than he had been before, as if he had moved it closer to his mouth. "That's nonsense," she thought. She strolled around, looking at a few more scenes in the diorama showcases. Suddenly, a hand grabbed her shoulder, and she jumped. It was just Dad. "Boy, you're a little jumpy," he said with a laugh. "There's a ramen place around the corner from here. Want to go get some lunch?"

"Sure," Ireeni said. She began following her dad out of the exhibit. As she passed the Neanderthal one last time, her eye spotted something truly inexplicable. A huge bite had been taken out of the meat in the cave man's hand!

Name ____________________

Mischief at the Museum

In a story, details that **foreshadow** are clues about what might happen later in the story. Foreshadowing can help you make predictions about the story as you read. Authors use foreshadowing to help readers make predictions and to build suspense in the story.

When a character is concerned or intrigued by something specific, that can provide a clue about what may happen later.

When a character notices unusual details, this can provide a clue.

Answer the items about the story you read.

1. Describe what is being foreshadowed throughout the story, or what the author wants readers to figure out.

____

2. What happens in the first paragraph that is an example of foreshadowing?

____

____

3. Write two additional details from the story that foreshadow.

____

____

____

4. What conclusion do you think Ireeni will draw at the end of the story? Explain why you think so.

____

____

____

Name ______________________________

Answer the items.

1. Explain what foreshadowing is in a story.

____

____

2. How can foreshadowing help you predict if something good or bad will happen later in the story?

____

____

____

3. How can foreshadowing help you analyze the plot of a story?

____

____

____

4. Explain the connection between details a character notices and events that take place in a story.

____

____

____

5. Explain why an author may choose to foreshadow events in a story.

____

____

Name ____________________

When you **summarize** a story, you use your own words to state the most important details from the story. A summary provides a short version of the story. Do the following when you summarize:

Provide as many of the following details as possible: **who**, **what**, **where**, **when**, **why**, and **how**

Include details from the story rather than your own opinions.

Include only the most important details in the summary. Leave minor details out of the summary.

Read the story. Then answer the items.

As the villagers cheered for Lady Jane, who'd just chased away a mountain troll, Sir Bolland wished just once a crowd would cheer for him. He went to the wizard, Kerzak, who offered to conjure a dragon. "It will be a cowardly dragon that's easy to defeat," Kerzak said. "You'll be a hero." Sir Bolland liked the sound of that! Kerzak mixed a potion, recited a spell, and poof—a dragon appeared in the sky! Sir Bolland stepped outside. The villagers watched as he drew his sword. Flames shot from the dragon's mouth, instantly melting the sword. Sir Bolland gulped. Kerzak quickly recited another spell, and the dragon disappeared. "Sorry," the wizard whispered to Sir Bolland. "The dragon wasn't as cowardly as I'd planned." The villagers praised Kerzak as a hero. Feeling more terrible than ever, Sir Bolland shuffled home. On his way, a young boy cried for help. He was stuck in a tree. Sir Bolland reached up and carried the boy, gently putting him down. The boy called Sir Bolland a hero.

1. Write a paragraph to summarize the plot of the story.

____

____

____

____

2. How does Sir Bolland feel at the beginning of the story? Explain why he feels this way.

____

____

Name ____________________

The RV Fiasco

Riley and I were over the moon when Mom and Dad said we were renting an RV for a camping trip. Mom researched nearby areas and finally zeroed in on a campground up in the mountains, about five hours away from our home. We packed everything we'd need—sleeping bags, tents, coolers, chairs, sunscreen, and about a million other things—into the RV and headed off to the mountains.

Arriving at the campsite, Dad drove past a small office building but then hit the brakes when he saw someone run out and wave for him to stop. Apparently, we needed to stop to register for our campsite.

After registering at the front office, Dad drove the RV down to the camping area and parked. "Riley, Sean, you need to help set up the site," Mom said. We all pitched in, dragging out our camp chairs, coolers, and other supplies, and soon we were ready to kick back and relax. Sitting at the picnic table, I popped open a bag of chips.

"Let's get some music going," Dad said. "Hey, where's the electrical hook-up?"

"Oh, boy," Mom said. "We're in the tents-only area, where there's no electricity. We're not even supposed to be in this area with an RV."

Twenty minutes later, we'd broken camp and packed everything back in the RV. Mom drove around the campgrounds until we spotted other RVs and then

pulled to a stop. After we unpacked everything, I sniffed and was immediately slammed with the most horrible stench I'd ever smelled in my entire life. "We're right near the dumpsters!" I groaned.

We quickly shoved everything back into the RV, and drove to a different spot, where, after making sure there were no bad smells, or any other problems, we unpacked all the gear—again—and set up our campsite—again. If only that were the end of the story, but it isn't! When Mom tried to plug in the extension cord, she couldn't find the electrical hook-up, and that's because it was on the other side of the RV! We'd parked in the wrong direction. Dad climbed back in the RV and started to turn it around. Pop! There must have been a sharp rock because now the RV had a flat tire.

"What do we do now—call a tow company?" Mom asked.

Dad was quiet for a moment and then finally just laughed. "Tomorrow. Right now, it's time to start enjoying this camping trip. Let's get a fire started!"

Name ____________________

The RV Fiasco

When you **summarize** a story, you use your own words to state the most important details from the story. A summary is always shorter than the story being summarized. It tells what the story is mostly about.

You can write one sentence to summarize each paragraph in a story.

You can write one sentence to summarize a portion of dialogue in a story.

Answer the items about the story you read.

1. Who are the characters in the story?

____

2. What is the conflict in the story?

____

____

3. Write a paragraph to summarize the events in the story.

____

____

____

____

____

____

____

____

____

____

Name ______________________________

Answer the items.

1. Explain how to summarize a story.

____

____

____

2. How can reading a summary help people to better understand a story?

____

____

3. Why do you think it's best to leave minor details out of a summary?

____

____

____

Read the paragraph. Then summarize it.

4. Mason and Sowra were standing in the crowd, waiting to see their dad jump out of the plane, along with a bunch of other skydivers. This wasn't his first jump, but they were as excited as ever. They always loved watching him skydive. After about an hour of waiting, they could see the plane approaching in the distance. Then, people started jumping out! Their dad was wearing a bright neon green skydiving suit, so the children couldn't miss him. As Sowra watched her dad flatten out his body and spread out his limbs, she couldn't help but think of a flying squirrel. Mason was taking pictures with his digital camera. After a few seconds, which felt like an eternity, the children's dad opened up his parachute. He glided down to the earth smoothly. He looked so happy. Eventually, he landed in a nearby field, laughing heartily as he rolled up inside his parachute on the ground. He gave the children tight hugs when he saw them.

____

____

____

Name ______________________________

You can **make inferences** as you read a story. When you make an inference, you use background information and clues in the text to figure out details that the author does not state directly. This is an example of an inference:

What I read: Gilbert goes to work each day, where he puts on an apron and specializes in making soups, roasts, and desserts.

Inference I can make: Gilbert is a chef.

Read the sentence. Then mark the sentence that tells an inference you can make.

1. Indra wishes she could order the dessert with peanut butter, but she doesn't want to end up with a rash, so she orders the vanilla pudding instead.
   Ⓐ Indra doesn't like peanut butter.
   Ⓑ Indra is allergic to peanuts.

2. When Jose looked at his dinner and frowned, his mom shook her head and said, "See, I told you we'd be eating soon."
   Ⓐ Jose ate a snack just before dinner.
   Ⓑ Jose doesn't like what's being served.

Read the sentences. Then write an inference you can make.

3. Mom handed the spoon to Marco and told him to mix the batter slowly; otherwise, it would splatter all over the place. After mixing for a moment, Marco looked at the counter and groaned.

   ____

   ____

4. When Dad was making pancakes, Emily asked if she could crack open the eggs for the batter. She cracked open two eggs and let them plop into the bowl. Then she asked her dad a question. "Hey, Dad, it's okay if some eggshells are in the pancakes, right?" "Let's just make a new batch of pancake batter," said Dad.

   ____

   ____

Name ______________________________

You can **make inferences** as you read a story. When you make an inference, you use background information and clues in the text to figure out details that the author does not state directly. You can make inferences about characters, settings, events, and pictures.

Example: When you read a story and figure out on your own why a character probably acted a certain way, you are making an inference.

Read the paragraph. Then answer the questions.

Commander Boltworth landed his spacecraft on the surface of the planet. His navigator, Rex, stood up and said, "I'll make sure there's oxygen since I don't need to breathe in order to survive." Rex rolled out onto the icy surface. He lifted his metallic arm and opened a small hatch in his hand that had a thermometer-like tip. He took air samples and reported back that it was safe for Boltworth to come out. The commander stepped out cautiously and shivered. A group of beings that appeared alien stood nearby. They were about three feet tall. They were black and white with pointy beaks and wings. They waddled when they walked. When the commander tried to speak to the beings, they just ignored him. The commander was confused. "Earth is supposed to have intelligent life," he said. "Where is it?"

1. What inference can you make about Rex? Tell how you made this inference.

____

____

2. What inference can you make about Commander Boltworth? Tell how you know this.

____

____

3. What are the "beings that appeared alien"? Explain how you made this inference.

____

____

____

Name ______________________________

A Visit to the Family Farm

As the car went over the top of the hill, Phoebe and Tanner caught a wide view of the entire valley, which seemed to go on forever. Phoebe was three years older than Tanner, old enough to remember the last time they'd left the city to visit their cousins at the family farm in upstate New York.

As the car pulled into the driveway, Holden and Summer came running excitedly out the front door. Aunt Carol and Uncle Travis came out, and after a round of warm hugs and hellos, everyone helped carry bags in the house.

Walking into Summer's room, Phoebe saw brushes, pencils, and stacks of sketchbooks. The walls were plastered with paintings, and there were several spots on the floor where it appeared as if paint had dripped and someone had tried, unsuccessfully, to clean it up.

Later, the four cousins rode bikes around the farm and up to the top of a steep hill. "Ready?" Summer asked as she squeezed her brakes to make sure they were working. She flew down the hill, zipping around bushes and jumping over small bumps. Holden went next, racing down after his sister. Phoebe and Tanner looked at each other. Phoebe inhaled deeply and then pushed off. Her younger brother was right behind her.

Back down at the bottom, Tanner pumped his fist. "That was awesome!" he said. "We couldn't do that in the city."

By the evening, Phoebe and Tanner were starving. Uncle Travis prepared an elaborate dinner for everyone. "Now, I don't know if I told you this," he announced just before dinner, "but we're vegetarians, so I hope you don't mind tofu, Brussels sprouts, and other veggies." It was obvious that Uncle Travis had worked hard on the dinner.

The dinner was served buffet style. Before putting food on his plate, Tanner studied the strange, springy cubes of tofu. He decided not to take any. As everyone else ate, Tanner quietly pushed his food around with his fork, hoping his parents would think that he was eating the vegetables.

Uncle Travis said he hoped everyone liked the food, glancing at Tanner, who quickly stopped playing and stuffed a forkful into his mouth. He gave a thumbs up, and Uncle Travis smiled. Tanner gulped down the food and drank a huge swig of water. Then he looked at Phoebe, who smiled as she scooped out a second helping for herself.

Phoebe and Tanner had a blast visiting their relatives that week. They were sad to leave and couldn't wait until their next visit to the farm.

Name ____________________

A Visit to the Family Farm

When you **make inferences** as you read, you figure out details that are not provided in the story. You can use background knowledge, clues in the text, and visual information to make inferences.

You can make inferences about the following things:

characters' traits and emotions

plot and setting

reasons that certain things happen in the story

Answer the questions about the story you read.

1. What is Summer's hobby? Explain why you think so.

____

____

2. Why do you think that Tanner says they couldn't do the same biking activity in the city?

____

____

3. How does Tanner feel about the dinner? Explain why you think so.

____

____

____

4. Why do you think Tanner stuffs food in his mouth when Uncle Travis looks at him?

____

____

5. How does Phoebe feel about the dinner? Explain why you think so.

____

Name ______________________________

Answer the items.

1. Explain what an inference is.

____

____

2. Explain how your own background knowledge can help you make inferences as you read a story.

____

____

3. How is making an inference different from guessing?

____

____

4. State the story elements or details that you can make inferences about.

____

____

Read the paragraph. Then write an inference you can make.

5. Whenever students forget their P.E. uniforms, Mr. Sop, the P.E. teacher, makes them sit on the bleachers for the entire class period. Today, Suzy brought homework to do as she sits on the bleachers.

____

6. Morgan was babysitting her little brother, Ryan, who was only six years old. She asked Ryan if he was hungry, and he said, "No, I snacked on some trail mix a little while ago." Later, Morgan saw an opened package of trail mix on the table. It said that the ingredients were chocolate chips, peanuts, raisins, cashews, and sunflower seeds, but Morgan didn't see any chocolate chips in the package at all. She saw all the other ingredients in the mix, though.

____

Name ______________________________

When you **predict** as you read a story, you analyze details in the story to try to determine what will happen later. You use your own background knowledge and clues in the text to make predictions.

Sometimes, you may not accurately predict what happens later. Any prediction is a good prediction if it is based on details in the text.

Read the paragraph. Then answer the questions.

Brad was obsessed with taking photos. Everywhere he went, he saw scenes and images that he wanted to snap photos of. When Brad found out that his school had Camera Club, which met every Thursday, he decided to go to one of the meetings. The club's director, Mrs. Arias, told Brad that he needed to have his own digital camera, the only requirement for joining. Brad already knew that he wanted a Zakawn-P680, the most awesome camera being sold. He also knew that it was going to cost at least $100 and that he had only $47 saved up from his allowance money. When he got home that day, Brad said, "Can you get the camera for me, Mom? I don't have enough money."

"Well, Brad," she said, "I have told you for months that I am willing to increase your allowance if you are willing to take on more chores around the house, but you've never wanted to take me up on my offer. Why don't you start doing more chores now?"

"But, Mom," he argued, "I want the camera right now! I don't want to wait until I've done chores and saved up enough money! I'm begging you to get the camera now."

1. How do you think Brad's mom is going to respond? Explain why you think so.

____

____

2. What do you think Brad will do if his mom responds how you predicted? Explain why.

____

____

3. What would you do if you were in Brad's situation? Explain why.

____

____

Name ______________________________

Off the Trail!

When Emerson and his dad arrived at the information board at the trail head, they took a map to use on their hike. "I don't even know if we need a map," said Emerson's dad, "because we'll be following the trail the entire time. Besides, we're just going up a mountain, so as long we keep walking up, we'll reach the top." They headed up the trail, excited for the view they were sure to see from the top.

After twenty minutes of hiking, Emerson saw a massive boulder alongside the trail, and his eyes opened wide. He loved climbing on boulders. He threw down his backpack and climbed up onto it.

As Emerson climbed, his dad told stories about spending a summer hiking in Alaska. "One time, we got lost in the wilderness for hours. Luckily, we climbed a hill and spotted our car from high up, so we were able to find our way back."

Emerson and his dad continued up the steep trail, stopping every now and then to drink water or watch an animal. After a particularly steep section, the trail passed by an open field. Nestled between the tall trees were boulders of all shapes and sizes. An enormous one was deeper in the woods, far from the trail. It was too good to pass by, so Emerson insisted on hiking to it. Emerson's dad didn't want to stray from the trail. "Please, Dad!" Emerson begged. Reluctantly, his dad agreed. Pushing aside branches and stepping over roots and rocks, they made their way to the big boulder. After Emerson climbed for a while, he and his dad wanted to get back on the trail.

They hadn't gone far when they realized they couldn't find the trail. Emerson's dad scanned the map and the surrounding forest, looking for signs of the trail, but he didn't see any.

"This is bad," he said. After about forty minutes of being lost, Emerson started to get tired and hungry—and worried.

Suddenly, his dad had an idea. "Let's keep walking up! The top of the mountain is rather narrow. We can look for the trail from there." Up they went, pushing their way through the thick, thorny brush. Finally, they found themselves on a flat, grassy area overlooking a wide valley. Not far from them, they could see where the trail came out.

Emerson looked down at his scratches from the thorns and grinned sheepishly. "Hiking is a lot more fun when you stay on the trail!"

Name ______________________________

Off the Trail!

When you **predict** as you read a story, you analyze details in the story and state what you think is likely to happen later. You use your own background knowledge and clues in the text to make predictions. The following types of details may provide clues that help you make predictions:

certain habits of characters	**certain problems or conflicts**
the story's title	**characters' spoken words or thoughts**

Answer the questions about the story you read.

1. Did the title help you predict what the story would be about? Explain why or why not.

____

____

2. What clues in the story may have helped you predict that Emerson and his dad would lose the trail?

____

____

3. Emerson loves to climb boulders. How does this detail help you make predictions about the story?

____

____

4. What do you think will happen the next time Emerson and his dad go hiking?

____

____

5. Did anything in the story help you predict how they'd solve their problem? Explain.

____

____

Name ____________________

Answer the items.

1. Explain how you make predictions as you read.

2. How does analyzing a story help you predict?

3. How do the characters' actions and words in a story provide clues that help you make predictions?

4. How does your own background knowledge help you make predictions as you read?

5. How is a prediction different from a guess?

Read the paragraph. Then write a prediction for something that will happen after.

6. After school, instead of doing homework, Denny went to the mall with his older sister. He was going to do his homework as soon as he got home, but his friend Josh came over to hang out. Denny decided to do his homework after dinner. But Mom served dinner later than usual, and Denny felt tired after eating. He decided to take a shower to wake himself up and do his homework assignment later, in pajamas.

Name ______________________________________

When you think about **cause and effect** in a story, you analyze the events to determine the reasons why they happen. A **cause** is a reason why something happens. An **effect** is what happens as a result.

These are some ways cause and effect are shown in a story:

The setting or environment makes a character feel or act a certain way.

A character's actions cause certain events to happen.

An event in the story causes a reaction.

Read the sentence. Circle it if it's about a cause and an effect.

1. It was a perfect day to go to the beach and lie out in the sun.
2. A huge wave crashed and sent Iggy tumbling in the wet sand.
3. Miguel spent over an hour collecting shells and smooth stones.
4. Ryu was upset after a wave rolled up the beach and destroyed his sand castle.
5. Poor Dad fell asleep on the beach, and now he has a painful sunburn!

Match each cause with the correct effect.

6.

cause	**effect**
Tori stepped on a pointed rock. •	• Tori got knocked over.
Tori forgot to put a bandage on her injury. •	• Tori made some new friends.
Tori didn't see the wave coming. •	• The cut on Tori's foot became infected.
Tori wandered over to some other kids. •	• Tori's foot was injured.

Read the sentence. Circle the cause and underline the effect.

7. The weather was perfect, so many families decided to go to the beach.
8. Mom set up an umbrella because the sun was scorching and bright.

Name ________________________________

When you think about **cause and effect** in a story, it helps you to better understand the plot of the story. Events in a story can cause other things to happen as a result. The plot of a story is made up of a long line of events that happen for a reason.

Read the paragraph. Then answer the items.

Dad insisted we leave two hours early for the airport because last year he left late for a business trip and missed his flight. We quickly packed all our luggage into the trunk and set out in the afternoon. There was a ton of traffic. Sitting in the car, I felt really anxious. Would we miss our flight? We got to the airport much later than Dad had hoped. Luckily, the lines weren't long, though, and we were in the terminal with plenty of time to spare. Mom realized that during the rush to pack, she'd forgotten her book. She went into a bookstore to get a new one. While she was in there, a voice announced that our flight was boarding. Mom came rushing out of the store. "No time for a book!" she cried. "Let's go!"

1. Explain what caused Dad to have the family leave two hours early.

____

____

2. Write one effect that resulted from the family packing so quickly.

____

____

3. What caused the narrator to feel anxious?

____

____

4. What happened when the voice announced the flight was boarding? Tell why.

____

____

Name ______________________________

Giant Mutant Frog!

It was a beautiful day, so Violet, Phan, and Teddy went to their neighborhood park to play on the playground. After running around, climbing on equipment, and practicing the monkey bars, the three friends had worked up an appetite, so Violet grabbed her backpack and found a picnic table near the pond. There was a small splash as a small frog with spots leaped out of sight and into the water. Nearby, a dragonfly buzzed as it flew away.

Violet opened her backpack and took out the snacks and drinks she'd packed.

"I love nectarines," Phan said. "Thanks, Violet!"

Teddy held up a bottle of blue liquid and examined the label. "Nitro Blast Extreme Power Mega-Quencher. What is this drink?" he asked. Violet laughed and said it was some sort of vitamin water her older brother had bought. As Teddy opened the bottle, something fluttered near his head. He jumped, and the bottle went tumbling out of his hand.

"It's just a butterfly, Teddy," Phan said, laughing hysterically.

Teddy grinned sheepishly. "I thought it was a bee."

By now, the bottle had rolled down to the edge of the pond, and its bright blue contents emptied into the water. Teddy sighed, but Violet just laughed. "I doubt you're missing anything, Teddy. That stuff looked kind of suspicious anyway—I wouldn't have been surprised if it had transformed you into a frog!"

Everyone laughed, but then something caught Phan's eye. The look of surprise and confusion on his face caused Violet and Teddy to turn around, and when they saw what he was observing, they gasped. The entire pond was now a bright, shimmering blue!

Violet stepped closer to get a better look, but when she got to the edge, water bubbled furiously, and she frantically jumped back as a gigantic form rose up from the pond. Water cascaded down. The form had two large bulging eyes.

"I-it's the frog with spots," Teddy stuttered, "b-but it's really, really big!"

"RIBBIT!" The frog's long tongue shot out and grabbed Violet's backpack, swallowing it in one big gulp!

"Run!" Violet shouted. The giant mutant frog hopped, casting the entire park in shadow as it soared overhead. It landed, flattening a mailbox, and then hopped again, disappearing out of sight. The friends never saw that frog again.

Name ____________________

Giant Mutant Frog!

Analyzing **cause and effect** in a story can help you to better understand the story. When something happens in a story, it can cause other things to happen as a result. The plot of a story is made up of a long line of events that happen for a reason. These are some ways cause and effect are shown in a story:

The setting or environment makes a character feel or act a certain way.

A character's actions cause certain events to happen.

An event in the story causes a character to feel or act a certain way.

Answer the items about the story you read.

1. Explain what caused the children to work up an appetite.

____

2. Explain what caused Teddy to drop the bottle and why Phan and Violet laughed at Teddy about it.

____

____

3. Write two effects of the drink spilling into the pond.

____

____

4. How would the story be different if the friends sat at a picnic table that wasn't near the pond?

____

____

5. How did the children's actions affect the frog? How did the frog react?

____

____

Name ________________________________

Answer the items.

1. How does analyzing cause and effect help you to better understand a story?

2. In your own words, explain what a cause is and what an effect is.

3. Explain how cause and effect helps to create events in the plot of a story.

Read the paragraphs. Then answer the item.

4. “Imogen, stop feeding the raccoons in the backyard!” demanded Dad, pointing to some slices of bread sitting on the back porch. “It’s not a joke. The more you do it, the more they’ll hang around.” Imogen liked seeing the raccoons in the backyard, though.

“But, Dad,” she argued, “I only throw food that nobody in this house is going to eat. So, isn’t it better to give it to the raccoons than to waste it?”

“I see your reasoning, Imogen, but you’re actually doing more harm than good to the raccoons.” Imogen frowned because she didn’t understand, so Dad continued. ”When you feed them, they stop trying as hard to get food on their own. More raccoons will show up, and they’ll expect you to feed them. When you don’t, they may go hungry.” Imogen finally understood. She agreed to no longer feed the raccoons.

That evening, she looked onto the back porch. There were five more raccoons than usual out there. “Oh no, what have I done?” Imogen thought to herself.

Write one cause from the story. Then write its effect.

Name ______________________________

When you **compare and contrast** elements in a story, it helps you to better understand the story. To compare (analyze similarities) and contrast (analyze differences), you must carefully consider the details in the story. You can compare and contrast different stories. You can compare and contrast characters in a story. Look at these details:

characters' traits	**characters' spoken words and thoughts**
characters' actions	**characters' struggles**

Read *Story 1* and *Story 2*. Then answer the items.

Story 1

Krag gulped as he spotted the danger ahead. He was heading back home to his family's cave after a two-day hunting journey when a Tyrannosaurus rex popped into view. The dinosaur hadn't seen Krag yet, but there were no boulders for Krag to hide behind in this open land. Worried that the T. rex would smell the meat he was carrying and attack, Krag stood motionless, considering leaving the food behind.

Story 2

Mitchell rushed to make it to the bakery before it closed at six o'clock. His mom had ordered a birthday cake last week for his dad's surprise party, which was tonight. Mitchell parked in front of the bakery five minutes before closing time. Then he noticed Mrs. Namu, his neighbor, standing in front of the bakery. She was nice, but she was very talkative, and he knew he'd never make it inside on time if she stopped him to chat. He sat in the car for a minute, frozen and confused, wondering what to do.

1. Write three sentences that compare the main characters from Story 1 and Story 2.

____

____

____

2. Write one important way that the stories are different.

____

Name ______________________________

When you **compare and contrast** elements within a story, you analyze details that show similarities and differences. These are elements that you can compare and contrast in a story:

characters

events

settings or places described

Read the paragraph. Then answer the items.

Nora went to the art museum with her dad. They walked through cool air-conditioned corridors, which felt great compared to the sweltering, humid summer air outdoors. The art museum was crowded with people. There were so many beautiful paintings and statues, Nora didn't know where to look. Although Nora and her dad had to weave their way around lots of bodies, it was a calm environment because everyone was so quiet, with their eyes fixed upon the art. "Ready to go?" Nora's dad asked after a few hours of strolling around. Nora nodded, and they headed outside, where Nora immediately felt beads of sweat dripping down her neck and forehead. The busy sidewalk was packed with people rushing in opposite directions. It reminded Nora of a highway, except there were speeding pedestrians instead of speeding cars. Buses and cars on the street swooshed by continuously. Colorful signs, flashing traffic lights, and bright cones confused Nora, and she didn't know what her eyes should focus on. She just stayed close to her dad as they weaved among the other pedestrians. She hoped the walk home would be fast.

1. Contrast the settings inside and outside of the museum.

____

____

2. Compare the settings inside and outside the museum.

____

____

3. Write one way that Nora acts similarly inside and outside of the museum.

____

Name ____________________

Thinking About Nepal

Today I went hiking with my parents at a local nature preserve near the city we live in. The trail was made of concrete and went through a wooded area. The most eye-catching sight on this hike was the long line of fallen leaves that lined the trail. Once in a while, I would see a tiny squirrel zoom across the trail. I felt like a giant around them, and I think they were probably afraid of us.

Although I enjoyed the hike, the continuous need to look out for bicyclists coming up behind us was an unwelcome distraction. We had to make sure that we weren't walking in the center of the path. The hiking area was pretty, but it was also flat, neat, and not very physically challenging. As we walked along, I couldn't help but think about the trip we took earlier this year to Nepal, where we did a lot of hiking.

Hiking in Nepal was thrilling and tiring. We stayed in Kathmandu, Nepal's busy capital. Every morning, we would wake up, eat a hearty breakfast, and meet with a Sherpa. The Sherpa was a Nepalese man who took us to different hiking areas in the Himalayas, the breathtaking, world-famous Asian system of mountain ranges. We went on rocky trails in valleys along rivers and climbed steep trails up to Himalayan peaks. When I hiked in Nepal, I felt like I was an explorer on a magnificent adventure. In Nepal, we didn't have to look out for people on bikes. Rarely, we would see other hikers and Sherpas on our hikes, but for the most part, we were on our own, and it was so quiet that we could hear ourselves breathing heavily from the exercise. Hiking in the Himalayas made me feel like a tiny ant among the gigantic, humongous hills.

We took a lot of photos in Nepal, and my dad got a really great shot of me after we had just conquered one particularly challenging peak. When we got back from the local nature preserve, I pulled out that photo and looked at it for a few moments. I really enjoyed that trip to Nepal.

Name ______________________________

Thinking About Nepal

When you **compare and contrast** elements within a story, you analyze details that show similarities and differences. These are elements that you can compare and contrast in a story: **character**, **setting**, and **events** in the plot.

You can use visual information to help you compare and contrast elements.

Answer the items about the story you read.

1. Write four words from the story that describe hiking in Nepal but do not describe hiking near the narrator's home.

   ______________________ ______________________

   ______________________ ______________________

2. Write four words from the story that describe hiking near the narrator's home but do not describe hiking in Nepal.

   ______________________ ______________________

   ______________________ ______________________

3. How does the narrator use size to describe how he feels in each setting?

   ____

   ____

4. Contrast the feelings the narrator has in each setting.

   ____

   ____

5. How does the visual information demonstrate the differences between the two settings described in the story?

   ____

   ____

Name ______________________________

Answer the items.

1. Explain how to compare and contrast elements in a story.

____

____

2. How can visual information help you to compare and contrast details in a story?

____

____

3. When you compare and contrast details in a story, how does this help you to better understand the story?

____

____

Read the paragraph. Then answer the items.

Last year, Mr. Gold's sixth-grade class decided to play a friendly prank on Mrs. Dool's fifth-grade class. The sixth graders replaced all of the markers in the fifth-grade classroom with markers that were dried out and didn't work anymore. For an entire school day, the fifth graders tried to use the old markers. Then the students became fed up! This year, Mrs. Dool wanted her students to prank the sixth graders. The fifth graders hid a tablet in Mrs. Dool's classroom. At certain times during the day, the fifth graders played a weird old song from a playlist saved on the tablet. Until the sixth graders found the tablet, they had to listen to the weird songs throughout the day! This prank lasted for three entire school days. It was hilarious!

4. Write two details from the story to compare the two pranks.

____

____

5. Write two details from the story to contrast the two pranks.

____

____

Name ______________________________

A **dialogue** is a conversation that takes place between characters in a story. Dialogue can provide significant details about the story.

Ask these questions as you analyze a story's dialogue:

Does the dialogue provide details about the setting?

Does the dialogue provide details about the characters?

Does the dialogue provide details about the plot?

Read the dialogue. Then answer the questions.

Dad scratched his head. "What row was it?" he asked.
"Try to remember," Mom said. "These bags are getting heavy."
"It's definitely parked near the spot where people return the carts," Jia said.
"But I see three of those, " said Mom.

1. Based on the dialogue, where do you think the story takes place?

____

2. Who are the characters, and how do they know each other?

____

3. What is the conflict in the story?

____

Read the dialogue. Then answer the item.

4. "Don't forget the paper plates and napkins," Kelly said. "Oh, and ice."
"You don't need to be bossy, Kelly," Fitz said. "Mom gave *me* the list."
"Just because you're in college, it doesn't mean you can't forget things," Kelly said.
"Let's just get this done," Fitz said. "The guests will be at our house soon."

Explain who Kelly and Fitz are and what they're doing.

____

____

Name ______________________________

Family Fun Challenge!

"Point the television camera my way!" demanded Marcus Starr. "Make sure you can see the colorful nets, slides, pipes, trampolines, pools, lights, and padded contraptions behind me! And, how does my hair look? Is it okay?" Marcus muttered. "Anderson, get me a mirror, please." A young man hurried over with a small hand-held mirror and held it while Marcus examined himself and frowned. "That makeup artist put way too much powder on my face again—I look ridiculous."

"Get ready, Mr. Starr," said Anderson, "we go live in five, four, three, two, and..."

A huge grin appeared on Marcus Starr's face as he spoke into the camera. "Hello, Everyone, and welcome to another exciting episode of Family Fun Challenge, where families like yours compete for a chance to win $10,000, but only if they can conquer the unconquerable, the death-defying, the hair-raising Family Fun Challenge Obstacle Course! The rules are simple, folks—get through the entire course without falling in the mud, but watch out and make sure you don't get bonked! Are you ready to meet tonight's contestants? In red, all the way from Indiana, we have the Brenson Family!"

Mrs. Brenson pumped her fist in the air. "We don't bruise, and we don't lose!"

"I'm a plumber, so I'm not afraid of a few pipes and some water!" Mr. Brenson said with a competitive edge.

"And in blue," Marcus said, "we have a family from right here in sunny LA—let's hear it for the Kim Family!"

The two Kim children looked at the Brenson children and, with big grins, said, "You're going down!"

Jake Brenson went on the obstacle course first, making his way across the balancing beams, past the swinging padded arms that were trying to knock him into the mud, and past the ropes.

"He's like a ninja!" Marcus shouted.

"That stuff is more slippery than it looks," said Mr. Kim after he'd taken a shot at the course.

"Look at Mom freaking out!" said Julie Kim, shaking her head and laughing as her mom swung on the ropes, screaming the entire time.

On the way home, Mr. Brenson said, "That was fun, but winning $10,000 would have been even more fun."

Name ______________________________

Family Fun Challenge!

A **dialogue** is a conversation that takes place between characters in a story. Dialogue can provide significant details about the story.

Dialogue may provide details about the following:

character traits	reasons for characters' actions
setting	conflicts or challenges characters face
plot	characters' plans or intentions

Answer the items about the story you read.

1. Write three character traits that describe Marcus Starr.

   ____________ ____________ ____________

2. What does the dialogue at the beginning tell you about the story?

   ____
   ____
   ____

3. What does Marcus compare Jake Brenson to? Why does Marcus do this?

   ____
   ____

4. Why does Julie Kim think that her mom is "freaking out"?

   ____
   ____

5. Write one important detail from the story that the dialogue provides.

   ____
   ____

Name ____________________

Answer the items.

1. Explain what dialogue is.

____

____

2. Explain how dialogue can provide significant information about characters in a story.

____

____

____

3. Explain how dialogue can provide significant information about plot.

____

____

____

Read the dialogue. Then answer the items.

"If you borrowed my yoga mat, it's fine!" Ruby said sternly. "Just be honest!"

"I didn't borrow it," insisted Joaquin. "You don't believe your own brother? I don't even do yoga, you know that."

"I know you use my yoga mat as a foot pillow, Joaquin! I've seen y... " Ruby paused. "Hey, do you hear that thumping noise?" Joaquin and Ruby went into their sister Liv's room. "Hey! Don't use my yoga mat to squish a spider!" Ruby shrieked.

4. Describe the conflicts that the characters struggle with in the story.

____

____

5. Explain how the dialogue provides significant details in the story.

____

____

Name ____________________

An **idiom** is a phrase or an expression. It is a form of figurative language, which has a meaning that is not literal. Use the context of the surrounding words and phrases to figure out the meaning of an idiom. Here is an example of an idiom in a sentence:

It's raining cats and dogs, so we won't go for a walk today.

The idiom is underlined. It means that it's raining a lot.

Read the pair of sentences, which contains an underlined idiom. Write what you think the idiom means. Then explain why you think so.

1. AJ was much quieter than usual. His mom couldn't tell what was on his mind, so she said, "A penny for your thoughts?"

2. "The ball is in your court," Erin said. "I don't care what movie we watch."

3. "What if the doctor says I need a shot?" Paul asked, clearly worried. "We'll cross that bridge when we get to it," Mom said.

4. "I wish I could go," Kwon said with a cough. "But I'm feeling under the weather."

5. Priya's brother ate the last cookie and then lost the book she'd let him borrow. When he broke her phone, it was the last straw, and she lost her temper.

Name ______________________________

An **idiom** is a phrase or an expression that has a figurative meaning, or a meaning that is not literal. If you take an idiom's meaning literally, it will not make sense.

Example: When a woman says she's **in over her head**, she doesn't mean she's underwater. She means that she can't handle everything that needs to be done.

Read the paragraph, which contains underlined idioms. Then answer the questions.

Leo was in a pickle. He had a big test coming up, and he hadn't made time to study. The night before the test, he decided that he needed to put his nose to the grindstone. He read his books and his notes. He looked at old homework assignments and quizzes and studied as much as he could.

1. **in a pickle**
   What do you think this idiom means? Explain why you think so.

   ____

   ____

2. **put his nose to the grindstone**
   What do you think this idiom means? Explain why you think so.

   ____

   ____

Read the paragraph. Then answer the question.

Francine begged her brother Alfie to be quiet so she could study for her test, but he wouldn't cooperate with her at all. First, he played a song on his recorder. Then, he turned the television volume up really high. He thought it was funny. Later, Alfie was trying to listen to a song on his phone, and he asked Francine to quiet down. But she made more noise. "See, you're getting a taste of your own medicine," said Francine.

3. **a taste of your own medicine**
   What do you think this idiom means? Explain why you think so.

   ____

   ____

Name ________________________________

Our Pet Gator

To be honest, "pet" isn't an accurate word for Cletus, the gator who's lived in our yard for the past several years. He's more a member of the family, really. One morning, Pop and I walked outside, and there he was, just a young gator who'd obviously been through a lot: he was malnourished, injured, skittish... the whole nine yards.

We live right on the bayou, where the water is full of gators, so we're not strangers to having an occasional gator show up behind our house. But this gator was clearly different. He was very young and needed serious help.

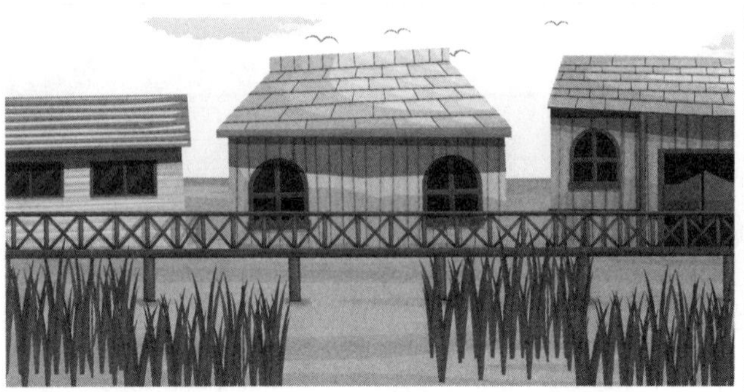

Pop guessed that somebody got it into their head that keeping a gator as a pet would be a good idea. Then, when that person realized that the gator was going to get big and strong and need thorough care, he or she released it into the wild. Pop shook his head. "Some folks just bite off more than they can chew and give up."

The chances of us getting Cletus back to the point where he could survive and hunt on his own were slim to none. Pop used to work for the Park Service, often tracking and tagging gators, so he knew we could help the poor creature. We kept him outside, and he usually just stayed in the bayou. We fed him every day, so he just stayed near our house. We'd often hang out with our neighbors, playing yard games and boiling craw fish. And Cletus would swim in the bayou, which is pretty much part of our backyard. He would float around happily, looking like he was smiling and like he was on cloud nine, snapping at dragonflies and birds occasionally. Whenever we cooked and had bits that we didn't use, we'd throw them to Cletus.

The years have gone by, and Cletus has become a local celebrity. Every year, we send a picture to the local newspaper to celebrate his birthday. Well, we don't know his exact birthday, but we went out on a limb and estimated when it is. As Cletus's fame has grown, so has his body, by leaps and bounds. Last year, he hit a whopping six feet in length. Now, he's a happy alligator, and I can't imagine life without him.

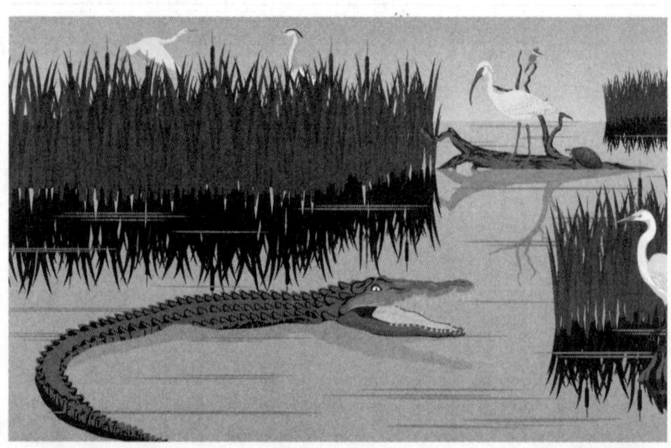

Name ____________________

Our Pet Gator

An **idiom** is a phrase or expression. When you read an **idiom**, you don't take the meaning literally. Use the context of other words and sentences to figure out the meaning of an idiom.

Authors use idioms to add humor to the story.

Authors also use idioms to make the narrator and characters' dialogue sound natural. Many people use idioms when they speak.

Answer the questions about the story you read.

1. Which idiom means "everything possible"?
   Ⓐ on cloud nine
   Ⓑ leaps and bounds
   Ⓒ the whole nine yards
   Ⓓ out on a limb

2. Pop said the people who had Cletus first must have bitten off more than they could chew. What did he mean by that? Explain how you know.

   ____

   ____

   ____

3. **on cloud nine**
   What do you think this idiom means? Explain why you think so.

   ____

   ____

4. **we went out on a limb**
   What do you think this idiom means? Explain why you think so.

   ____

   ____

Name ____________________

Answer the questions.

1. What is an idiom?

____

____

2. How do idioms make the dialogue in a story realistic?

____

____

Read the pair of sentences. Then write **yes** or **no** to tell whether or not it has an idiom.

3. Chris's dog, Sue, is very energetic, and she always wants Chris to pay attention to her. Chris often takes Sue on extra long walks so she will run out of steam. ____________

4. Piper met her cousin Junior for the first time at the family reunion. But Piper found Junior to be quite rude, so the cousins got off on the wrong foot. ____________

5. Brandon had received a gift card from his grandparents, which he could use at his favorite store. But then he lost the card, and he was extremely disappointed. ____________

Read the paragraph. Then answer the question.

6. Melanie's mom and dad were both working on Tuesday night, so Melanie was going to be home alone. Melanie's mom made a lasagna ahead of time and told Melanie that she just needed to heat it up for dinner. Melanie cut a square of lasagna and put it on a plate, but she didn't want to eat lasagna by itself. So Melanie went the extra mile and cut up some vegetables for a salad. She also toasted some bread rolls.

went the extra mile
What do you think this idiom means? Explain why you think so.

____

____

Name ______________________________

In a story, **symbolism** is anything that stands for something else, such as a big idea or something that is happening in the world. An animal, object, or color can be a symbol. Details in the story help to show what the symbol stands for.

When looking for symbolism in a story, ask yourself these questions:

Does the story draw a comparison between an animal, object, or color and an important idea?

Does the story mention a certain animal, object, or color more than once?

Does a particular animal, object, or color appear at important parts of the story?

Read the story. Then answer the items.

Sir Kensington was the bravest knight in the land. He owned a magnificent sword and had a fierce lion painted on his armor. One day, the king summoned Sir Kensington. The knight came right away. Chest puffed out, he strode past a large statue of a lion and entered the throne room. The king told him that a dragon was terrorizing the kingdom, and that he needed a brave knight to put a stop to it. Sir Kensington held his head high. "Your Majesty, I shall defeat the dragon!" As the knight rode off to fight the dragon, a sense of fear swept over him. How big and fierce would this dragon prove to be? Looking up, Sir Kensington noticed a strange cloud. "That cloud looks like a lion!" he gasped. With renewed courage, he galloped forward.

1. In the story, a ______ is a symbol.
   Ⓐ sword
   Ⓑ cloud
   Ⓒ knight
   Ⓓ lion

2. What details in the story show that this symbol stands for bravery and courage?

____

____

____

3. Why is the symbol important to the story?

____

Name ____________________

Disaster Relief

Day 1

I decided to start keeping a journal because I have a lot to say, and my parents said that writing it all down would be a good idea. Mostly what I have to say is that life right now is roses because Mom has been home for over a month. She's in the Army National Guard, so sometimes she gets deployed to different areas of the country when there's an emergency. I like seeing Mom in her uniform. It has American flag patches on each arm. The one on her left arm looks normal, but the one on her right arm is backwards. Mom said that's deliberate because the blue area with the stars should always be facing toward the front of the soldier who's wearing it. She said the two patches are meant to resemble the two sides of a real flag flying in the breeze.

Day 2

We learned about bald eagles in school today. The Founding Fathers chose it as our national symbol. Not all of the Founding Fathers agreed, though. Benjamin Franklin felt that the turkey would be a better symbol for our country. Personally, I think that turkeys are cute, but a bald eagle is definitely more appropriate for a national symbol. When it's soaring high in the sky, it's free, without boundaries or limits. It spreads its wings as wide as it can, having the entire spacious sky as is its playground. There is nothing as free as the soaring bald eagle, in my opinion.

Day 3

Bad news! In another state, there was a catastrophic hurricane that resulted in lots of flooding, so Mom's being deployed to help with disaster relief. I feel sorry for all those people, but I'm miserable because I don't want Mom to leave.

Day 4

Mom left early this morning. I cried as she hugged Dad and me goodbye. After she left, I went out to the backyard to think. Of everyone I know, why did it have to be my mom who constantly left to help other people? As I stood in the yard, I saw a large bird soaring high above. I could see its white head, and that's when I realized it was a bald eagle. I watched it circle for a few minutes, until it drifted out of sight. When I went inside, I found myself feeling really proud of Mom.

Name ______________________________

Disaster Relief

When an author uses **symbolism**, the author uses an animal, object, color, or image to represent something else, such as a big idea or something happening in the world. An author uses symbolism to draw a connection between the symbol and what it represents. Details in the story support this connection.

When looking for symbolism in a story, ask yourself these questions:

Does the story draw a comparison between an animal, object, or color and an important idea?

Does the story mention a certain animal, object, or color more than once?

Answer the items about the story you read.

1. Explain what the two patches on the mom's uniform represent.

____

____

____

2. What does a bald eagle symbolize in the story? Explain how details support this.

____

____

____

3. Why do you think the Founding Fathers chose a bald eagle instead of a turkey to be a national symbol for America?

____

____

4. Why does the sight of the soaring bald eagle make the narrator feel proud of her mom?

____

____

Name ____________________

Answer the items.

1. Explain what symbolism is.

2. How can recognizing symbolism in a story help you to better understand the story?

3. Write one question you can ask yourself when you're thinking about symbolism in a story.

4. Explain why authors use symbolism in a story.

Read the paragraph. Then answer the question.

5. "Look at that spider, Mac," said Grandma. Mac paused the movie to look up at the corner of the room where Grandma was pointing. He appeared disgusted.

"Oh, gross," he said, "let's get rid of it, quick."

"It's spinning and weaving its home," said Grandma. "It's entitled to make its own place in this world, isn't it?" Mac shrugged as Grandma continued. "It's chosen where to spin its web. It's chosen how tightly and how strongly to weave the strings. It's even chosen how big to make the web. Every choice the spider makes about the web, and each new string it weaves affects its life. It affects how much food it catches and how safe it will be." Mac didn't understand. "We all of us, big or small, weave our lives with our choices. Every choice we make is an important one, even if it seems insignificant."

Mac finally understood Grandma's point. "And now, Grandma, can we make the choice to continue our movie?" he said with a grin. Grandma nodded.

What do you think the spider web could represent in this story? Explain why.

Name ____________________

A **historical fiction** story takes place in the past. Some of the events, characters, or settings may have been real, but the story is fictional.

These are important things to remember about historical fiction:

The setting is real or realistic.

The characters do things that people really did in the past.

The story provides factual details about how people lived in the past.

Read the pair of sentences. Circle it if it could be from a historical fiction story.

1. Nigel saw the newspaper article and gasped. Two brothers had just flown the world's first airplane!

2. Shali was writing a report on the Wright Brothers. She searched the internet for information and was amazed by what she found out.

3. It was 1919, and Mason needed a way to earn money. Having been a pilot during World War I, he began traveling around the country, performing aerial stunts for crowds.

Read the paragraph. Then answer the items.

A young journalist named Emmet stood among the crowd, which bristled with excitement. The strange man who'd arrived in Monday's stagecoach stood at the top of the hill, hoping to be the first person to fly. Strapped to his back was a pair of wings that looked just like those of a bird. He ran, flapped, and leaped! For a brief moment, Emmet thought he had the scoop of the century. That feeling quickly faded away, though, as the man tripped, stumbled, and rolled down the hill. Emmet sighed and went into the telegraph office to wire the disappointing story to the newspaper.

4. What details suggest that this story is historical fiction?

____

____

5. Write one thing that might be different if the story's setting were the present time.

____

Name ____________________

His Majesty's Sense of Humor

Will gulped as yet another poor, unemployed jester shuffled out of the throne room, looking utterly defeated. Like many other jesters, Will had traveled as fast as he could, which was by horseback, to the castle to audition for the role of court jester. Apparently, the king had become dissatisfied with the previous jester and sent him away, and now His Majesty was seeking a new one, someone who could make him laugh.

Will learned that the king needed a new jester when a royal messenger came to his village and announced it to the crowd in the village square, which was how everyone got their news.

Will was very nervous. He had heard the king reject seven jesters now. In fact, he was sorely offended by one of the jesters, whom he had thrown in prison.

Will had all of the basic skills that jesters were expected to have: singing, juggling, acrobatics, dancing, and telling jokes and stories. But he was still terribly poor—a position in the king's court would mean plenty of food and a roof over his head. And, if Will proved to be talented enough, perhaps he would also earn some money.

Suddenly, the door to the throne room burst open. A guard stepped from the throne room, pushing out a sad-looking jester. Then the guard motioned for Will to enter.

Taking a deep breath, Will stepped inside and bowed before the king. Then he stood up and stared at the floor. He stood like this, in silence, for a few moments, and then suddenly and cheerily exclaimed, "Greetings, Your Majesty! Will Winters at your service, and it is my honor to make your acquaintance, though I must say, you are quite a bit smaller than I'd ever imagined. It looks as if you haven't eaten in days!" Will reached down and lifted a bit of fuzz from the red carpet. He held it up for all to see and continued to speak to it. "May I ask why you are all the way down there? Should you not be seated on your royal throne?" Will then looked up at the king and pretended to be surprised. "Your Majesty! An impostor is seated on your throne, and if I may say so, he has the appearance of a rather bored and serious sort of person."

There was silence in the throne room as the king looked at Will. Suddenly, the king burst into laughter. "Finally," he boomed. "Someone who isn't afraid to poke fun at me! Will Winters, you shall be my new court jester!"

Name ______________________________

His Majesty's Sense of Humor

A **historical fiction** story takes place in the past. Even though the story may seem true, it's fictional. These things are common in historical fiction:

The story mentions objects or things that people used in the past.

The story is about things that were realistic in the past.

The story gives details about things people did in the past.

Answer the items about the story you read.

1. What details suggest that this story takes place in the past?

____

____

____

2. How did jesters get paid?

____

____

3. Write two details from the story that might be different if the story took place today.

____

____

____

4. Write one way that royal jesters of the past are similar to comedians today.

____

5. If you were a king or a queen hundreds of years ago, would you have hired a jester? Explain why or why not.

____

Name ____________________________________

Answer the items.

1. Explain what makes a story a historical fiction.

____

____

2. How is historical fiction different from other genres?

____

____

3. Is it possible to learn facts about the past from reading a historical fiction story? Explain your answer.

____

____

____

Read the paragraphs. Then answer the item.

4. Maximus drove home as fast as he possibly could. He parked in the driveway and took the big box out of the trunk. He couldn't wait to take it inside to surprise his family. "Papa!" his children and wife shouted when he walked through the door.

"This is a surprise for you all," he said. Maximus took the object he'd just bought out of the box. He took the wire and plugged it into the wall. Then he adjusted the antennas and turned a dial. The flat surface started to make sounds and show pictures. "It's one of these new things called a television!" he said.

His family loved the surprise. "It's too bad all the pictures are black and white," said Maximus's son. "I wish the television could show things in color." After the family had watched television for an hour, Maximus's wife said she was going to heat up the leftovers from yesterday for tonight's dinner. "I'll put the leftovers in the oven now, so it should be all heated up in about a half an hour," she said.

"I'm so hungry, I wish there was a way to heat it up faster," said Maximus's son.

Write two details from the story that show that it is historical fiction.

____

____

Name ________________________________

A **realistic fiction** story is about events that can actually happen. The setting is usually in the present and in a place that could be real. The details in a realistic fiction story are consistent with conditions in the real world.

This is a description of a realistic fiction story:

> A boy has to miss his best friend's birthday party because he has the flu.

This is a description of story that is not realistic fiction:

> A boy has to miss his best friend's birthday party because he has transformed into a giant bug.

Read the pair of sentences. Circle the pair that is from a realistic fiction story.

1. Min looked out the car's window at the big bear lumbering through the woods. "I wonder what he's thinking," Min thought.

2. A large bear drank some water from the stream. A strange feeling came over the bear and, to his shock, he suddenly knew how to speak Russian, Japanese, and English.

3. Jose did a research report on grizzly bears. He wrote about their diet, habitat, behavior, appearance, and other aspects of their lives.

Read the pair of sentences. Then state whether or not it is from a realistic fiction story. Explain your answer.

4. All of the bear leaders got together at a conference. They were discussing a persistent problem that their communities had been dealing with: humans invading their territories.

____

____

5. The nature expert had spent five days alone in the woods when he stumbled upon a baby bear that had fallen into a hole. She could hear the baby bear whimpering and decided to help the poor creature out, as it was probably weak, hungry, and thirsty.

____

____

Name ____

A Common Language

When Caneze's grandfather moved to the United States last month, the family threw a big party, but Caneze didn't spend much time with him that day. He didn't speak English, so how could she have any sort of conversation with him? Caneze spent most of that day in the den, texting her best friend, Maya, and watching her cousins play video games. There was a huge art competition coming up at school, and Caneze and Maya were planning to compete.

"I wish you'd spent time with your grandfather instead of your phone, Caneze," Mom said on the way home.

"But I don't even know him," Caneze said, "and he doesn't speak any English."

"And you don't speak any Ukrainian, Caneze, but he'd love to get to know you. I think you may find that you two have a lot in common."

Two weeks later, Caneze came home from school in the afternoon to find her grandfather sitting at the kitchen table with Mom. On the table sat some books. The old man smiled warmly at Caneze, and she smiled back as she sat down at the table. As Grandpa and Mom spoke in Ukrainian, Caneze let her mind wander. An idea for a picture came to her, so she fetched her sketchbook. Sitting at the table, she sketched while the adults talked. Then Caneze heard Mom say, "I have to run out for a few minutes. You can stay here with Grandpa."

Caneze suddenly felt unsure and shy. What would the two of them talk about? "This is going to be awkward," she thought. She gave Grandpa a polite smile and then returned to the lines and shapes she'd drawn on the page.

She could sense Grandpa watching her. "This is a sketchbook," Caneze said, pointing at her page. The old man nodded. Then he stood up and walked away, returning a moment later with a laptop. He typed as Caneze sketched. After a few minutes, Grandpa tapped Caneze on the shoulder and pointed to the laptop screen. So Caneze scooted her chair closer to his so she could see better. The open page was an online portfolio. Caneze could tell from the name that it was Grandpa's portfolio.

"This is beautiful—I didn't know you were an artist," Caneze said. Caneze showed her grandfather some of her own work. He smiled, giving her a thumbs-up. Later, when Mom returned, neither Caneze nor Grandpa seemed to notice. They were too busy drawing together.

Name ________________________________

A Common Language

A **realistic fiction** story is about things that can actually happen.
Even though it's a fictional story, it is believable.
These are important details to remember about realistic fiction:

The events usually take place in the present time.

The characters have problems that real people deal with.

The characters' actions and dialogue are realistic and believable.

Answer the items about the story you read.

1. Describe in detail Caneze's problem in the story. Can real people have this problem?

____

____

____

____

2. Write three details from the story that suggest that this story takes place in the present.

____

____

3. How does Caneze feel at first when she's alone with her Grandpa? Are her feelings realistic? Explain why or why not.

____

____

4. Explain why this story is realistic fiction.

____

____

5. Have you ever been in a situation similar to Caneze's? yes no

Name ______________________

Review

Answer the items.

1. Explain what makes a story realistic fiction.

____

____

2. How is realistic fiction different from other genres?

____

____

3. Write about a problem that a character might have in a realistic fiction story.

____

____

4. Write about a problem that a character would not have in a realistic fiction story.

____

____

Read the paragraph. Then answer the item.

5. Wida was getting ready for school when she saw something that seriously concerned her in the mirror. "Oh my goodness, I have a gray hair!" she exclaimed to herself. "No way, I'm only twelve years old!" She took some tweezers and plucked out the gray hair, and she tried not to think about it again for the rest of the day. At school, though, she couldn't forget it. She told all her friends about the gray hair at lunch. As her friend Tammy was listening, her eyes became fixed on Wida's head. "What are you looking at, Tammy?" Wida asked. "Not another gray hair?" Tammy nodded. Now Wida was really freaking out. At dinner that night, she told her mom, who was a nurse, the whole story. Her mom said that this was nothing to worry about at all and that it was actually not that unusual. Wida felt relieved.

   Write two details from the story that show that it is realistic fiction.

____

____

Name ____________________________________

A **myth** is a fictional story about supernatural events, or events that could not happen in the real world. A myth has characters with supernatural powers, such as gods, goddesses, and monsters. A myth often has a hero. These are additional details to remember about a myth:

The setting is ancient.

It can take place on Earth or in a place similar to Earth.

It may explain how something was created or why something in the world is a certain way.

It is told as if it is historical fact, even though it is not true.

Read the paragraph. Then answer the questions.

Now we have only one sun above Earth, but long ago, ten suns lived above Earth. They took turns going across the sky, one at a time. One day, however, they decided to stay in the sky together. Blinding light filled the sky. The heat dried wells and burned fields. At the same time, three monsters appeared in the land. Emperor Yao was miserable seeing his usually peaceful empire in such turmoil. He called upon Yi, the world's greatest archer, to help. Yi pulled back the string and let his first arrow fly. A flash filled the sky, and one of the suns was gone. One-by-one, Yi shot down eight more suns until there was just one left in the sky. Then he set out to defeat the monsters. One monster had an enormous tooth, which Yi shattered with an arrow. Next, Yi defeated a giant monster bird, and finally, he destroyed a vicious sea monster that had been terrorizing fishing villages. The empire was once again at peace.

1. Who is the hero in the story? Explain how you know.

____

____

2. What details make this story a myth?

____

____

3. What does this myth explain about the world?

____

Name ______________________________

Bellerophon and Pegasus

In the city of Corinth, a young man named Bellerophon was so strong and wise that he was almost like a god. In fact, it was rumored that he was the son of the sea god, Poseidon.

There was one thing in the world that Bellerophon wanted more than anything else, and that was the winged horse, Pegasus, which nobody had ever been able to tame. An oracle advised Bellerophon to go to the goddess Athena's temple, which he did. There, he received a golden bridle from Athena.

Bellerophon spied Pegasus drinking from a spring outside of Corinth and approached cautiously. When the winged horse saw Bellerophon with the bridle, it showed no sign of fear and allowed the young man to place the bridle over its head. Bellerophon was now master of the magical creature. Dressed in bronze armor, Bellerophon soared through the sky on Pegasus.

Years later, while visiting the home of King Proetus, Bellerophon accidentally offended the king, who became furious. King Proetus wanted to punish Bellerophon. Knowing that it would anger the gods if he were to harm a guest in his house, Proetus asked Bellerophon to deliver a letter to the King of Lycea. Little did Bellerophon know that the letter asked the Lycian king to punish Bellerophon brutally. The Lycian King, however, feared the gods' wrath as much as Proetus did. Rather than harming Bellerophon, the Lycian king sent him on a dangerous mission that nobody could possibly accomplish: defeating the Chimaera, a dreadful, fire-breathing monster—part lion, part goat, and part serpent.

Bellerophon found the Chimaera. Mounted on the back of Pegasus in the sky, Bellerophon fired a spear into the fearsome monster.

By taming Pegasus and defeating the Chimaera, Bellerophon gained a heroic reputation among the gods and was widely respected. He started to become very proud. One day, Bellerophon tried to fly to the top of Mount Olympus and live among the gods. The gods were outraged by this, and Pegasus sensed this. The horse threw off his master and joined the other horses in the gods' stables atop the mountain. Bellerophon survived the fall, but he lived the rest of his life in misery, hating the gods.

Twice the pride, double the fall.

Name ____________________

Belleraphon and Pegasus

A **myth** is a fictional story about supernatural events, or events that could not happen in the real world. A myth has characters with supernatural powers, such as gods, goddesses, and monsters. A myth often has a heroic figure. These are additional details to remember about a myth:

It can take place on Earth or in a place similar to Earth.

It may have a lesson or a moral.

It is told as if it is historical fact, even though it is not true.

Answer the items about the story you read.

1. Write one way that the setting is similar to Earth.

____

2. What makes Bellerophon the heroic figure in the story?

____

____

3. Write two details from the story that demonstrate that it is a myth.

____

____

4. What does the moral at the end of the story mean?

____

____

____

5. Do you think that Bellerophon is a supernatural being? Explain why or why not.

____

____

Name ____________________

Answer the items.

1. Mark the story idea that could be used to write a myth.
   Ⓐ Everyone in the village was preparing for the New Year's feast. In a few hours, the village would be ringing in the new year and the turn of the century: the year 1900!
   Ⓑ Buddy was excited and nervous because he was about to start taking driving lessons. He had never driven a space shuttle before, but now that he was twelve years old, it was time that he learned. The driving age for space vehicles had been lowered to twelve back in the year 2091.
   Ⓒ Vera had never tried to order a gift online before, but she received an e-gift for her birthday, so she decided to give it a try.
   Ⓓ Demula, who is a woman by day and a statue by night, has only forty days to travel to the goddess Shakria's temple and ask for help. Demula's village had recently been attacked by giant flies.

2. Write three details to remember about myths.

____

____

Read the paragraph. State whether or not it is a myth.
Then explain why or why not.

3. Hundreds of years ago, when there were no flavors, the Cookers used to leave their castles in the sky to visit the people living on the planet below. The Cookers loved the people, and they thought of the people as their pets. The Cookers made all of the food that the people ate. The Cookers were giants, and they'd bring arm loads of food from their castles. All of the food was beige, and it all tasted like water. The people were always happy to receive the food, and they had never eaten anything else. They had a good relationship with the Cookers, until one day, when a person decided to start cooking his own food. The person used some plants that grew on the planet. The person sprinkled and chopped and grated ingredients. When this person tasted the food, his eyes grew wide. He loved the food he had made and vowed to never eat the Cookers' food again. He started sharing the food he cooked with the other people, and they all made the same vow. The Cookers became furious. They decided to never bring food down from the sky to the people on the planet ever again.

____

____

Answer Key

✱ These answers will vary. Examples are given.

Page 7

Name ______________________

Nonfiction
Main Idea and Details
1

The **main idea** of a text is what the text is mostly about. Authors typically introduce the main idea early in the text.

The **supporting details** provide more information about the main idea.

Below is the first paragraph of an article. Read the paragraph. Then answer the question.

1. Have you ever seen a meerkat? They are adorable, squirrel-sized animals with big dark eyes and delicate, pointy faces. They live in the deserts and plains of the southern part of Africa. Meerkats work extremely well together and divvy up special jobs among them.

What is the main idea?

✱ Meerkats work well together because they all have special jobs.

Below are details from the rest of the article from number 1. Put an **X** next to the details that support the main idea.

2. Does it support the main idea?	Supporting Details
	Meerkats live in large social groups called mobs.
X	Each member contributes to the mob with a special job that may vary from day to day.
X	For example, all the adult meerkats take turns caring for the young.
X	Other meerkats have the task of looking for insects and spiders to feed the mob.
	Meerkats occasionally eat lizards and small birds.
	They spend nights in burrows, safe from predators.
X	The most important job is that of the sentry, who finds a high spot to look out for predators.

© Evan-Moor Corp. • EMC 2426 • Reading Comprehension Fundamentals 7

Page 8

Name ______________________

Nonfiction
Main Idea and Details
2

The **main idea** is the most important idea in the text. It's the idea the author most wants to express.

Supporting details, such as examples, facts, reasons, and visual information, can provide more information about the main idea. Photos, diagrams, and graphs are examples of visual information. These signal words and phrases can help you identify supporting details in the text: **also, for example, as well, for instance, such as, in addition, furthermore**

Read the paragraph. Then answer the items.

Some robotic machines are programmed to do specific jobs repeatedly, like putting together the parts of a car. In addition to this, some robots are programmed to act like humans and do human jobs. Scientists have constructed robots that can communicate with us and do different tasks, such as take and deliver food orders. Some are also designed to keep young children and the elderly company. In Japan, for example, robots are employed to watch kids while the parents shop at a department store. There are robots who assist guests at a hotel in Japan, as well. The aim is for some robots to take over even more jobs that were once only done by humans. Who knows? Maybe someday a robot will do your chores at home!

1. What is the main idea of the text?
✱ Scientists are making human-like robots to do human tasks.

2. Write three signal words or phrases from the text.
✱ such as — also — as well

3. Write three details from the text that support the main idea.
✱ In Japan, robots keep children company. Robots assist guests at a hotel. Robots deliver food.

4. Write an example of a type of visual information that could be included in this text.
✱ a photo of a robot assisting people

8 Reading Comprehension Fundamentals • EMC 2426 • © Evan-Moor Corp.

Page 10

Name ______________________

Nonfiction
Main Idea and Details
3

Hydroponics: Feeding Our Future

The **main idea** is the most important idea in a text.

Supporting details provide more information about the main idea. Supporting details can be facts, reasons, and visual information. Signal words and phrases often introduce supporting details.

Authors may use headings to organize the supporting details in a text. The text under each heading has its own main idea and supporting details.

Answer the items about the text you read.

1. What is the main idea of the text?
✱ Hydroponics may be the best way to feed future generations.

2. Write four signal words or phrases from the text.
✱ for instance — also — for example — as well

3. Write three supporting details from the text.
✱ Hydroponics does not require a lot of land. Hydroponics uses water efficiently. Hydroponics can get a lot of food to people quickly.

4. What is the main idea of the section with the heading "People"?
✱ Hydroponics can use people's resources efficiently so more people have food to eat.

5. Explain how the photograph supports the main ideas in the text.
✱ It shows vegetables being grown with an efficient use of space, on racks.

10 Reading Comprehension Fundamentals • EMC 2426 • © Evan-Moor Corp.

Page 11

Name ______________________

Nonfiction
Main Idea and Details
Review

Answer the items.

1. Explain what a main idea and supporting details are.
✱ A main idea is the most important idea in a text and what the text is mostly about. Supporting details tell more about the main idea. They can be facts, examples, pictures, and reasons.

2. Write four signal words or phrases that can introduce supporting details in a text.
✱ for instance — such as — in addition — as well

3. Explain how facts and examples can support a main idea.
✱ Facts and examples tell us more about the main idea and help us to better understand it.

4. Explain why authors sometimes use headings in a text.
✱ Headings help to organize supporting details in a text.

5. Explain how a text can use visual information to support a main idea. Describe an example.
✱ Visual information in graphs and diagrams can provide details not stated directly in the text. For example, a text with the main idea that more Americans buy white bread than whole grain bread may include a graph that shows how much of each bread people buy each month.

© Evan-Moor Corp. • EMC 2426 • Reading Comprehension Fundamentals 11

Page 12

Name ______________________

Nonfiction
Text Features and Visual Information
1

Text features are parts of texts, signs, charts, and other informational sources. Text features provide additional information about the text or the topic and can help an author emphasize a particular part of the text.

These are common types of text features:

the title of the text	numbers and bullet points in a list
bold words and headings	pictures and captions

Read the flyer. Then answer the items.

Don't Waste Food!

Did you know that one-third of all food is wasted? That's a shame when so many people go hungry each day. Here are some tips to help you decrease food waste:

Compost. Let unwanted food break down and use it in the garden to grow more food.

Get a Doggy Bag. Save uneaten food for later, give it to a pet, or give it to someone you know who doesn't have much to eat.

Buy Less. Only buy foods you know you and your family will eat.

Eat Less. Start with less on your plate. You may find that you get full and can save the rest for later.

1. State two text features used in this flyer.
✱ A title and bold words are used in the flyer.

2. What is the purpose of the bold words? Explain what follows the bold words.
✱ They suggest in few words how to decrease food waste. After the bold words there are further explanations about the suggestions.

3. Does the information in the flyer support the title?
✱ Yes. The focus of the flyer is to tell us how to avoid wasting food.

12 Reading Comprehension Fundamentals • EMC 2426 • © Evan-Moor Corp.

Page 13

Name ______________________

Nonfiction
Text Features and Visual Information
2

Authors use different kinds of **visual information** in a text. Pictures, photographs, graphs, and charts are types of visual information. Visual information elaborates on the information presented in the text. Sometimes, visual information provides additional information that was not stated directly in the text.

Read the paragraph and look at the chart. Then answer the items.

Over 30% of the world's frogs and toads have an official status of "threatened" or "near threatened." Much of this is due to capturing frogs and toads for the pet trade, as well as systematic deforestation of their habitats. The oophaga lehmanni, also known as the Lehmann's poison frog or red-banded poison frog, is critically endangered, for example. Its distribution, throughout areas in its native Columbia, is scattered and continues to decline.

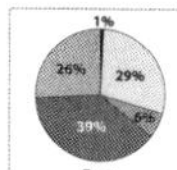

Frogs

Extinct	1%
Near-threatened	29%
Least Concern	39%
Data deficient	28%

1. What information does the pie chart provide?
✱ It shows what percentages of frogs and toads are threatened or at low risk.

2. How does the key below the pie chart help you to better understand the pie chart?
✱ It clearly states what the different shades and percentages represent on the chart.

3. How does the pie chart support what the text states?
✱ The text states that some frogs and toads are threatened, and the chart shows how many.

4. Write one fact you learned from the pie chart or the text.
✱ The Lehmann's poison frog is also known as the red-banded poison frog.

© Evan-Moor Corp. • EMC 2426 • Reading Comprehension Fundamentals 13

Page 15

Name ______________________

Nonfiction
Text Features and Visual Information
3

A Wave You Don't Want to Ride: The Tsunami

Text features can help an author convey an important message in few words or help an author emphasize important parts of a text. These are some types of text features: a text's title, headings, bold or italicized words, numbers in a list, and bullet points.

Visual information shows details about a text's subject. Visual information is any kind of picture or image and includes the following: illustrations, photos, diagrams, graphs, maps, labels, and captions.

Pay attention to text features and visual information as you read.

Answer the items about the text you read.

1. How does the title of the text help you to prepare to read the information?
✱ The title tells me right from the start that I'd be reading a text about waves called tsunamis.

2. State the types of text features and visual information used in the text.
There is a diagram with labels. There is a title. There are bold headings.

3. Explain how the visual information supports what the text states.
✱ The diagram shows an earthquake's shaking energy creating a tsunami, as the text describes.

4. Why do you think the author includes bold headings in the text?
✱ They help the author organize the information in few words. The headings are clear and explicit.

5. How may the bold headings help readers remember facts?
✱ They may help you remember by categorizing.

© Evan-Moor Corp. • EMC 2426 • Reading Comprehension Fundamentals 15

Page 16

Name ______________________

Nonfiction
Text Features and Visual Information
Review

Answer the items.

1. Explain why authors use text features and visual information in a text.
✱ Authors use text features to emphasize important ideas and share a message in few words. They use visual information to provide more details about a topic.

2. State three types of text features and three types of visual information.
✱ bold words — headings — title — photos — captions — diagrams

3. Explain how visual information can help you to better understand a text.
✱ It can show you examples or more details about the topic. Labels help make the facts more clear.

Read the paragraph. Then answer the item.

4. High above Athens, Greece, sits the ancient city known as the Acropolis. In Greek, Acropolis means "city at the top." It was built on the highest point in that area many centuries ago to keep people safe from invaders. Among the many ancient structures in Acropolis is the renowned Parthenon. This massive marble temple was built in dedication to the goddess Athena, the patron goddess of Athens.

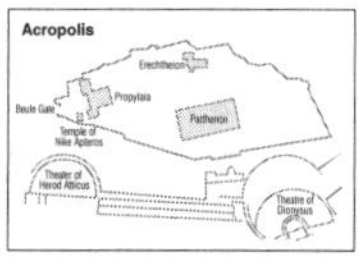

Write two other ancient structures in Acropolis, according to the map.
✱ The Theater of Herod Atticus and the Temple of Nike Apteros are also in Acropolis.

16 Reading Comprehension Fundamentals • EMC 2426 • © Evan-Moor Corp.

Page 17

Name ______________________

Nonfiction
Description
1

Authors use different kinds of text structures to convey information. When an author writes a text with a **description** structure, the author uses descriptive details, examples, and reasons to support the main idea.

A text with a description structure may include pictures or diagrams with captions that provide readers with additional details about the topic.

Read the paragraph. Then answer the items.

Scorpions can be dangerous, but have you ever stopped to think about their attributes? Scorpions are very adaptable creatures. They live in all kinds of environments throughout the world—from damp forests to grasslands and hot, dry deserts. Scorpions mostly eat insects but can eat other prey, such as reptiles, birds, and rodents. And when all forms of food are scarce, they can slow down their metabolisms and ingest as little as one insect a year! Slowing their metabolisms also enables them to use very little oxygen. It's no wonder that these adaptable creatures have been around since before the age of the dinosaurs!

In addition to fighting and eating different kinds of prey, scorpions fight and eat each other.

1. State the main idea of the paragraph in your own words.
✱ Scorpions have survived a long time because they can adapt their attributes.

2. In your own words, state two details from the text that support the main idea.
✱ Scorpions can enable themselves to use little oxygen. Scorpions have a varied diet.

3. What information do the photograph and caption provide about scorpions?
✱ They show two scorpions fighting and explain that scorpions will even prey on each other.

4. Explain why the author refers to scorpions as "adaptable."
✱ They are able to change in order to survive.

© Evan-Moor Corp. • EMC 2426 • Reading Comprehension Fundamentals 17

*** These answers will vary. Examples are given.**

Page 19

Name ____________

Nonfiction
Description
2

Adapting to Antarctica's Harsh Environment

An author may use a **description** text structure to write an informational text. In a text with a description structure, the author uses descriptive details, examples, and reasons to support the main idea. The title may help you determine what the main idea is. Descriptive details can help a reader form a mental image.

Visual information can demonstrate the descriptive details from the text.

Answer the items about the text you read.

1. Write the main idea of the text in your own words.
   Antarctica has many animals with adaptations that allow them to survive in its harsh climate.
2. Write three adaptations that animals in Antarctica have.
   * Penguins and seals can see in deep water. Seals use their blubber for nourishment when they're hungry. Penguins have downy feathers.
3. Write one descriptive detail from the text that supports the main idea.
   * Emperor penguins have scale-like feathers that help keep out wind and water.
4. Why do you think the author refers to sea spiders and sea pigs as "strange and unusual"?
   * The photos show that they have features that are different from those of animals we usually see.
5. What details from the text support the idea that Antarctica's environment is harsh?
   * Antarctica is a desert. It is freezing cold. It is windy and icy.

© Evan-Moor Corp. • EMC 2426 • Reading Comprehension Fundamentals 19

Page 20

Name ____________

Nonfiction
Description
Review

Answer the questions.

1. How do descriptive details support the main idea of a nonfiction text?
   * These details elaborate on the main idea. They provide examples and explanations, or evidence.
2. Why would an author choose to use a description text structure for a nonfiction text?
   * The author's purpose may be to inform or help a reader form a mental image of a topic.
3. Why is it important for an author to support a main idea with details, reasons, examples, and visual information?
   * If the author doesn't support the main idea, then the main idea doesn't seem credible.

Read the paragraph. Then answer the items.

Plastic bags are everywhere. Each year, about 500 billion to one trillion are consumed. They can be handy, especially if people recycle and reuse them. But, unfortunately, they end up in places where they do harm, as well. Millions of bags end up in the garbage and eventually line landfills. It could take hundreds of years for these bags to decompose, and as they do, they release toxins into the earth and bodies of water. These pollutants are not only harmful to us, but to wildlife as well. Additionally, plastic bags end up in the oceans where they pose a threat to sea life. For example, fish get caught in them and die trying to break free. Also, animals like seagulls and turtles choke on them or ingest them, which ultimately kills the animals.

4. Write the main idea of the text in your own words.
   * Many plastic bags end up not being reused and cause harm to the environment.
5. Write three words or phrases that support the main idea.
   * toxins   pollutants   turtles choke

20 Reading Comprehension Fundamentals • EMC 2426 • © Evan-Moor Corp.

Page 21

Name ____________

Nonfiction
Cause and Effect
1

A text with a **cause-and-effect** structure states the reason that something happens. When a **cause** happens, it leads to an **effect**. You can analyze the details in a text to determine causes and effects.

An event can cause multiple effects. Similarly, an effect may have multiple causes.

Read the paragraph. Then answer the items.

Ann Lowe was the first African American fashion designer. Born in 1898, in Alabama, Ann learned to sew from her grandmother and mother. When Ann was a teenager, her mother died, leaving Ann to run her mom's dressmaking business. It wasn't long before Ann set off to New York to study fashion design. Ann's designs got a lot of attention and caught the eye of Jacqueline Bouvier. Jacqueline hired Ann to create 15 dresses for her wedding to John F. Kennedy (who would later become president of the United States). This was an exceptional occurrence, as Jacqueline was one of the world's most admired style icons whose clothing choices were noticed by many. Ann created 15 dresses, including the wedding gown, for the wedding, which took place in 1953. The dresses are still remembered to this day for their elegance. Although this was a high profile designing job that should have resulted in a profit for Ann, she lost money doing this job. Ten days before the wedding, a pipe burst in her New York studio, destroying 10 of the 15 dresses! Ann bought new material and summoned all of her seamstresses to work around the clock to remake the dresses. They finished the dresses in time, but all the extra fabric and hours of employing the seamstresses were costly for Ann.

1. What do you think caused Ann to become interested in fashion design at a young age?
   * She learned to sew from her grandmother and mother. She took over a dressmaking business.
2. What was the result of Ann's dresses getting a lot of attention?
   * Her dresses caught the eye of Jacqueline Bouvier, who hired Ann to create dresses for a wedding.
3. Explain what caused Ann to lose money on a famous job that should have paid well.
   * She had to remake the ruined dresses.

© Evan-Moor Corp. • EMC 2426 • Reading Comprehension Fundamentals 21

Page 22

Name ____________

Nonfiction
Cause and Effect
2

A text with a **cause-and-effect** structure states the reason that something happens. When a **cause** happens, it leads to an **effect**.

These signal words and phrases can help you to identify cause-and-effect relationships discussed in a nonfiction text:

create	**reason**	**make**	**cause**
because	**due to**	**effect**	**result**

Read the paragraph. Then answer the items.

The High Plains Aquifer, a large underground basin of water that lies under eight U.S. states, has provided farmers with water for over a century, but this water reserve is starting to diminish as a result of overuse and environmental changes. The aquifer ranges from South Dakota to Texas and is used for about thirty percent of U.S. farming and irrigation. The amount of water is decreasing because farmers pump water from the aquifer at unsustainable rates. One reason for this is that we have a lot more land dedicated to agriculture than we did a few decades ago. Additionally, we no longer get enough rainfall or melting snow to refill the aquifer. The overuse, coupled with drought and a changing climate, means that the water is being used faster than it can be replenished, and the effects of this are negative. One result is that rivers that count on the aquifer, like the Republican River in Nebraska, are shrinking. Moreover, many farmers' wells are drying up, and they don't have enough water to irrigate crops or provide water to livestock. Farmers are losing money, and food prices are slowly rising. Conservation efforts may help to prevent the disappearance of the aquifer.

1. Write three cause-and-effect signal words or phrases from the text.
   * reason   effect   because
2. In your own words, state two reasons why the High Plains Aquifer is diminishing.
   * The water is being used at an unsustainable rate by farmers. We get less rainfall.
3. If the aquifer dries up completely, what effect could that have on the U.S.?
   * The crops will become more expensive.

22 Reading Comprehension Fundamentals • EMC 2426 • © Evan-Moor Corp.

Page 24

Name ____________

Nonfiction
Cause and Effect
3

Could Rice Be a Dwindling Staple?

A text with a **cause-and-effect** structure states the reason that something happens. When a **cause** happens, it leads to an **effect**. You can analyze the details in a text to determine causes and effects.

An event can cause multiple effects. Similarly, an effect may have multiple causes.

Answer the items about the text you read.

1. Write one sentence to explain a cause-and-effect relationship discussed in the text.
   * The text focuses on how climate change affects the growth of rice plants in Asia.
2. What is the result of growing rice plants in standing water.
   * It prevents pests and weeds from interfering with the rice plant growth.
3. Explain how climate change can cause rice plants to suffer from heat stress. Then describe the effects of heat stress on rice plants and rice yields.
   * If the climate is too hot, it may cause the plant to become sterile. This can make the plant yield very little rice or no rice at all.
4. Why would a farmer choose to manage different crops differently?
   * A farmer can use different methods to make the plants yield more grains.
5. What is a possible outcome for people if Asia stops growing rice entirely? Explain why you think so.
   * People would go hungry. Rice is a staple, and Asia grows 90 percent of it.

24 Reading Comprehension Fundamentals • EMC 2426 • © Evan-Moor Corp.

Page 25

Name ____________

Nonfiction
Cause and Effect
Review

Answer the items.

1. What does a text with a cause-and-effect structure explain?
   * It explains the reasons that certain things happen or the results of certain events.
2. Explain why it's important to be able to identify causes and effects in nonfiction texts.
   * If you can identify them, you can understand and explain why things are the way they are.
3. How can cause-and-effect signal words and phrases help you to identify and understand cause-and-effect relationships being discussed in a text?
   * The signal words and phrases stand out and indicate what a cause is and what it leads to. They guide you as you read and analyze a text.

Read the paragraph. Then answer the questions.

Some people stretch their bodies before and after a workout. There are a few reasons to stretch before a workout. It can loosen your muscles, which can in turn help you to prevent a muscle injury. Stretching before a workout may also lead to better physical performance during the workout and less soreness after the workout. Stretching after a workout can also help reduce soreness. Another effect of stretching after a workout is muscle relaxation. Some experts debate whether dynamic stretching (a slow stretch combined with constant movement) is better or worse than static stretching (a stretch in which the person stays still). However, many experts agree that both types of stretching can be beneficial.

4. What are the benefits of stretching before a workout?
   * It can make you perform better. It can prevent you from being sore.
5. What could happen to you if you forget to stretch before and after a workout?
   * You could be in a lot of pain, with sore muscles.

© Evan-Moor Corp. • EMC 2426 • Reading Comprehension Fundamentals 25

Page 26

Name ____________

Nonfiction
Compare and Contrast
1

An author may use a **compare-and-contrast** text structure to write an informational text. The text explains the similarities and differences between two or more things. Sometimes an author uses signal words in the text. Look for compare-and-contrast signal words as you read.

compare:	**alike**	**too**	**also**	**both**	**similar**
contrast:	**different**	**yet**	**but**	**while**	**rather**

Photos and pictures in a text can help show similarities and differences.

Read the paragraph. Then answer the items.

Most of the similarities among the various kinds of snakes are obvious. All snakes are long and covered in scales. Also, they all shed their skin as they grow, and none of them have eyelids. The way snakes bear their young, however, marks some big differences. Most snakes are oviparous, meaning they lay eggs. Just about all oviparous snakes lay their eggs somewhere warm, such as in a nest of leaves or a hole in the ground, and leave their eggs to hatch. Yet a few kinds of oviparous snakes, such as pythons and king cobras, coil up on their eggs until the eggs hatch. While most snakes are oviparous, not all snakes lay eggs. Some are viviparous, meaning they give birth to live young. Among viviparous snakes are Anacondas, most vipers, and many sea snakes.

1. Write three compare-and-contrast signal words or phrases from the text.
   * also   yet   while
2. In your own words, explain the difference between oviparous and viviparous snakes.
   * Oviparous snakes lay eggs, while viviparous snakes have live births.
3. Contrast how Anacondas and king cobras give birth to their young.
   * Anacondas give birth to live snakes, but king cobras are oviparous, so they lay eggs and coil on them until they hatch.

26 Reading Comprehension Fundamentals • EMC 2426 • © Evan-Moor Corp.

Page 27

Name ____________

Nonfiction
Compare and Contrast
2

A text with a **compare-and-contrast** text structure explains the similarities and differences between two or more things. Sometimes an author uses comparative and superlative adjectives to compare and contrast.

These are examples of comparative and superlative adjectives:
uglier, ugliest, more nutritious, most nutritious, less eager, least eager

Read the paragraph. Then answer the items.

Both running and swimming are great ways to get an aerobic workout. Neither requires special equipment; however, running is more convenient for people who do not live near a pool. With running, you can get up and go anywhere. You are not limited to a pool, a lake, or an ocean. Although, running is harder on your joints than swimming is. When you run, you pound your bones and joints on the pavement. Swimming is a more gentle exercise for people who may have knee or back problems, because the water provides a cushion around their limbs. Swimming also works just about every major muscle group in the body. Running does as well.

1. Explain the reasons why a person may choose to run instead of swim for exercise.
   * If you don't live near a pool, you may want to run. You aren't limited by the water's boundaries.
2. Explain the reasons why a person may choose to swim instead of run for exercise.
   * If you have joint pain or health issues with your bones, you'd want to swim because it's gentler.
3. Compare the benefits of swimming and running.
   * Both exercise your entire body. You don't need special equipment for either.

Read the sentence. Then write **compare** or **contrast** to tell what the sentence does.

4. You sweat when swimming, just as you do when running. compare
5. Shoes affect performance in running but not in swimming. contrast

© Evan-Moor Corp. • EMC 2426 • Reading Comprehension Fundamentals 27

Page 29

Name ____________

Nonfiction
Compare and Contrast
3

Electric Cars vs. Gasoline Cars

A text with a **compare-and-contrast** text structure explains the similarities and differences between two or more things.

Consider the features of the two things being discussed in the text. Visual information may provide additional details that can help you to compare and contrast.

Answer the items about the text you read.

1. Write two benefits of electric cars that gasoline cars don't have.
   * They're better for the environment. They are cheaper to take care of.
2. Write two benefits of gasoline cars that electric cars don't have.
   * Gasoline cars don't take up to six hours to refuel. Gas cars can go farther without refueling.
3. Why does the author state that gasoline cars are "traditional"?
   * Gasoline cars have been sold for a lot longer than electric cars.
4. Explain the reasons why electric cars are cheaper to care for than gas cars.
   Electric cars have fewer parts and are more energy efficient.
5. Write one similarity or difference between gas and electric cars that you can determine from the photographs.
   * They both have an opening that allows a pipe or tube to enter to provide fuel or electricity.

© Evan-Moor Corp. • EMC 2426 • Reading Comprehension Fundamentals 29

* These answers will vary. Examples are given.

Page 30

Nonfiction
Compare and Contrast
Review

Name ____________________

Answer the items.

1. Write two comparison signal words.
* similar both
2. Write two contrast signal words.
* yet different
3. Explain why it's necessary to analyze details in a text in order to compare and contrast details from the text.
* You have to look at details closely and think about the features of the things you are comparing and contrasting.
4. Explain how visual information can help you compare and contrast things you read about.
* Visual information can show details that the text didn't state. Images can show how two things are similar or different.

Read the paragraph. Then answer the question.

5. Seals and sea lions may have some similarities in appearance, but they are different animals with entirely different behaviors. Sea lions have small floppy ears while seals merely have holes in their heads. Sea lions have skin-covered front flippers, but seals have furry front feet. Typically, sea lions are louder and noisier than seals. Furthermore, seals tend to be less social than sea lions. Finally, seals are more adapted to living in water than on land, so they don't move as well as sea lions do on land.

   Is the main idea of the paragraph comparing or contrasting two things? Explain how you know.
* It is contrasting two things. The text states differences in appearance and behavior.

30 Reading Comprehension Fundamentals • EMC 2426 • © Evan-Moor Corp.

Page 31

Nonfiction
Sequence
1

Name ____________________

An author may use a **sequence** text structure to write an informational text. In a sequence text, the author describes details in the order they happen. The details may be events, steps in a process, or stages in a cycle.

Look for these signal words and phrases to identify the order of details:

before after next then finally last first second at last

Read the paragraph. Then answer the items.

Doctor William Key, also known as Doc, showed the world that animals need patience and respect. He was born into slavery in 1833. As a young boy, he clearly had a special way with animals, especially horses. After the Civil War, Doc became free from slavery, and in the late 1800s, he became a renowned veterinarian and businessman. In 1889, Doc's beloved horse died after giving birth to a weak foal. Doc expected the foal to die but lovingly took good care of it and named it Jim. Doc even let Jim sleep with him! To Doc's surprise, Jim started to get stronger and followed doc everywhere. Doc noticed that Jim was extremely intelligent, so he decided to try an experiment. First, he taught Jim the letters of the alphabet. When Jim chose the right letter, Doc rewarded him with sugar or apples. Then he used the same method to teach Jim to recognize colors. Jim eventually learned how to make change from a cash register! Finally, Doc decided to share the success of his experiment with others. He and Jim performed all over the country, showing millions that treating animals with love and respect can do wonders. In no time, Doc and Jim became very famous.

1. Explain how you can determine that this text has a sequence text structure.
* There are sequence signal words. The text tells about events in the order they happened.
2. Write three events from the text in your own words. Write them in the order they happened.
* The Civil War ended, and Doc was free from slavery. He cared for a foal named Jim. Doc taught Jim the letters of the alphabet.

© Evan-Moor Corp. • EMC 2426 • Reading Comprehension Fundamentals 31

Page 33

Nonfiction
Sequence
2

Name ____________________

How to Make a Mini Hovercraft

An author may use a **sequence** text structure to write an informational text. In a sequence text, the author describes details in the order they happen. The details may be events, steps in a process, or stages in a cycle.

Look for signal words that tell the order of details in the text.

Answer the items about the text you read.

1. Explain how you can tell that this text has a sequence text structure.
* There are sequence signal words. The text tells about a process with steps that go in order.
2. What would happen if you were to blow through the hole in the CD before attaching the balloon to the plastic nozzle? Explain why you think so.
* The air you blew through the CD hole would just float away, and the hovercraft project would fail. The steps need to be followed in order for it to work.
3. Why does the author suggest that you duct tape the nozzle to the CD before you blow air into the balloon?
* The duct tape makes the connection airtight. The author is trying to help make the project easier.
4. Why do you need to put the hovercraft into a certain position before you use it?
* The hovercraft will not work if it's not in the correct position first.

© Evan-Moor Corp. • EMC 2426 • Reading Comprehension Fundamentals 33

Page 34

Nonfiction
Sequence
Review

Name ____________________

Answer the items.

1. Why would an author choose to write a text with a sequence text structure?
* In some texts, the order of details matters a lot. If an author writes about a process or an event, the author may think the order of details matters.
2. Write three sequence signal words.
* first then second
3. Why do you think it's important to follow steps in the order they're given when you're reading a how-to text, or a text that details a process?
* If you don't follow the steps in order, you may not get the result you want.

Read the paragraph. Then answer the question.

4. Did you know that a monkey once sued a man in court? Well... that is kind of true. In 2011, a British photographer named David Slater traveled to Indonesia and took some selfies on his camera with a macaque. Interestingly, the macaque actually pressed the shutter on the camera, which is a piece that can block the lens and move to allow pictures to be taken. Because the macaque did this, some people believe that the macaque (not David) was the creator of the photos. Years later, David tried to sue some websites for using the photos without paying him, but the sites refused to stop using the photos, claiming that they belonged to the macaque. The story got even more complicated when, the following year, the People for the Ethical Treatment of Animals, or PETA, sued David Slater on behalf of the monkey. They claimed that the macaque owned the copyright to the photos. In 2017, the court case was settled.

   What events happened before PETA sued David on behalf of the macaque monkey?
* David let a macaque help create photos with his camera, so people thought the macaque created the photos. They didn't stop using the photos, so David sued the sites using the photos.

34 Reading Comprehension Fundamentals • EMC 2426 • © Evan-Moor Corp.

Page 35

Nonfiction
Problem and Solution
1

Name ____________________

An author may use a **problem-and-solution** text structure to write an informational text. In a problem-and-solution text, the author describes a problem in detail. Then the author describes solutions or ideas to solve the problem.

Read the paragraphs. Then answer the items.

The Great Pacific Garbage Patch is a soupy collection of floating litter in the North Pacific Ocean. Although there are some large objects in the patch, such as plastic bottles, shoes, and fishing gear, most of the patch consists of tiny pieces of plastic called microplastics. This plastic has been broken down into tiny pieces and is harmful to marine wildlife. For example, albatross think the minute bits of plastic are eggs and feed them to their chicks, ultimately killing them. Bigger pieces of plastic are harmful too. Many marine animals, such a turtles and seals, ingest plastic and die because their bodies cannot process it. The garbage patch also affects the growth of plankton and algae, which disturbs the entire marine food chain.

One would think cleaning up the patch would be an easy solution; however, it's too large, and most of the plastic pieces are too small to remove without killing important sea organisms in the process. Most scientists agree that our best solution is to eliminate the use of disposable plastics. Local and national organizations work to make people aware of the impact that plastics in the sea have so people can make wiser choices and use biodegradable or reusable items instead. For example, a zoo in Washington has launched an exhibit of huge sea creature sculptures made entirely out of plastic items found along the Oregon coast to raise awareness. Some organizations work with companies to transition from plastic to reusable materials.

1. In your own words, describe the problem in the text.
* The Great Pacific Garbage Patch is made of a lot of plastic and poses a threat to animals.
2. Explain why raising awareness of this problem is a solution to the problem.
* People can solve the problem by using materials that are biodegradable or reusable. More people will try to help if there is an increased awareness.

© Evan-Moor Corp. • EMC 2426 • Reading Comprehension Fundamentals 35

Page 37

Nonfiction
Problem and Solution
2

Name ____________________

Where Have All the Bees Gone?

An author may use a **problem-and-solution** text structure to write an informational text. In a problem-and-solution text, the author describes a problem. Then the author describes solutions or possible solutions to the problem.

Sometimes the author provides background information about the problem to get readers to consider why the problem is relevant and why they should care about finding a solution.

Answer the items about the text you read.

1. Why is it a concern that bee populations are decreasing?
* Bees help us to grow crops and flowers. The bees are disappearing rather quickly.
2. Why does the author use facts and percentages to help illustrate the problem?
* The facts help prove that this is a real problem and convey how serious or severe the problem is.
3. The text states that this problem is prevalent in Europe, Hawaii, and the U.S. mainland. Why is this significant?
* It illustrates that the bee problem is widespread and not simply a minor problem in one area.
4. State two examples the author provides to show that actions are being taken to solve this problem.
* The Obama administration has designated land for bee conservation. Scientists are trying to make a miticide to kill mites and save bees.
5. Explain how the problem discussed in the text is relevant to you personally.
* Answers will vary.

© Evan-Moor Corp. • EMC 2426 • Reading Comprehension Fundamentals 37

Page 38

Nonfiction
Problem and Solution
Review

Name ____________________

Answer the questions.

1. What is the purpose of a text with a problem-and-solution structure?
* It describes a problem and details what steps can be taken or are taken to solve it.
2. How can facts and percentages from scientific studies help show how serious a problem actually is?
* They can tell us the rate or depth of the problem, which may help us actively search for solutions.
3. How does an author get a reader to care about solving a problem?
* The author may state how people would benefit if the problem were solved.

Read the text. Then answer the item.

4. Technology and the Internet can be great resources to help you get information. But some online sources are unreliable. Some sites appear to provide news or educational information, but they deliberately impart information that is inaccurate. Some people refer to the information on these sites as "fake news." Fake news sites are a problem, particularly when you are trying to do research or become well informed about a particular issue. The good news is that there are many reliable sources of information on the Internet. If you have a difficult time distinguishing reliable sources from the unreliable ones, here are some solutions to your problem.

   Visit multiple sites to fact-check the original facts you read. If the same facts are repeated on several sites, this could suggest that the facts are accurate.

   Keep a list of sites you know to be reliable. You can visit these sites more frequently than unfamiliar ones.

   Analyze each site. If a site is missing key information, don't rely on the site. You can also see if a website cites reliable sources from which it gets its own information.

   Explain how you can tell that this text has a problem-and-solution structure.
* The text discusses the problem of fake news sites. The text suggests ways to deal with the problem.

38 Reading Comprehension Fundamentals • EMC 2426 • © Evan-Moor Corp.

Page 39

Nonfiction
Vocabulary
1

Name ____________________

When you read, you may come across unfamiliar **vocabulary**. Clues in a text can help you figure out a word's meaning. Do the following things to find clues in a text:

Look at the surrounding words. Think about what would make sense in the sentence.

Think about what you already know about the topic.

Read the sentences before the word. Read the sentences after the word.

Read the paragraph. Then answer the items.

Many arts and dance critics say that Martha Graham was the most influential dancer and choreographer of the twentieth century. She has a repertoire of over seventy years of dance pieces she choreographed in her inimitable style, known as the Graham Technique. This unique style was a radical change from the usual type of dance in the late 1920's. Instead of flowing, lyrical movement, Graham's style was angular, sometimes harsh, and deeply emotional. Graham developed her unique style by experimenting with the human form engaging in contraction and release. Graham died in 1991, but the Martha Graham Dance Company still performs and is a source of inspiration for dancers and visual artists.

1. Mark the meaning of the word *repertoire*.
   ● a range of skills and accomplishments
   Ⓑ a group of people who form a dance company
2. Explain why you chose the answer you did for number 1.
* The text says that Martha's "repertoire" includes pieces she choreographed. So it must be a range or collection of skills or work.
3. What do you think *inimitable* means? Explain why you think so.
* It means "unique." Graham's style is named after herself. She developed it. It was different from the ordinary type of dance at that time.

© Evan-Moor Corp. • EMC 2426 • Reading Comprehension Fundamentals 39

Page 40

Nonfiction
Vocabulary
2

Name ____________________

When you read, you may come across unfamiliar **vocabulary**. You can use information in the text to help you figure out a word's meaning. Check to see if the author provided a clue by providing the following:

a definition in the sentence before or after the word

a synonym, or a word that has the same meaning

an antonym, or a word that has the opposite meaning

Read the paragraph. Then answer the items.

Have you ever thought about what traveling would be like if the world were devoid of bridges to take us across rivers, straits, lakes, and valleys? Without bridges, transcontinental travel would be more challenging and time consuming. Bridges help us go over obstacles instead of having to go through them or around them. Engineers have been constructing bridges since ancient times. One ancient bridge is the beam bridge, in which a large beam rests on piers or big blocks below. Arch bridges made out of stone were also common in ancient times. Ancient bridge technology has been useful for centuries, but an unprecedented technology was used to create the suspension bridge in the 15th Century. This technology was new and creative for its time. The first simple suspension bridges were conceived by Thangtong Gyalpo in Tibet. He used ropes and chains to hold up the weight of the bridge. Today, suspension bridges like the Golden Gate Bridge use cables and towers.

1. What do you think *devoid* means? Explain why you think so.
* It means "without" or "lacking." The author says "without" in reference to the opening question.
2. Mark the meaning of the word *unprecedented*.
   Ⓐ traditional, being from ancient times
   ● having never been done or used before
3. Explain why you chose the answer you did for number 2.
* The text says that the technology was new and creative for its time.

40 Reading Comprehension Fundamentals • EMC 2426 • © Evan-Moor Corp.

* These answers will vary. Examples are given.

Page 42

Nonfiction
Vocabulary
3

Name ______________________

Government in Ancient Greece

When you read, you may come across unfamiliar **vocabulary**. You can use context clues in the text to help you figure out the meaning of **academic vocabulary** and **content-specific vocabulary**.

The term **academic vocabulary** refers to words used in texts about various topics and subject areas.

The term **content-specific vocabulary** refers to words used in texts about a specific topic or subject area.

Answer the items about the text you read.

1. What do you think *originated* means? Explain why you think so.
* It means "to be invented" or "began." The text says that things such as trial-by-jury and democracy began in Ancient Greece.

2. What do you think *instigate* means? Explain why you think so.
* It means "to start something." The new ruler started democracy, which was new.

3. What do you think a *proposal* is, as it is used in the text? Explain why you think so.
* A proposal is a question or an idea up for discussion. The text gives examples of proposals.

4. Mark the meaning of the word *obligation*.
   - Ⓐ something that is an option
   - ● something that is required

5. Write a definition for the word *ballot*. Explain how you know the meaning.
* It's a tool or a means for jurors to vote. Each ballot conveyed a different option a juror could choose.

42 Reading Comprehension Fundamentals • EMC 2426 • © Evan-Moor Corp.

Page 43

Nonfiction
Vocabulary
Review

Name ______________________

Answer the items.

1. Explain why it is important to try to figure out the meaning of unfamiliar words in a text.
* Knowing all the words in a text helps you to better understand the text and its topic.

2. Write two things you can do if you come across an unfamiliar word.
* You can see if the author included a definition before or after the word. You can look for antonyms or synonyms, which are clues.

3. Explain the difference between academic vocabulary and content-specific vocabulary.
* Academic vocabulary is in texts about everything. Content-specific words apply to certain topics.

4. Explain how background knowledge can help you figure out the meaning of unfamiliar words.
* If you already know facts about a topic, it may help you picture the meaning of a word.

Read the paragraph. Then write a definition for the underlined word.

5. Seismologists study earthquakes and try to develop ways to predict when and where they will happen. Unfortunately, this is impossible at the present time, and the best we can do is predict whether or not an earthquake will get worse after it's already started. It is also currently impossible to prevent earthquakes. It is inevitable that Earth will experience more earthquakes in the future, but there is one upside to this. More earthquakes means seismologists will have more opportunities to study them. Even though they can't predict earthquakes now, it is inevitable that earthquakes will keep happening. So, perhaps one day, all of the research may lead us to a point where we can predict them.

* Inevitable means "unstoppable or certain."

© Evan-Moor Corp. • EMC 2426 • Reading Comprehension Fundamentals 43

Page 44

Nonfiction
Summarize
1

Name ______________________

When you **summarize** a text, you use your own words to state its most important details. You should not include your personal opinions in a summary.
Do the following when you summarize:

Write the main idea of each paragraph in a single sentence.

Provide as many of the following details as possible:
who, what, where, when, why, and **how**

Read the paragraph. Then complete the chart with details from the paragraph.

The Ringling Bros. and Barnum & Bailey Circus was a traveling circus that started in 1919. For decades, huge crowds anxiously waited for the circus, known as "The Greatest Show on Earth," to come to their town or city. The show featured wild animals doing tricks. Tigers would leap through hoops of fire and elephants would stand on their back feet. There were also displays of human strength, such as acrobats building human pyramids, riding bikes on high wires, or flying through the air from one swinging trapeze to another. In the last three decades or so, however, popularity for the circus has dwindled. Some experts say that may be because other forms of human entertainment, like video games and television, have taken the circus' place. But the biggest cause for the circus' demise is the publics' awareness of cruelty toward animals. Many believe the animals were mistreated and abused. In May 2017, the Ringling Bros. and Barnum & Bailey Circus performed for the last time.

*	
Who or what is the topic?	The Ringling Bros. and Barnum & Bailey Circus
When?	It began in 1919 and ended in 2017.
What happened?	Its popularity dwindled and it shut down.
Why or how?	It was criticized for cruelty to animals.

44 Reading Comprehension Fundamentals • EMC 2426 • © Evan-Moor Corp.

Page 45

Nonfiction
Summarize
2

Name ______________________

When you **summarize** a text, you use your own words to state its most important details. The purpose of a summary is to provide a short version of the text.
Do the following when you summarize:

Write the main idea of each paragraph in a single sentence.

Provide as many of the following details as possible:
who, what, where, when, why, and **how**

Read the paragraph. Then answer the questions.

Marc Chagall was a famous artist known for his dream-like, colorful paintings. He was born in 1887 in Belarus, a country west of Russia. He became interested in art at an early age and began his formal training in painting at the age of 19. He quickly began developing his own emotional and poetic style that was a departure from the popular art of the time. After a move to Paris in 1911, Chagall settled in an artist's colony outside of Paris, where he lived and worked with other influential artists of the time. Despite the fact that his work was unusual, Chagall enjoyed some success and showed his work in public venues. He moved around a lot, at one point spending seven years in the U.S. before returning to France. Chagall's remaining years in France were amazing. He painted and worked with ceramics, sculpture, and stained glass. Commissions for his work took him all over the world. By the time of his death at the age of 97 in 1985, Marc Chagall had received many honors. He and his legacy of work are still celebrated today.

1. What is the main idea of the text?
* Marc Chagall was a famous artist who received many honors and is still celebrated today.

2. What details support the author's statement that Chagall's remaining years in France were amazing?
* Chagall worked with paint, sculpture, ceramics, and stained glass. He was hired all over the world and received many honors.

© Evan-Moor Corp. • EMC 2426 • Reading Comprehension Fundamentals 45

Page 47

Nonfiction
Summarize
3

Name ______________________

Education in Colonial America

When you **summarize** a text, you use your own words to state its most important details. You should not include your personal opinions in a summary.
Do the following when you summarize:

Write the main idea of each paragraph in a single sentence.

Provide as many of the following details as possible:
who, what, where, when, why, and **how**

Answer the items about the text you read.

1. In your own words, state the main idea of the text.
* Education in colonial America was different in some ways from education today.

2. Summarize the text. For each paragraph in the text, write one sentence that tells the most important details.
* Education in the colonies was somewhat different from now. Some kids worked, and some kids got an education. Education depended on where a family lived. Colonial students learned reading and writing using hornbooks. When students got older, they either went to college, studied the arts, or learned a trade. Over time, education in America changed and became regulated.

3. Write two ways that education in the colonies was different from education today.
* Education in colonial America was not as regulated. Boys and girls learned different skills.

© Evan-Moor Corp. • EMC 2426 • Reading Comprehension Fundamentals 47

Page 48

Nonfiction
Summarize
Review

Name ______________________

Answer the items.

1. Explain how to summarize a text.
* Write the most important details in your own words without stating your own opinion.

2. Write the six one-word details that you should try to include in a summary, if possible.

   who what where
   when why how

3. Why is it best to leave your personal opinions out of a summary?
* It would be incorrect to include opinions. A summary states what the text states, only shorter.

4. A summary is always shorter than the original text it summarizes. Explain why.
* The summary states only the most important details, not all of the original details.

Read the paragraph. Then answer the item.

5. Did you know that a cat can be a hero? In 2015, a cat named Major Tom saved his owner's life. Major Tom and his owner, Grant MacDonald, were aboard a yacht called the *Osprey*, about 40 miles (64 km) off the coast of Australia, when the boat started to flood. It was the middle of the night, and MacDonald was fast asleep. Major Tom was aware of the flooding and did everything he could to wake up MacDonald. Major Tom head-butted MacDonald and made continuous noise until he finally woke up and realized that he had to abandon the yacht using the life raft. Major Tom saved his owner's life!

Write one sentence to summarize the text.
* Cats can be heroes that save lives, which is illustrated by the story of the heroic cat Major Tom and his owner, Grant MacDonald.

48 Reading Comprehension Fundamentals • EMC 2426 • © Evan-Moor Corp.

Page 49

Nonfiction
Predict
1

Name ______________________

When you **predict**, you think of what will probably happen next. You can make a prediction about something that hasn't happened yet. Or, you can make a prediction about details in the text that will be revealed later.

As you read farther in the text, your prediction will often be correct. But it may also be incorrect. That's okay. Sometimes an author wants to surprise you.

What is important is that you think about the text and consider what is likely to happen.

Read the text. Then answer the items.

Cheetah and Dog Buddies

When animals get stressed out, zoo caretakers worry about them. For years, zoos have been pairing cheetahs with dogs to help cheetahs relieve stress. This is almost always done when the cheetah is a cub and the dog is a puppy. The relationship is usually symbiotic, meaning that both the cheetah and the dog benefit from spending time together. The best part is that the cheetah and dog usually become fast friends, growing up together, playing, and being inseparable. Some people are critical of pairing cheetahs and dogs because they think this relationship would never happen in nature. However, both cheetahs and dogs are intelligent and capable of forming lasting bonds, so zoos feel that these relationships do more good than harm to the animals.

1. How did the title help you predict what the text would be about?
* I predicted that I'd read about cheetahs and dogs that get along. The word "buddies" was a clue.

2. Predict what will happen if a new cheetah is born at a zoo and shows signs of stress.
* I predict that the zoo would adopt a puppy to pair with the cheetah to relieve its stress.

3. Predict what would happen if an adult cheetah were to see an adult dog in the wild.
* I predict that the cheetah would attack the dog.

© Evan-Moor Corp. • EMC 2426 • Reading Comprehension Fundamentals 49

Page 51

Nonfiction
Predict
2

Name ______________________

Tiny Houses

When you **predict**, you think of what will happen next. You can predict as you read. Use what you read and your own background information to predict what will happen later. A prediction is always about what will happen later.

Ask these questions to help you make predictions:

What are all the possible things that can happen?

What information tells me what will likely happen?

Answer the items about the text you read.

1. Do you predict that the number of people who are interested in tiny houses will increase or decrease in the future? Explain your answer.
* The number will increase. More people are searching for information about tiny houses.

2. If the price of tiny houses rises to the price of other houses, how will this affect the number of people buying tiny houses? Explain why you think so.
* The number of people buying tiny houses will decrease. Their low price is part of their draw.

3. Explain how the title and headings helped you predict what you would read next.
* The title tells that the text is about tiny houses. The headings are clues about what follows.

4. Do you think the number of tiny house communities will increase or decrease in the future? Explain your answer.
* They will increase. The text says that more tiny house communities were being planned in the year 2015.

© Evan-Moor Corp. • EMC 2426 • Reading Comprehension Fundamentals 51

Page 52

Nonfiction
Predict
Review

Name ______________________

Answer the items.

1. Explain how you can make predictions as you read a text.
* You can use background information and clues in the text. You can ask yourself certain questions.

2. Explain the difference between a prediction and a guess.
* A guess is not necessarily based on evidence in the text or clues, yet a prediction is.

Read the paragraph. Then answer the item.

3. Desalinization is the process of turning salty seawater into drinkable water by removing the salt. It is predicted that desalinization may happen on a large scale by the 2030s. Currently, it is estimated that about 10% of the world's population does not have access to clean drinking water. This is a serious problem. Worse still, this percentage could rise as climate changes lead to more water vapor forming, leaving less actual water.

Predict the effect that large-scale desalinization will have on the world's population.
* The effect will be positive. More people will have access to clean drinking water.

4. Indigenous populations in South America have declined significantly in the last few centuries. Brazil is home to a number of "uncontacted tribes," or tribes that have not been impacted greatly by other cultures. In 1988, Brazil arranged in its constitution for large areas of forest to be safely reserved for indigenous people. About 12.5% of Brazil's total land was designated for about 450,000 indigenous people, which has helped them to increase their population. Of the entire indigenous population in Brazil, 60% live in the Amazon. The areas where they live are protected, so most farmers, landowners, and land developers do not frequent these parts of the Amazon.

Predict what would happen to Brazil's indigenous population if Brazil's constitution were to no longer protect certain areas of the Amazon.
* Brazil's indigenous population will start to decrease again.

52 Reading Comprehension Fundamentals • EMC 2426 • © Evan-Moor Corp.

*** These answers will vary. Examples are given.**

Page 53

Name ____________

Nonfiction
Fact and Opinion
1

Some nonfiction texts contain both **facts** and **opinions**.

A fact is information that can be proven true. Research findings and data help us determine facts that are true.

An opinion is what a person thinks, feels, or believes about something. An opinion is a person's judgment. People can have different opinions about a single topic.

Read the paragraph. Then answer the items.

Research has shown that dark chocolate, which is made from the seed of the cacao tree, has nutrients that are beneficial to your health. Consumed in moderation, dark chocolate can help lower the risk of heart disease. Dark chocolate has also been proven to help lower high blood pressure. Dark chocolate has half the sugar and four times the fiber of milk chocolate. Dark chocolate also has fewer calories. Milk chocolate contains less of the cacao bean than dark chocolate, and milk chocolate also contains milk, sugar, and cream. That's what makes it so creamy and delicious. There is no denying that dark chocolate is better for you than milk chocolate, but dark chocolate has a bitter and unappealing taste. Dark chocolate simply doesn't taste as good as milk chocolate.

1. Write one sentence from the text that states an opinion. Use quotation marks.
   * "Dark chocolate simply doesn't taste as good as milk chocolate."
2. Write one sentence from the text that appears to state a fact. Use quotation marks.
   * "Dark chocolate also has fewer calories."
3. The author mentions research. Do the facts in the text support what the research shows? Explain your answer.
   * The research supports the fact that dark chocolate is healthier than milk chocolate. Research can show that facts are true.

© Evan-Moor Corp. • EMC 2426 • Reading Comprehension Fundamentals 53

Page 55

Name ____________

Nonfiction
Fact and Opinion
2

Bizarre Deep-Sea Creatures

Authors can include both **facts** and **opinions** in a nonfiction text. A fact is information that can be proven true. You can find a fact in multiple sources. An opinion is what someone thinks, feels, or believes. A person can disagree with another person's opinion.

Fact: Humans are mammals.

Opinion: Humans are better than animals.

Answer the items about the text you read.

1. Explain how the title tells you the author's opinion about deep-sea creatures.
   * The title tells you that the author thinks deep-sea creatures are bizarre, or strange.
2. Write three details from the text that tell the author's opinion.
   * The deep sea is a dark, spooky place. The Dumbo octopus is a cute creature. The red handfish is a strange-looking fish.
3. Write three details from the text that appear to be facts.
   * The red handfish was found in the waters of Australia. The bioluminescent octopus was found in the Gulf of Maine. Scientists had to come up with a new species of crab for the yeti crab.
4. Do the photos make you agree with the author's opinion that these deep-sea creatures are bizarre and strange-looking? Explain your opinion.
   * Answers will vary.

© Evan-Moor Corp. • EMC 2426 • Reading Comprehension Fundamentals 55

Page 56

Name ____________

Nonfiction
Fact and Opinion
Review

Answer the items.

1. Explain the difference between facts and opinions.
   * Facts are statements or pieces of information that are true and can be confirmed with research. Opinions are judgments, unique to a person.
2. How do you identify whether a statement shares a fact or an opinion?
   * Authors often refer to research or numbers when they state facts. A judgment statement is easy to identify. It's not necessarily true or false.

Read the paragraph. Then answer the items.

We all know that teachers assign students grades. Should students also be able to grade their teachers? Some people think so. Schools around the U.S. are already involved in programs that help assess a teacher's performance. In some schools, students complete questionnaires that ask them to evaluate their teachers. The questions are not only about academics. Some questions are about communication skills. For example, some questions ask how well the students feel that their teacher is connecting with them and how comfortable the students feel approaching their teacher with questions. One concern that some educators have about asking students to grade a teacher is whether or not students will be fair and honest about their teacher's performance.

3. Does this text include both opinions and facts? Explain your answer.
   * It uses facts. The text states no opinions and discusses only what is happening in the U.S. now.
4. Write a statement that shares your opinion about this topic.
   * Answers will vary.

56 Reading Comprehension Fundamentals • EMC 2426 • © Evan-Moor Corp.

Page 57

Name ____________

Nonfiction
Make Inferences
1

You can **make inferences** as you read a text to better understand it. When you make an inference, you use background knowledge and clues in the text to figure out something that is not directly stated.

Even though you don't read an inference directly, it is a detail that you believe is true based on the information you have.

Read the paragraph. Then answer the questions.

People who live in areas with mountain lions have to make certain considerations that other people do not have to make. For example, pet owners living in such areas may want to consider keeping their dogs and cats indoors. Additionally, people may want to consider doing activities such as bike riding and jogging in areas that don't have mountain lions. Mountain lions are known for pouncing on moving objects. Mountain lions attack prey and anything that they think is invading their territory. Still, it's important to remember that it is not in a mountain lion's nature to attack a human, which is why attacks on humans happen so rarely. Mountain lions typically prey on smaller animals.

1. Why should some pet owners consider keeping their domestic dogs and cats indoors?
   * Mountain lions prey on small animals.
2. How would we know if it were in a mountain lion's nature to prey on humans?
   * Attacks on humans would be more frequent.

Read the paragraph. Then answer the item.

3. Ticks are organisms that live on the outside of animals, including dogs and cats. When they bite, ticks irritate an animal's skin. Ticks can get carried into houses by pets, posing a threat to humans in addition to animals. Shampoo your pets with medicated ingredients provided by a veterinarian, and give your pets oral medications regularly.

   Explain what the medications mentioned in the text probably do. Then explain how giving your pets these medications would benefit you.
   * The medications probably kill ticks. It would help you by keeping ticks out of the house.

© Evan-Moor Corp. • EMC 2426 • Reading Comprehension Fundamentals 57

Page 58

Name ____________

Nonfiction
Make Inferences
2

You can **make inferences** when you read a text. Making inferences will help you to understand it better. Inferring is figuring out something that the author didn't tell you. It is "reading between the lines" in order to find out why something happens.

Read the paragraph. Then answer the items.

Many people are affected by a condition that causes them to sneeze uncontrollably when they are suddenly exposed to bright sunlight, such as when leaving a dark movie theater. This genetic condition is known as the photic sneeze reflex. Although an episode of uncontrolled sneezing might prove embarrassing, it is generally harmless. There are situations in which it can be dangerous, however. Imagine a pilot in flight experiencing such an episode and losing control, even for a few seconds.

1. Why does the author suggest that a pilot in flight experiencing a photic sneezing episode could cause a dangerous situation? Explain how this is possible.
   * Sneezing may be distracting or cause the pilot to close his or her eyes.
2. Write two scenarios or situations that could bring about a photic sneezing episode.
   * stepping outside from a dim museum
   a cloudy day that suddenly becomes sunny

Read the paragraph. Then answer the question.

3. Many people suffer with hay fever, an allergic disorder. People with hay fever may have a runny nose, itchy throat, and watery eyes, and they may cough and sneeze often. Pollen and other plant substances can cause hay fever to flare up. There are two types of hay fever: seasonal (flaring up at a certain time of the year) and perennial (flaring up all year round).

   How would you know if you have seasonal or perennial hay fever?
   * If you sneeze, cough, and have other symptoms all year round, you have perennial hay fever.

58 Reading Comprehension Fundamentals • EMC 2426 • © Evan-Moor Corp.

Page 60

Name ____________

Nonfiction
Make Inferences
3

Trademarks

You can **make inferences** as you read a text to better understand it. When you make an inference, you use knowledge and clues in the text to figure out something that is not directly stated in the text.

Even though you don't read an inference directly, it is a detail that you believe is likely to be true based on the information you do have.

Answer the items about the text you read.

1. The author states that before you register a trademark, you need to do a search to find out if it is available. What does the author most likely mean by the phrase "do a search"?
   - Ⓐ Drive on the highway.
   - ● Do research online.
   - Ⓒ Look in an encyclopedia.
   - Ⓓ Watch television.
2. A company with the trademark name "Koco-berreez" sells chocolate covered fruits. Which category would its trademark fall into? Explain how you know.
   * It would be Fanciful because the name seems made up and doesn't have another meaning.
3. Which category of strength would the trademark name "Bank of Oregon" fall into? Explain how you know.
   * It would fall into the Descriptive category. It states a geographic location and the service, a bank.
4. Describe the features of an unsuccessful trademark. Explain why you think a trademark like this would be unsuccessful.
   * It would be generic. It would not be memorable or recognizable. The text says that a successful trademark is unique and recognized right away.

60 Reading Comprehension Fundamentals • EMC 2426 • © Evan-Moor Corp.

Page 61

Name ____________

Nonfiction
Make Inferences
Review

Answer the items.

1. Explain how to make inferences as you read a text.
   * You use background knowledge and details in the text to figure out other details that the author did not state directly.
2. Explain how making an inference is different from guessing as you read a text.
   * A guess may not be based on evidence in the text, but an inference is based on details that you read in the text.
3. Why do you think that making inferences is an important skill?
   * It helps you learn more and understand more about a particular topic.

Read the paragraph. Then make an inference to answer the question.

4. Hot chocolate is a favorite treat for many people. If you're worried about burning your tongue when you drink it, pour some milk straight from the refrigerator into your hot chocolate mug.

   What effect would the author's suggestion have on the hot chocolate?
   * The hot chocolate would become cooler.
5. Instead of munching on chips, try snacking on nuts or sunflower seeds, which are also crunchy. Replace sugary candy with dried fruit or fruit yogurt, which can be naturally sweet. You can also add vegetables to meals that are already your favorites.

   What is the purpose of the text that this paragraph is from?
   * The purpose is to give the reader tips on how to eat more nutritiously.

© Evan-Moor Corp. • EMC 2426 • Reading Comprehension Fundamentals 61

Page 62

Name ____________

Nonfiction
Author's Purpose
1

Authors always have a **purpose** for writing a text. These are reasons authors write:

- **to inform**, or tell facts
- **to entertain**, or tell an interesting story
- **to persuade**, or give opinions
- **to teach**, or give instructions about how to do something

Read the paragraph. Then answer the question.

1. The State Hermitage Museum in Saint Petersburg, Russia, is one of the world's oldest and largest museums. It is a sprawling complex of interconnected buildings that house a vast collection of paintings and artwork, which in the 18th century belonged to Catherine the Great. At that time, cats guarded the artwork against rats and mice. Dozens of cats still live in the museum's basement, serving the same purpose.

   What is the author's purpose for writing this paragraph? Explain how you know.
   * The purpose is to inform. The text mentions facts rather than opinions or instructions.

Read the paragraph. Then answer the questions.

The cats at the Hermitage Museum live a charmed life, nesting in baskets and blankets placed in the basement. Still, things need to change. Some people drop off their unwanted cats at the museum, possibly believing that the museum is a cat shelter of some kind. It's not right to abandon a pet, and people need to stop doing this. Someone should write a letter to the authorities in Saint Petersburg urging them to take action against this practice.

2. What is the author's purpose for writing this paragraph? Explain how you know.
   * The purpose is to persuade. The text uses the word "should" and offers opinions.
3. How can you tell that the purpose is not to teach?
   * There are no instructions or steps to follow.

62 Reading Comprehension Fundamentals • EMC 2426 • © Evan-Moor Corp.

Page 64

Name ____________

Nonfiction
Author's Purpose
2

Deserts of Australia

Authors always have a **purpose** for writing a text. These are reasons authors write:

- **to inform**, or tell facts
- **to entertain**, or tell an interesting story
- **to persuade**, or give opinions
- **to teach**, or give instructions about how to do something

As you read, ask, "What does the author want me to think about or know?" This can help you to identify the author's purpose.

Answer the items about the text you read.

1. What is the author's purpose for writing this text? Explain how you know.
   * The purpose is to inform. There are many facts, including measurements of distances, throughout the text.
2. How can you tell that the purpose is not to entertain?
   * Most entertaining stories do not have so many facts and numbers. The text is very informative.
3. Write two details from the text that support your answer to number one.
   * The Tanami Desert is considered one of the most isolated places on Earth. The Great Victoria Desert is the largest desert in Australia.
4. How does the main idea of the text illustrate the author's purpose?
   * The main idea is that Australia has remote areas that make up the Outback. This is a fact.

64 Reading Comprehension Fundamentals • EMC 2426 • © Evan-Moor Corp.

* These answers will vary. Examples are given.

Page 65

Name ____________ Nonfiction — Author's Purpose — Review

Answer the items.

1. Write four purposes that authors may have for writing a text.
to inform — to persuade
to entertain — to teach

2. Explain how you can identify the author's purpose when you read a text.
* You can look for clues such as facts or opinions. You can ask what the author wants you to know.

3. How can knowing an author's purpose help you to better understand a text?
* It can help you identify the main idea. If you know the author's purpose, you are likely to remember details that you read.

Read the paragraph. Then answer the items.

Have you ever taken pictures on your smart phone but then wished you had them on your computer? It's easy to move pictures from your phone to your computer. One way you can do it is by following these simple steps. First, go into the gallery or storage area of your phone, where your photos are saved. Next, look for a menu. Most smart phone galleries have a menu that you can go into and see various options. Select the "share" option. At this point, you can click on as many of your saved photos as you want. Choose the photos you want to move. Somewhere on your phone's screen, you will see the word *share*—press it. Next, email yourself the photos. Finally, sign in to your email account on your computer, open the email from your smart phone, and download the photos to your computer.

4. What is the author's purpose for writing this text? Explain how you know.
* It's to teach. There are detailed steps on what you should do to move photos to your computer.

5. Write one detail from the text that supports your answer to number four.
* Next, email yourself the photos.

© Evan-Moor Corp. • EMC 2426 • Reading Comprehension Fundamentals 65

Page 66

Name ____________ Nonfiction — Expository Nonfiction — 1

The purpose of **expository nonfiction** text is to inform the reader about a topic, which may be a person, place, thing, event, or idea. Expository nonfiction informs by giving facts and providing explanations.

Expository texts state a main idea and provide facts that support it. You can find expository nonfiction in textbooks, on websites, and in other types of resources.

Read the paragraph. Then answer the items.

A heat wave is defined as record-high temperatures persisting for five or more consecutive days. A heat wave is especially dangerous in a city, where the air is stagnant. In this case, a heat wave is a mix of polluted air and extreme heat. The poor air quality can create many health problems for people. In addition, the concrete in a city retains heat during the day, gradually releasing that heat at night. These higher nighttime temperatures produce what is called the "urban heat island effect."

1. Explain how you can tell that the author's purpose for writing this text is to inform.
* It has a main idea and facts. The author explains what urban heat island effect is.

2. Write the text's main idea.
* A heat wave is when there are high temperatures for days, and it's particularly dangerous in a city.

3. State details from the text that help you understand why a heat wave in a city is especially dangerous.
* The poor air quality can lead to health problems. Heat released by concrete at night makes night temperatures high.

4. Did you know about urban heat island effect before you read this text?
* Answers will vary.

66 Reading Comprehension Fundamentals • EMC 2426 • © Evan-Moor Corp.

Page 68

Name ____________ Nonfiction — Expository Nonfiction — 2

Augusta Savage

The purpose of **expository nonfiction** text is to inform the reader about a topic, which may be a person, place, thing, event, or idea. Expository nonfiction informs by giving facts.

When you read expository nonfiction, try to identify the main idea and supporting details to better understand the text.

Answer the items about the text you read.

1. Explain what makes this an expository text.
* It tells about dates, events, and other facts about Augusta's work and life.

2. Write the text's main idea.
* Augusta Savage was a talented artist who spent her life trying to help African American artists.

3. Describe what you learned from reading this text.
* I learned who Augusta Savage was and how she helped artists. I learned about the Harlem Community Art Center.

4. Write one sentence from the text that appears to state a fact. Use quotation marks.
* "As an adult, Augusta moved to New York City to study art."

5. Write two things Augusta accomplished during her lifetime.
* She started the Savage Studio of Arts and Crafts. She sculpted a bust of W. E. B. DuBois for the New York Public Library.

68 Reading Comprehension Fundamentals • EMC 2426 • © Evan-Moor Corp.

Page 69

Name ____________ Nonfiction — Expository Nonfiction — Review

Answer the items.

1. What is the purpose of expository nonfiction text? Why would you read an expository nonfiction text?
* The purpose is to inform by providing facts and explanations. You read it to learn about a topic.

2. Write two types of resources in which you can find expository nonfiction text.
* You can find expository nonfiction on websites and in textbooks.

3. How do you think expository nonfiction is different from persuasive nonfiction?
* Expository nonfiction provides more facts while persuasive nonfiction may provide more opinions.

Read the paragraph. Then answer the items.

Lobsters are crustaceans, which means they have an exoskeleton, or outer skeleton. Their exoskeleton is usually hard. However, their exoskeletons do not grow as their bodies grow, so lobsters shed their hard outer shell at times, exposing a soft, new exoskeleton. It takes time for the new exoskeleton to harden, so lobsters are at risk until this happens. Lobsters have ten legs, as shrimp and crabs do. Lobsters rely on feeling and touching to catch prey. Some deep-sea lobsters are blind. Lobsters have been known to eat other lobsters.

4. Explain what makes this an expository text.
* It provides many facts about lobsters without using opinions.

5. Write a fact that you learned from the text.
* Lobsters have been known to eat other lobsters.

© Evan-Moor Corp. • EMC 2426 • Reading Comprehension Fundamentals 69

Page 70

Name ____________ Nonfiction — Persuasive Nonfiction — 1

The purpose of **persuasive nonfiction** text is to convince the reader to have a particular opinion about a topic. The author states an opinion and provides facts and reasons to persuade the reader to have the same opinion.
The opinion the author states is usually the main idea of the text.

When you read persuasive nonfiction text, analyze the author's arguments and reasoning to determine whether or not you agree.

Read the paragraph. Then answer the items.

All schools should require students to wear uniforms to benefit the school as well as the students. For one thing, having a standard uniform for all students would save students time every day because they wouldn't have to figure out what to wear each morning. Also, students would not have to worry about peer pressure to follow fashion trends if everybody at their school has to wear the same thing every day. Having uniforms would benefit schools because they wouldn't have issues with students not following school dress codes. In fact, requiring uniforms may eliminate the need for schools to have any dress code at all because the outfits that the school finds appropriate would be determined by the school. And many school uniforms are cute. If your school ever conducts a vote to see how many people are in favor of requiring student uniforms, raise your hand up high and vote for that fabulous option.

1. What is the main idea of the text?
* The author states that all schools should require students to wear standard uniforms.

2. What details does the author provide to support the main idea?
* Wearing uniforms would benefit students and schools. It would save students time each day.

3. Write a sentence from the text that states an opinion. Use quotation marks.
* "And many school uniforms are cute."

70 Reading Comprehension Fundamentals • EMC 2426 • © Evan-Moor Corp.

Page 72

Name ____________ Nonfiction — Persuasive Nonfiction — 2

Project-Based Learning

The purpose of **persuasive nonfiction** text is to convince the reader to have a particular opinion about a topic. The author states a viewpoint and provides facts and reasons to get the reader to view the topic in the same way.

A persuasive text usually favors one viewpoint.

You can find persuasive nonfiction text in advertisements, pamphlets, movie reviews, blogs, and many other sources.

Answer the items about the text you read.

1. Explain what makes this text persuasive nonfiction.
* The author clearly states a specific viewpoint. The author states opinions and facts that support only one viewpoint.

2. What is the author's opinion statement, or the main idea? Explain how you know.
* All educators should embrace PBL. The text states only positive things about PBL.

3. In your own words, write one opinion statement presented in the text.
* An important part of PBL is that failure is part of the learning process.

4. Do any of the facts the author provides support the opposite viewpoint, or the concerns with PBL? Explain your answer.
* No. All of the facts the author provides favor PBL and state positive potential results of it.

5. Do you agree with the opinion the author promotes in the text? Explain why or why not.
* Answers will vary.

72 Reading Comprehension Fundamentals • EMC 2426 • © Evan-Moor Corp.

Page 73

Name ____________ Nonfiction — Persuasive Nonfiction — Review

Answer the questions.

1. What is the purpose of persuasive nonfiction text?
* The author states an opinion and tries to convince the reader to have the same opinion.

2. How do facts and opinions help an author convince a reader?
* Facts are difficult to disagree with. If an author's opinions make sense to you, you'll be convinced.

Read the sentence. Then write **Y** on the line if the sentence is likely to be from a persuasive nonfiction text. Write **N** on the line if the sentence is probably not from a persuasive nonfiction text.

3. Don't feed animals at the park or in your yard because you are doing more harm than good by possibly making the animals dependent on the food you give them. Y
4. Some people do cardiovascular exercise, such as running, every day of the week. N
5. Some people think that only organic vegetables are nutritious, but you should buy and eat vegetables even if they're not organic because those are nutritious as well. Y

Read the paragraph. Then explain what makes this a persuasive nonfiction text.

6. Eleven years of age is not too young to get a smart phone. First of all, a smart phone can come in handy for doing school assignments. Students can type, email, and share assignments with a phone. Eleven years of age is a perfect time to get a cellphone because students have to do research for homework assignments and projects. Secondly, children can use a smart phone to easily communicate with relatives, such as grandparents, who live far away. Finally, there are a lot of online news sources that are meant for young audiences, so smart phones can help children to be well informed, which is important.
* This text has opinions. It favors only one viewpoint.

© Evan-Moor Corp. • EMC 2426 • Reading Comprehension Fundamentals 73

Page 74

Name ____________ Nonfiction — Narrative Nonfiction — 1

Narrative nonfiction tells a story about true events experienced by real people. Although narrative nonfiction has literary elements, such as setting, character, and plot, the text is nonfiction. Whenever you tell a true story about your own life or somebody else's life, it is narrative nonfiction.

A memoir is a type of narrative nonfiction. A memoir is a historical account of an event or time period, told by someone who really experienced the events in the story.

Read the memoir. Then answer the items.

When I was a young man, my parents thought it best for me to attend a boarding school in Mexico City. I agreed simply to please my dear mother, but I was not the most diligent student. Don't get me wrong. I enjoyed learning, but I did not enjoy studying. Luckily, I had an anxious roommate who would pace back and forth, studying for an exam by reading earnestly from the textbook. Meanwhile, I would lie in the top bunk, listening to him, receiving the information and capturing it in my mind, much as a voice recorder would. Sometimes, my roommate would mispronounce a word, and I would correct him. Other times, my attention would wane, and I would ask him to repeat. Invariably, on test day, I would hear my roommate's voice replaying in my mind. This is how I made top scores in school.

1. Explain what makes this narrative nonfiction.
* It is a memoir. It is an account of events that happened, told by the person they happened to.

2. What details can you infer about the person this memoir is about? Explain how you made these inferences.
* He is male, and he is probably an older man. He says "When I was a young man."

3. In what ways does this nonfiction text seem similar to a fictional story?
* It has a main character, who is the narrator. It has a setting and a happy ending.

74 Reading Comprehension Fundamentals • EMC 2426 • © Evan-Moor Corp.

Page 76

Name ____________ Nonfiction — Narrative Nonfiction — 2

Pup in Distress

Narrative nonfiction tells a story about true events experienced by real people. Although narrative nonfiction has literary elements, it is based on facts. The story's settings, characters, and events are true.
Narrative nonfiction reads like a story, unlike many other types of nonfiction, which read like an essay or a news article.

Answer the items about the text you read.

1. Explain what makes this narrative nonfiction.
* It tells a story about a true event that happened. The text has literary elements. The main character is Juan. The setting is California, near the ocean.

2. In what ways does this nonfiction text seem similar to a fictional story?
* It reads like a story, with words like "suddenly." There is a setting, a conflict, and a main character.

3. Write a fact about sea lions that you learned from the narrative nonfiction text.
* Sea lion mothers leave their pups for days to search for food in the sea.

4. How is this nonfiction text different from a news article or an essay?
* This text is like an interesting story. It doesn't state only facts like a news article would.

5. If you saw a sea lion pup in distress, as Juan did, would you react in the same way? Explain your answer.
* Answers will vary.

76 Reading Comprehension Fundamentals • EMC 2426 • © Evan-Moor Corp.

✱ These answers will vary. Examples are given.

Page 77

Name ______ Nonfiction Narrative Nonfiction Review

Answer the items.

1. Explain how narrative nonfiction is different from other types of nonfiction texts.
✱ Narrative nonfiction reads like a fictional story. It describes an event as a story would. It has literary elements, even though it's nonfiction.

2. What kinds of facts can you learn from narrative nonfiction text? Provide examples.
✱ You can learn dates and locations of events. You can learn about animals and make inferences about the person whom the story is about.

3. Do you think that a narrative nonfiction story can be just as interesting as a fiction story? Explain why or why not.
✱ Answers will vary.

Read the sentence. Then write **Y** on the line if the sentence is likely to be from a narrative nonfiction text. Write **N** on the line if the sentence is probably not from a narrative nonfiction text.

4. As he did every day, President George Washington gathered his long hair in his hands and pulled it back firmly at the back of his head before tying it with a ribbon. Y
5. The ideal weight for a healthy domestic cat is 10 pounds. N
6. Ramona decided to show all of her friends her superpowers, so she bent her knees and shot up straight into the air before flying away, high up in the sky. N
7. Queen Elizabeth snapped another picture of her children with her camera and remembered her parents warmly, for they gave her the camera as a wedding gift years ago in 1947. Y

© Evan-Moor Corp. • EMC 2426 • Reading Comprehension Fundamentals 77

Page 78

Name ______ Nonfiction Descriptive Nonfiction 1

Descriptive nonfiction provides descriptive sensory details about a topic. The topic can be a person, place, thing, or event. Descriptive nonfiction explains how the main topic **looks, feels, tastes, smells,** or **sounds.**

When you read descriptive nonfiction, you feel as if you are experiencing what the writer is describing.

Read the paragraph. Then answer the items.

Have you ever eaten a spicy curry? Curry is one of the most diverse foods because it can be made in so many different ways. Eating a curry is a delightful experience that can excite all of your senses. If you do not particularly enjoy hot, pungent food that burns your tongue slightly, you can have a curry that is sweet, bitter, or tangy. While some curries have a creamy, velvety texture, others have a chunky, thick texture. And other curries have a thin consistency. There are vegetable curries, meat curries, and tofu curries. Curries can be orange, yellow, green, red, brown, or multi-colored with a variety of hues. One distinct quality of a curry is its tantalizing smell, which often includes hints of coriander, turmeric, garlic, ginger, pepper, cumin, chili, and more! When a curry is being cooked, you hear spices being ground up, onions and garlic sizzling, and bubbling as the curry simmers and thickens. Whenever a new ingredient is added to the curry pot, you hear sizzling, you see steam rise, you smell a unique aroma, and this makes your mouth water for the delicious curry.

1. Write words or phrases that appeal to your senses and help describe curry.
✱ looks: orange, a variety of hues, steam rise
smells: coriander, turmeric, unique aroma, ginger
tastes: spicy, sweet, tangy, bitter
feels: velvety, chunky, creamy, thick
sounds: sizzling, spices being ground up, bubbling

2. Based on the descriptive text, would you want to eat a curry? Explain your answer.
✱ Answers will vary.

78 Reading Comprehension Fundamentals • EMC 2426 • © Evan-Moor Corp.

Page 80

Name ______ Nonfiction Descriptive Nonfiction 2

A Memorable Modern Building

Descriptive nonfiction provides details about a topic. The topic can be a person, place, thing, or event. Descriptive nonfiction provides sensory details, or details about how the main topic **looks, feels, tastes, smells,** or **sounds.**

The purpose of descriptive nonfiction is to help the reader form a mental image of the topic.

Answer the items about the text you read.

1. Explain what the Cleveland Clinic Lou Ruvo Center is and where it is located.
✱ It is a clinic for people with brain diseases. It is in Las Vegas, and it is a modern building.

2. How does the Lou Ruvo Center building illustrate deconstructivism in architecture?
✱ It looks fragmented. It has no symmetry. The architect made it that way intentionally.

3. Why did the architect make the building so unique?
✱ He wanted to create a building that would be memorable, talked about, and visited.

4. Write six words or phrases from the text that describe the building.
✱ bright; spotless, gleaming white; fragmented; from a science fiction; modern; soaring ceilings

5. Write two words or phrases you would use to describe the appearance of the building, after looking at the picture yourself.
✱ Answers will vary.

80 Reading Comprehension Fundamentals • EMC 2426 • © Evan-Moor Corp.

Page 81

Name ______ Nonfiction Descriptive Nonfiction Review

Answer the questions.

1. What is the purpose of descriptive nonfiction?
✱ It's to make readers feel like they're experiencing what the writer is describing and to give readers a mental image.

2. Why are sensory details an important part of descriptive nonfiction?
✱ They tell how something looks, sounds, smells, feels, and tastes, which helps give the reader a detailed mental image.

Read the paragraph. Then explain whether or not it is descriptive nonfiction.

3. There are over 260 different kinds of monkeys in the world. They are primates. They live all over the world. You can see them at the zoo. These animals are related to humans. They can use tools and play games.
✱ This is not a good example of descriptive nonfiction because it does not have sensory details. It doesn't help me form a mental image.

4. Making your own pasta is fun, but it is hard work. You have to stir and roll dough out, which can make your arms feel sore after a while. You have to make sure the dough is well mixed. When you work with the dough, put dry flour on your hands and on the surface you're working on. You can smell the yummy, buttery scent of dough in the air as you make it. You flatten the dough and push it through a pasta maker. The dough looks like spaghetti that you can eat as it comes out of the machine, but you can't eat it yet because it's raw. You can boil the noodles and eat them.
✱ This is a good descriptive text because it has details about how your arms feel, how the dough smells, and how the noodles look.

© Evan-Moor Corp. • EMC 2426 • Reading Comprehension Fundamentals 81

Page 82

Name ______ Fiction Character 1

Character is one of the most important elements of a story. When you analyze character traits, it helps you to better understand the story. A character with more than one trait is complex and realistic. These are some traits that describe characters:

curious	lethargic	cautious	fun-loving
gullible	vain	sweet	honest

Read the paragraph. Then answer the items.

Maddie and her brother Doug watched a movie that took place during the Middle Ages. Maddie kept pausing the movie, though, to ask questions and closely study the props and costumes on the screen. "What kind of weapon is that knight using?" she asked Doug, who just shrugged. "Yum, what kind of food are they eating?" she wondered aloud. "I wonder if the women really wore those dresses!" she exclaimed. "Enough, Maddie!" pleaded Doug. "I just want to watch the movie!" That's when Maddie realized that, perhaps, Doug wasn't as curious about the Middle Ages as she was, so she controlled herself and decided to wait until after the movie to find out more. Later, she went on the Internet and looked up books about medieval history.

1. On the lines, write two character traits that describe Maddie.
✱ curious; self-controlled

2. Explain why you wrote the traits you did.
✱ Maddie wanted to know more about the Middle Ages. She was able to stop herself from pausing the movie and wait until later to find out more.

Read the paragraph. Then write two character traits that describe Sebastian.

3. Sebastian was the obedient servant of the queen—as far as the queen knew. For years, he polished her slippers, swept the palace, and fetched her tea. But secretly, Sebastian didn't like the queen because she wasn't very kind. So, one day, he came up with a plan to remove her from the throne and replace her with a new queen.
✱ scheming; hardworking

82 Reading Comprehension Fundamentals • EMC 2426 • © Evan-Moor Corp.

Page 83

Name ______ Fiction Character 2

When you analyze a **character** in a story, it helps you to better understand the story. Consider these questions as you analyze a character:

- Why does the character do certain things?
- Why does the character feel a certain way?
- What is important to the character?
- Do you agree or disagree with the character's actions?

Read the paragraph. Then answer the items.

Mason had a tough time dealing with his little sister, Jasmine, at the beach last weekend. She accidentally stepped on the sand castle he'd been building, so he got annoyed. When Jasmine asked him to help open her water bottle, Mason refused. Later, he walked across her beach towel, dripping sand and water all over it. Jasmine complained, but Mason just shrugged. He still felt angry. Finally, their mom intervened and told Mason he was being very unkind to his sister. "I know you're upset with Jasmine for stepping on your sand castle," his mom said. "But you have to remember, she's just three years old. She didn't mean to do that." Mason sighed. His mom was right, and he actually felt really bad about how he had acted. After all, he was twelve years old, and Jasmine was only three. He went over to Jasmine and asked if she'd like to help him build a new sand castle. She said yes. It was as if she had already forgotten that Mason had been upset earlier.

1. What does Mason do to cause Jasmine to complain about him?
✱ He starts being mean to her. He doesn't help her open the water bottle. He messes up her towel.

2. Describe how Mason's feelings change during the story. Explain how and why.
✱ First he is annoyed. Then he feels angry. Next, he feels bad that he was unkind. His feelings change because his mom intervenes and reminds him that Jasmine is a lot younger than he is.

© Evan-Moor Corp. • EMC 2426 • Reading Comprehension Fundamentals 83

Page 85

Name ______ Fiction Character 3

Ranger Wayne

When you analyze a **character** in a story, it helps you to better understand the story. Consider the following as you analyze a character:

character traits	dialogue
characters' actions	characters' feelings

Answer the items about the story you read.

1. Which pair of traits best describes Ranger Wayne?
Ⓐ courageous and cheerful
Ⓑ angry and greedy
Ⓒ intelligent and lonely
● serious and knowledgeable

2. How are Owen's character traits different from Ranger Wayne's?
✱ Owen is sarcastic. He is not serious. Ranger Wayne is stern.

3. Does Ranger Wayne have appropriate traits for his job? Explain why or why not.
✱ Yes. He's teaching people how to survive, so he needs to be serious and have knowledge.

4. How do the differences between Ranger Wayne and Owen create conflict in the story?
✱ Ranger Wayne makes Owen feel nervous. When Owen doesn't take the lesson seriously, this challenges Ranger Wayne.

5. Explain why Ranger Wayne's last statement is funny, considering his character traits.
✱ He seems stern, but his joke about the cartoon bear shows that he has a sense of humor.

© Evan-Moor Corp. • EMC 2426 • Reading Comprehension Fundamentals 85

Page 86

Name ______ Fiction Character Review

Answer the items.

1. Explain why it is important to analyze character traits as you read a story.
✱ It helps you learn about the character and why the character does certain things in the story.

2. Why would an author write about a character who has more than one trait?
✱ It makes the character more complicated and realistic, like real people.

3. On the lines, write three character traits that you can think of.
✱ beautiful; generous; inquisitive

4. How do character traits help to shape the plot of a story?
✱ Traits can make characters to do things or feel a certain way. This can lead to conflicts or solutions.

Read the paragraph. Then answer the question.

5. On Friday evening, Avery and her dad made cookie dough. Then they put it in the fridge to bake the next day. Dixie, the babysitter, came over, and Avery's dad went to work. Then Avery said, "I'm going to surprise my dad and bake the cookies tonight." Dixie wasn't sure this was such a good idea. "I'm allowed to use the oven, and I don't need help," said Avery. She knew that her dad's rule was that she couldn't use the oven on her own, but she thought he'd be okay with it once he found out that she wanted to surprise him. She heated the oven and put in the dough. After a while, she and Dixie smelled something burning, and they saw smoke. All of the cookies were burned and inedible. Still, Avery refused to throw them out. "I'll cut off the worst burned bits, and we can still eat them. It'll be fine," she said. Dixie just shook her head.

Which trait do you think best describes Avery: thoughtful or headstrong? Explain your answer.
✱ She is headstrong. She broke the rule and ruined the cookies. She didn't want to admit it.

86 Reading Comprehension Fundamentals • EMC 2426 • © Evan-Moor Corp.

Page 87

Name ______ Fiction Setting 1

Setting is one of the most important elements of a story. When you think about the setting, it helps you to better understand the story. Think about how the setting influences the characters to do certain things.

As you read, ask these questions about setting:

- What descriptive details help you form a mental image of the setting?
- How do the characters feel in the setting?
- What do the characters do in the setting?

Read the paragraph. Then answer the items.

Kevin and his friends had been standing in line for just a few minutes, and they were already roasting from the sun's heat. Kevin could feel drips of sweat roll down his back, and his shirt was starting to stick to his body. The sidewalk in front of the Moonlight Roller Rink had a bike rack and a trash can, but no shade at all. Finally the doors opened, and people rushed in. Kevin smiled as the cool breeze from the air-conditioners hit him. The place was dimly-lit, with red walls. Bright speckles of light flashed from a disco ball that hung in the middle of the rink. As always, the music was loud, which Kevin loved. He could feel the thumping beat of the music pound against his chest and immediately felt happy. Being at the rink made him feel as though he could never run out of energy. The combination of the loud music, the exercise, and seeing all his friends made it his favorite place to go every Saturday. He found it exciting.

1. Contrast how Kevin feels outside the roller rink and inside it.
✱ Outside, he's uncomfortable and hot. Inside he is happy, energetic, and feeling cool.

2. Write three details from the text that show why Keven finds the rink exciting.
✱ It has loud music and bright lights. His friends are there. The music's beat makes him feel energetic.

© Evan-Moor Corp. • EMC 2426 • Reading Comprehension Fundamentals 87

*** These answers will vary. Examples are given.**

Page 88

Name ______________________

Fiction
Setting
2

When you analyze the **setting** of a story, it can help you to better understand the story. Think about how the setting influences the plot and conflict in the story. These are details you can analyze about a setting:

- descriptive words and phrases that help you form a mental image
- characters' actions, feelings, and dialogue
- clues that provide additional details

Read the paragraph. Then answer the question.

1. A chill ran down Devon's spine as she entered the dark and creepy room. The floor was slanted, and she felt like she was going to fall over. Spooky sounds filled the air. As the large group of people entered a pitch-black hallway, Devon felt a hand grasp her shoulder. Whew! It was her mom. After passing through a huge room filled with cobwebs, a fake mummy suddenly popped out of a coffin with an agonizing groan. Devon shrieked and bolted out of that room. She stepped through a door and breathed a sigh of relief as she realized that she was in the sunlight. "I'm never going into a haunted house again," she exclaimed to her mom, "even if it *is* Halloween!"

What clues tell you that the setting is a house that is actually not haunted?

* Devon gives a clue when she says "Halloween." The mummy is "fake." There's a large group.

Read the paragraph. Then answer the question.

2. When Augie first saw his new house, he was creeped out. Paint was peeling, windows were broken, and the roof sagged. Mom said it would be a great house after it was fixed up. Augie wasn't so sure. It reminded him of the haunted house in a movie he'd just seen. They went inside, and the first thing Augie saw was a humongous spider web on the staircase bannister. A moment later, he heard a loud creaking sound. "A ghost!" Augie cried, running back out. Dad laughed and said, "It's just a creaky door, Augie!"

How does the setting help to create the plot and conflict in the story?

* Augie's fear of the house creates conflict. If the house were nicer, the story would be different.

88 Reading Comprehension Fundamentals • EMC 2426 • © Evan-Moor Corp.

Page 90

Name ______________________

Fiction
Setting
3

The Flea Market

When you analyze the **setting** of a story, it can help you to better understand the story. Think about how the setting influences the plot and conflict in the story.

As you read, ask these questions about setting:

- What descriptive details help you form a mental image of the setting?
- What do the characters' actions, feelings, and dialogue tell you about the setting?
- How do different characters view the setting differently?

Answer the items about the story you read.

1. Contrast how Antwon and his mom view the setting.
* His mom sees the setting as a "wonderland of treasures." He sees it as a boring place that is hot, dusty, and tiring.
2. How has Destiny's view of the flea market changed?
* Destiny used to find the market boring. But now that she needs something unique, she likes the flea market, like her mom.
3. How does the setting help to create conflict in the story?
* Antwon finally complains and says he's had enough of the flea market. He gets glared at.
4. Write three descriptive words or phrases that help you form a mental image of the setting.
* dusty colorful tents busy

90 Reading Comprehension Fundamentals • EMC 2426 • © Evan-Moor Corp.

Page 91

Name ______________________

Fiction
Setting
Review

Answer the items.

1. Write a question you can ask yourself about the setting in a story.
* What descriptive words help me form a mental image of the setting?
2. How can understanding a setting help you to better understand characters' actions?
* The way a character feels in a setting can affect what a character chooses to do or say.
3. How can the setting affect the plot and conflict in a story?
* By affecting characters, the setting can lead to actions that cause events, conflicts, or resolutions.
4. Why is it important to recognize how different characters view a setting differently?
* It helps you to better understand the story. You may relate to how one character feels in the setting but not another character.

Read the paragraph. Then answer the question.

5. As soon as Dale got home from football practice, he turned on the television, turned on all the lights downstairs, and turned up the heat. It seemed as though his parents were still at work. Dale had just sat on the sofa when he heard stomping on the stairs and figured it was his older sister, Rachel. "You made it way too warm in here," she said, frowning and turning the heat off as she spoke.
"It was freezing when I got home," argued Dale. "I don't understand why you can't let me be comfortable." Rachel said she was roasting. Dale rolled his eyes and quietly decided that he would turn the heat back on as soon as Rachel went back upstairs.

How does the setting help to create conflict in the story?

* Dale and Rachel feel differently in the setting. He feels cold and wants the heat on. She feels hot.

© Evan-Moor Corp. • EMC 2426 • Reading Comprehension Fundamentals 91

Page 92

Name ______________________

Fiction
Plot
1

Plot is one of the most important elements of a story. When we talk about plot, we refer to the events in a story. These are important parts of a plot:

Exposition: The author gives information about character, setting, and conflict.
Rising action: The character tries to resolve the conflict. The conflict becomes complicated or the character fails.
Climax: This is the turning point or the most exciting part of the story.
Falling action and **Resolution:** The action is slower, and the conflict gets resolved.

Read the paragraph. Then answer the items.

Mr. Galloway looked at his overgrown lawn and sighed. As goats romped and grazed on the farm next door, long grass and weeds were taking over his own property. His lawnmower was broken. Hoping to fix it himself, he took apart the motor, but some of the parts were too badly worn to repair. Weeks went by, and the top of the grass reached the bottom of his kitchen window. He was desperate to shorten the lawn now, so he decided to bring the mower to a repair shop. As he loaded the mower into his truck, his neighbor wandered over and asked if he'd like to buy a goat. "He's a friendly goat," the neighbor said. "And, he'll take care of that grass for you in no time at all." Mr. Galloway agreed. Later that day, he relaxed on his front porch as his new pet goat grazed happily.

1. Describe the information provided in the exposition of the story.
* Mr. Galloway's lawn is overgrown, but his mower is broken. The setting is next to a farm with goats.
2. What happens during the story's climax?
* Mr. Galloway is desperate and puts the mower in the truck, when his neighbor offers him a goat.
3. How was the conflict in the story resolved?
* Mr. Galloway's new goat grazes on the lawn.

92 Reading Comprehension Fundamentals • EMC 2426 • © Evan-Moor Corp.

Page 93

Name ______________________

Fiction
Plot
2

When you analyze the **plot** of a story, you gain a better understanding of the story. An author arranges the events in the story so that the story is interesting. If a story doesn't keep moving and isn't interesting, you may not want to read the entire story. These are the elements of plot that keep the story moving:

- There is major conflict in the story.
- Characters' actions relate to the conflict. Characters keep the story moving by trying to solve the problem.
- There is a suspenseful climax or a surprising twist in the story.

Read the paragraph. Circle it if it has a complete plot.

1. Sophie's sister had a birthday coming up. Sophie couldn't think of a good gift for her sister. Sophie watched TV for three hours and then had dinner. She had ice cream for dessert. The next morning she forgot all about the birthday gift.
2. Zeke wanted to buy a book for his sister for her birthday. Unfortunately, he didn't have any money. He searched all over his house for loose change but found only a dollar. Then he noticed leaves in his neighbor's yard and offered to rake them up. He earned ten dollars by doing that job and was able to buy the book for his sister. *(circled)*
3. Rohi had an awesome birthday. She went camping with her family. At the campsite, she ate hot dogs and chips. Then everyone sang happy birthday to her, and she ate her favorite kind of cake: red velvet. She ended the day by sitting around a campfire with her whole family.

Read the paragraph. Then state what is missing from the plot. Explain how you know.

4. At first, Everly was excited for her birthday party, but then she became frustrated with her dad. She told him that she didn't want any grown-ups at her party. "Everly, if you want, you can just ignore me and your mom while your friends are here," her dad said, "but we are going to make sure that there is an adult in the room at all times." Everly thought her parents were being so unfair. She thought about calling off the party.

* Falling action and a resolution are missing. The plot has conflict, and it ends with the conflict.

© Evan-Moor Corp. • EMC 2426 • Reading Comprehension Fundamentals 93

Page 95

Name ______________________

Fiction
Plot
3

Run Free

Plot is what happens in a story. Conflict is an important part of a story's plot. Without conflict, a story would not be very interesting. These are five kinds of conflict that are common in literature:

Person vs. Person: A character struggles with another character.
Person vs. Nature: A character struggles with environmental issues, such as the weather or a natural disaster.
Person vs. Self: A character struggles with a decision or his or her own thoughts.
Person vs. Technology: A character struggles with a machine, which has non-human traits.
Person vs. Society: A character struggles with the rules of a large group.

Answer the items about the story you read.

1. What do you find out in the story's exposition?
* Roxy thinks she's bad at sports. The conflict is that she is signed up for cross country.
2. What kind of conflict does Roxy struggle with most in the story: Person vs. Person, or Person vs. Self? Explain your answer.
* Person vs. self, because she struggles with her own thoughts about embarrassing herself.
3. Explain how the events in the story relate to the conflict.
* Roxy's getting new shoes deals with the conflict of running. Roxy challenges herself with Buster.
4. Describe the conflict's resolution.
* Roxy runs each day, going farther and farther. She looks forward to running now.

© Evan-Moor Corp. • EMC 2426 • Reading Comprehension Fundamentals 95

Page 96

Name ______________________

Fiction
Plot
Review

Answer the items.

1. Explain why plot is an important story element.
* Plot is necessary for a story. Without plot, there would be no events and no story.
2. What would a story be like if there were no conflict? Explain why you think so.
* It would be boring because most events in a story relate to the conflict.
3. Explain what each kind of conflict is:
* Person vs. Person: a character vs. another character
* Person vs. Self: a character struggles with thoughts
* Person vs. Nature: a character struggles with nature
* Person vs. Technology: a character vs. a machine
* Person vs. Society: a character vs. a group with rules
4. Explain what an exposition is in a story.
* It's the part of the story that provides details about character, setting, and conflict.
5. Explain what rising action is in a story.
* It's when the story gets more exciting or complex.
6. Explain what a story's climax is.
* It's a turning point, or the most suspenseful part.
7. Explain what falling action and resolution are in a story.
* It's when the story's problem is getting solved.

96 Reading Comprehension Fundamentals • EMC 2426 • © Evan-Moor Corp.

Page 97

Name ______________________

Fiction
Theme
1

Theme is an important story element. It is a message or lesson in a story. A theme can be personal. That means that different individuals may take away different messages after reading the same story. These are some possible story themes:

- A true friend is loyal.
- Material things cannot make you as happy as love and kindness.
- The most important possession you have is your honor.

Read the paragraph. Then answer the items.

The handlebars shook as Zinnia rocketed down the steep trail. The last time she'd raced this course, Zinnia braked too hard, missed a turn, and tumbled into a creek. Luckily, she only ended up with some scrapes, but the incident had shaken her. Worry flooded her head, but she shook it off—she must stay focused! Zinnia saw the turn approaching. Visions of crashing flashed before her eyes, and she did everything she could to push them out. It was one crash, no reason to think it would happen again. She pumped her brakes gently. Slowing down just enough, she eased through the turn and then shot down toward the finish line. Zinnia cried out, "Yes!"

1. What is a possible theme of this story?
Ⓐ It is always unwise to attempt things that scare you.
● If you fall, you can pick yourself up and try again.
Ⓒ Be a good sport when you compete against others.
Ⓓ Allow fear to rule your life.
2. Explain why you chose the answer you did for number 1.
* Zinnia was worried because of her memory of crashing, but she proved that you can overcome fear. You can try again and succeed.
3. Write a detail from the story that helps to show why Zinnia is able to succeed and make it past the turn.
* She pushed the discouraging visions out.

© Evan-Moor Corp. • EMC 2426 • Reading Comprehension Fundamentals 97

Page 98

Name ______________________

Fiction
Theme
2

Theme is a message or lesson in a story. A story can have multiple themes. Themes usually relate to important topics that the author wants to explore, such as these:

chaos and order	**war**	**loyalty**
isolation	**darkness and light**	**love**

As you read, think about the message that you take away from the story. This can help you identify a theme in the story.

Read the paragraph. Then answer the items.

The sixth-grade badminton team had practice twice a week. The coach, Mr. Jackson, was also the coach of the eighth-grade girls' volleyball team and the eighth-grade boys' rugby team. At every badminton practice, Mr. Jackson let the sixth graders know that their team was his least favorite to coach. "Yeah, I got stuck with the little sixth graders again this year," he said into his cellphone one afternoon, to whomever he was speaking to. He said it loudly, while all the sixth graders were warming up, so they could clearly hear him. After the phone call, Mr. Jackson told the students that badminton practice would be over in five minutes. The students complained and asked why it was ending so early. Mr. Jackson said, "It's not a big deal. You're only in sixth grade. Nobody cares about the sixth-grade games. It's the eighth graders that everyone cares about. Their games are important." The team felt deflated after that. Some of them wanted to quit the team, but then they decided that they weren't going to let Mr. Jackson's negative attitude affect their school year.

1. What is a possible theme of this story?
● Words can be a powerful tool for bad or for good.
Ⓑ Sports and clubs are more serious the older you get.
Ⓒ Coaches should only work with students at a single grade level.
Ⓓ Sometimes, quitting is the only choice that you have.
2. Explain why you chose the answer you did for number 1.
* The coach's words had an effect on the students.
3. Write another possible theme for the story.
* You shouldn't let others' negativity get you down.

98 Reading Comprehension Fundamentals • EMC 2426 • © Evan-Moor Corp.

***** These answers will vary. Examples are given.

Page 100

Fiction
Theme
3

Name ______

An Interview with a Zazneraldernol Citizen

The **theme** is the message or lesson in a story. Sometimes, the theme is obvious. A theme can also be personal. That means that different individuals may take away different messages after reading the same story.
Ask these questions as you think about a story's theme:

What is the main conflict in the story?
Does a character in the story struggle with a particular issue?
Does a character learn a lesson in the story?

Answer the items about the story you read.

1. What is the theme of the story?
   Ⓐ People who boast a lot are better than others.
   Ⓑ There are many good reasons to be boastful.
   ● Being boastful will win you few friends.
   Ⓓ Boasting a lot is a good way to get people to like you.
2. How do people feel about Bertha? Explain why.
   * They try to avoid her. They don't like her because she boasts and complains a lot.
3. How and why does Aziza's attitude toward Bertha change during the interview?
   * Aziza starts to get annoyed with Bertha. She gets cut off by Bertha. She finds Bertha to be boastful.
4. Write two details from the story that help to demonstrate the theme.
   * Bertha brags about staying with royalty and presidents. She says she's smarter than the smartest person on Earth.
5. Do you think that Aziza ended the interview appropriately? Explain your opinion.
   * Answers will vary.

100 Reading Comprehension Fundamentals • EMC 2426 • © Evan-Moor Corp.

Page 101

Fiction
Theme
Review

Name ______

Answer the items.

1. Explain what a theme is in a story.
   * A theme is an important message or lesson that you take away from the story.
2. Explain how themes can be personal, or unique, for different people who read the same story.
   * A story can have more than one theme. Different people may relate to different parts of the story.
3. Explain how you can identify themes in a story.
   * You can think about the issues characters struggle with or the conflict in the story.
4. Why do you think theme is an important story element?
   * Characters in every story deal with conflicts. All stories explore particular issues and topics.

Read the paragraph. Then answer the items.

Amal took a bow, and the entire auditorium applauded her. She was beaming, smiling from ear-to-ear, as roses were flung onto the stage for her. She picked them up, bowed again, and left the stage. "That was a perfect piano recital, Amal," said her Aunt Clarice. Amal thought back to four years ago, when she was eight years old and had just started taking piano lessons. She didn't play well at all. But she practiced every single day and never gave up, even when it became harder to make time to practice. Now, she was a local celebrity. The mayor even came to one of her recitals.

5. Write a possible theme for the story.
   * The more you practice, the better you become.
6. Explain why you think this is a theme in the story.
   * Amal remembers when she didn't play well.

© Evan-Moor Corp. • EMC 2426 • Reading Comprehension Fundamentals 101

Page 102

Fiction
Point of View
1

Name ______

A story is written from the narrator's **point of view**. There are three major points of view: **first person**, **second person**, and **third person**.

first person: The narrator is in the story and says "I" and "me" while telling the story.
second person: The narrator speaks to the reader and says "you" while telling the story.
third person: The narrator is not in the story and tells a story about the actions of others.

An **omniscient** narrator knows what the main character and other characters think, feel, and plan to do and may know what will happen later in the story.
A **limited** narrator knows only what the main character thinks, feels, and plans to do and does not know what will happen later.

Read the paragraph. Then answer the questions.

Tara was delighted to be opening her birthday presents. "Exactly what I've been wishing for," she thought when she opened the headband-making kit from her uncle. "Yes!" she declared when she unwrapped the phone cover. "This is awesome," Tara thought about her new pen. Then she saw her Aunt Milly's gift: two tickets to a musical show. "Oh, no," she thought silently, unable to hide her disappointment.
"I don't think she likes my gift," thought Aunt Milly. A moment later, Aunt Milly had a change of heart. "Actually, Tara has never been to a musical before," she thought. "It won't hurt her to try a new experience, and she may love it." Little did Aunt Milly know, but her positive thoughts paid off. Tara used the tickets and ended up loving musicals.

1. Is the story written in the first, second, or third person point of view? Explain how you know.
   * It's the third person point of view. The narrator talks about the main characters by name.
2. Is the narrator omniscient or limited? Explain how you know.
   * The narrator is omniscient. The author knows everyone's thoughts and what will happen later.

102 Reading Comprehension Fundamentals • EMC 2426 • © Evan-Moor Corp.

Page 104

Fiction
Point of View
2

Name ______

A Day in My Life

Point of view is an important element in a story. The narrator's perspective, or view, frames the story. Often, the reader knows only what the narrator knows.
When you think about point of view, ask the following questions:

Is the story told in the first, second, or third person point of view?
Is the narrator omniscient or limited?
What details do I know because the narrator told me?
Do I agree with or recognize the narrator's perspective?

Answer the questions about the story you read.

1. What point of view is the story told in: first, second, or third person? Explain how you know.
   * It's the first person. The main character is in the story and says "I" while telling the story.
2. Is the narrator omniscient or limited? Explain how you know.
   * He's limited. He doesn't know where the kids go every day. He only knows his own thoughts.
3. How might the story be different if it were told from Mom's first-person point of view?
   * It would focus on the struggle of catching the dog to give it a bath. The main character wouldn't have hidden and knows where the kids go daily.
4. What might the title be if the story were told in the third person point of view?
   * A Day in Freddy's Life
5. Before you had read the ending of the story, were you able to tell that the story was being told from a dog's perspective? Explain why or why not.
   * Answers will vary.

104 Reading Comprehension Fundamentals • EMC 2426 • © Evan-Moor Corp.

Page 105

Fiction
Point of View
Review

Name ______

Answer the items.

1. Explain why point of view is an important element in a story.
   * It is a major part of the story because it's how the story is seen and told by the narrator.
2. Explain the difference between a narrator who is omniscient and a narrator who is limited.
   * An omniscient narrator knows what happens later and what all characters think. A limited narrator knows the main character's thoughts.
3. Explain how a narrator's perspective can make some events in the story more of a focus than other events.
   * The reader sees details about events that the narrator thinks are most important.

Read the paragraph. Then answer the item.

4. Uncle Vernon took me sailing last weekend. I had never been sailing before, and I was a bit nervous. I helped him raise up the sail and untie the boat. After a little while, we were on the open ocean. I noticed that the waves were rougher and more choppy the farther out we sailed, and the wind had picked up. Soon, it started to get really rough and choppy out there. The boat went up and down so violently that it felt like we were on a roller coaster at one point. I wondered if Uncle Vernon had ever sailed in weather like this before or if he was nervous. He didn't appear to be nervous. He calmly said that it was time to turn the boat around and head back to shore.

   What point of view is this story written in? Include whether the narrator is omniscient or limited. Then explain how you know the point of view.
   * It's the first person limited point of view. The main character says "I" to tell the story and does not know the uncle's thoughts or abilities.

© Evan-Moor Corp. • EMC 2426 • Reading Comprehension Fundamentals 105

Page 106

Fiction
Vocabulary
1

Name ______

When you come across unfamiliar **vocabulary** in a story, you can use context clues to figure out the meanings of the words you don't know.

Look at the surrounding words. Think about what would make sense in the sentence.
Think about what you know about the topic.
Try replacing the word with a word you already know that may have a similar meaning.

Read the paragraph. Then answer the items.

The wall shook as monotonous dance music blasted from Erika's room. The music never changed. The beat, the tones, the pitches—it was just the same sounds over and over again. Sitting in his bedroom, Dave looked at his oboe and sighed. It was inconceivable for him to practice with that repetitive music playing, so he didn't even know why he was thinking about it. Perhaps he was still hoping to practice because he knew he had a band concert coming up in a few weeks. But Erika played the same music every single day. Dave was in a real predicament, so he was worried.

1. Mark the meaning of the word *monotonous*.
   Ⓐ unique and unusual
   ● repetitive and unchanging
2. Explain why you chose the answer you did for number 1.
   * The text says that the music is repetitive and that the same sounds play over and over again.
3. What do you think *inconceivable* means? Explain why you think so.
   * I think it means unthinkable or impossible. Dave can't practice the oboe with the loud music.
4. What do you think *predicament* means? Explain why you think so.
   * It means a tricky situation. Dave was worried. He had a problem but didn't know how to fix it.

106 Reading Comprehension Fundamentals • EMC 2426 • © Evan-Moor Corp.

Page 108

Fiction
Vocabulary
2

Name ______

Kitchen Champ

When you come across unfamiliar **vocabulary** in a story, you can use context clues to figure out the meanings of the words you don't know.

Look at the surrounding words, and think about what would make sense in the sentence.
Think about what you know about the topic.
Try replacing the word with a word you already know that may have a similar meaning.
Pictures can help you figure out what a word means.

Answer the items about the story you read.

1. Mark the definition of the word *culinary*.
   Ⓐ related to household management
   ● related to the kitchen and cooking
2. What do you think *sear* means? Explain how the picture helped you know.
   * It means to heat and make the surface look charred. The picture shows charred salmon.
3. What do you think *dubious* means? Explain why you think so.
   * I think it means doubtful or uncertain. Gabe and Sam doubted the foods they saw on the counter.
4. What do you think *improvise* means? Explain why you think so.
   * It means to make decisions quickly. Instead of planning, Dad wants Sam to improvise.
5. What do you think *devise* means? Explain why you think so.
   * It means to create or to design something. Before cooking, the family devises meals to make.

108 Reading Comprehension Fundamentals • EMC 2426 • © Evan-Moor Corp.

Page 109

Fiction
Vocabulary
Review

Name ______

Answer the items.

1. Explain how you can use context clues to figure out a word's meaning.
   * You can look at the words that come before and after the word you don't know for clues. You can think about what you know about the topic.
2. Explain how pictures can help you figure out a word's meaning.
   * A picture may show a characteristic of an object that provides a clue to the word's meaning.

Read the paragraph. Then answer the item.

3. My older brother, Hugh, is 22 years old. He has a job and lives at home with Mom, Dad, and me. Last summer, he went on a three-week-long trip to Florida with his friends. He asked me to take care of his plant, which he keeps in his room, while he is away. He loves that plant, and he takes really good care of it so it stays green, strong, and healthy. "Make sure you water it every other day," Hugh told me. "The soil can't become dry because it's not good for the plant." I promised Hugh that I'd take care of it. The three weeks that Hugh was gone went by quickly. I went with Mom and Dad to pick him up from the airport. Hugh greeted us with a big smile and gave us each a tight hug. "I missed you guys," he said. In the car, he was all smiles and chatty. "How's my plant doing?" he finally asked me. I froze. Oh. My. Goodness. I had completely forgotten about Hugh's plant. I never went into his room during the three weeks that he was gone. I gulped. I stuttered. I felt my face becoming red. I finally told Hugh that I hadn't watered the plant at all. His countenance immediately changed. Whereas before he was smiley, now he frowned and looked half angry and half sad.

   What do you think a person's *countenance* is? Explain why you think so.
   * It is a person's facial expressions or appearance. The narrator talks about countenance and talks about smiling, frowning, and looking sad.

© Evan-Moor Corp. • EMC 2426 • Reading Comprehension Fundamentals 109

Page 110

Fiction
Foreshadowing
1

Name ______

In a story, details that **foreshadow** are clues about what might happen later in the story. Foreshadowing can help you make predictions about the story as you read.

Example:

If the main character sees a crow several times in the story, and something bad always happens right after the main character sees a crow, this is an example of foreshadowing. The next time the character sees a crow, you can predict that something bad is likely to happen.

Read the paragraph. Then answer the item.

1. Clara loved traveling the world by herself, hiking and sightseeing. Now she was in Mongolia. She'd heard about a scenic trail leading up a mountain to a plateau. From there, she would have a breathtaking view of the green plains below. One day, she decided to travel by camelback to search for the trail. It was a beautiful sunny day. Her camel was a mild-natured creature, gentle and calm. Clara heard birds tweet and saw happy, lazy yaks grazing as she traveled. In the distance, though, she saw a mountain peak that was enveloped in gray, evil-looking clouds. Abruptly, Clara came upon a wide trail. "This must be the trail I'm looking for," she thought. She observed that it led to the misty, dark mountain. She followed the trail for a while. Then she came upon an old woman walking along the trail. She had a walking stick, which a raven sat upon. Suddenly, the old woman turned to Clara and said, "I would not travel up that mountain alone, if I were you." As Clara rode on, the clouds grew darker. The more Clara stared at the mountain, her camel suddenly dug its heels into the ground. It refused to go any farther, grunting and spitting, protesting in any way it could. Clara decided to turn around and abandon her plan.

   Write three details from the story that foreshadow that the mountain may be dangerous.
   * It was a sunny day, but the mountain had dark clouds around it. The old woman told Clara not to go alone. The camel refused to go farther.

110 Reading Comprehension Fundamentals • EMC 2426 • © Evan-Moor Corp.

* These answers will vary. Examples are given.

Page 111

Name ______________________

Fiction
Foreshadowing
2

In a story, details that **foreshadow** are clues about what might happen later in the story. Foreshadowing can help you make predictions about the story as you read. Authors use foreshadowing to help readers make predictions and to build suspense in the story.

These are some questions to ask as you read and think about foreshadowing:

Do the words or pictures suggest something good or bad might happen?

Is a character wishful for something or nervous about something in particular?

Do the characters see or experience something that they have seen or experienced earlier in the story?

Read the paragraph. Then answer the question.

1. Miguel's best friend, Ashanti, said on the telephone that she was bringing over a humongous piece of cake, left over from her mom's party. But when Miguel saw the cake, it was only a teeny piece. He wasn't surprised at all. Ever since Miguel knew Ashanti, she would exaggerate about pretty much everything. She once convinced him to watch a movie, which she described as a short movie. Was it short? No! It was a three-and-a-half-hour-long movie. When they went bowling, Ashanti selected a bowling ball for Miguel while he was in the restroom. "It's really light. It's the perfect size for you," said Ashanti. Miguel immediately discovered that it was 16-pound ball, and it was too heavy for him to even lift. Miguel had been getting excited for his birthday, which was fast-approaching. Ashanti told him not to plan anything. "I know just what you'll want to do, the perfect activity for you," she said. "I'll plan a huge celebration. I'm your best friend, after all. It'll be the most fun birthday bash you've ever had." Miguel thought it was nice of Ashanti to offer. He really did want a huge birthday bash. When his birthday finally arrived, he went to Ashanti's house, where the party was supposed to be, but he was so disappointed. The only thing Ashanti had planned was to make some popcorn and play video games. To be fair, she did choose video games Miguel likes.

What details in the story foreshadow that Ashanti is going to disappoint Miguel with her plan for his birthday?

* Ashanti always exaggerates about everything. Miguel wanted a huge birthday bash. Ashanti said it would be the most fun birthday bash.

© Evan-Moor Corp. • EMC 2426 • Reading Comprehension Fundamentals 111

Page 113

Name ______________________

Fiction
Foreshadowing
3

Mischief at the Museum

In a story, details that **foreshadow** are clues about what might happen later in the story. Foreshadowing can help you make predictions about the story as you read. Authors use foreshadowing to help readers make predictions and to build suspense in the story.

When a character is concerned or intrigued by something specific, that can provide a clue about what may happen later.

When a character notices unusual details, this can provide a clue.

Answer the items about the story you read.

1. Describe what is being foreshadowed throughout the story, or what the author wants readers to figure out.
   * The Neanderthal is alive and can move around.
2. What happens in the first paragraph that is an example of foreshadowing?
   * The woman who works at the museum suggests that the Neanderthal can interact with people.
3. Write two additional details from the story that foreshadow.
   * Ireeni sees barefoot footprints, and the Neanderthal is barefoot. Ireenia sees movement in the corner of her eye in the Neanderthal area.
4. What conclusion do you think Ireeni will draw at the end of the story? Explain why you think so.
   * She will think that the Neanderthal is alive or real. Ireeni sees a bite taken out of the meat after she sees movement.

© Evan-Moor Corp. • EMC 2426 • Reading Comprehension Fundamentals 113

Page 114

Name ______________________

Fiction
Foreshadowing
Review

Answer the items.

1. Explain what foreshadowing is in a story.
   * It's a detail that provides a clue about what will happen later on in the story.
2. How can foreshadowing help you predict if something good or bad will happen later in the story?
   * It gives you clues. You may see happy images, such as cute animals, or negative images, such as dark clouds.
3. How can foreshadowing help you analyze the plot of a story?
   * It helps you think about the details in the story, to look for clues. Then you look closely for connections to events that come later in the story.
4. Explain the connection between details a character notices and events that take place in a story.
   * Sometimes the details that characters notice are described right before an event happens. The details can affect a character's actions, too.
5. Explain why an author may choose to foreshadow events in a story.
   * Sometimes authors use foreshadowing to make a story suspenseful.

114 Reading Comprehension Fundamentals • EMC 2426 • © Evan-Moor Corp.

Page 115

Name ______________________

Fiction
Summarize
1

When you **summarize** a story, you use your own words to state the most important details from the story. A summary provides a short version of the story. Do the following when you summarize:

Provide as many of the following details as possible: **who**, **what**, **where**, **when**, **why**, and **how**

Include details from the story rather than your own opinions.

Include only the most important details in the summary. Leave minor details out of the summary.

Read the story. Then answer the items.

As the villagers cheered for Lady Jane, who'd just chased away a mountain troll, Sir Bolland wished just once a crowd would cheer for him. He went to the wizard, Kerzak, who offered to conjure a dragon. "It will be a cowardly dragon that's easy to defeat," Kerzak said. "You'll be a hero." Sir Bolland liked the sound of that! Kerzak mixed a potion, recited a spell, and poof—a dragon appeared in the sky! Sir Bolland stepped outside. The villagers watched as he drew his sword. Flames shot from the dragon's mouth, instantly melting the sword. Sir Bolland gulped. Kerzak quickly recited another spell, and the dragon disappeared. "Sorry," the wizard whispered to Sir Bolland. "The dragon wasn't as cowardly as I'd planned." The villagers praised Kerzak as a hero. Feeling more terrible than ever, Sir Bolland shuffled home. On his way, a young boy cried for help. He was stuck in a tree. Sir Bolland reached up and carried the boy, gently putting him down. The boy called Sir Bolland a hero.

1. Write a paragraph to summarize the plot of the story.
   * Sir Bolland wants to be a hero. Kerzak, a wizard, tries to help Sir Bolland, but it doesn't go as planned. Later, Sir Bolland rescues a boy and is called a hero.
2. How does Sir Bolland feel at the beginning of the story? Explain why he feels this way.
   * He feels envious. He sees people cheer for Lady Jane and wishes they'd cheer for him.

© Evan-Moor Corp. • EMC 2426 • Reading Comprehension Fundamentals 115

Page 117

Name ______________________

Fiction
Summarize
2

The RV Fiasco

When you **summarize** a story, you use your own words to state the most important details from the story. A summary is always shorter than the story being summarized. It tells what the story is mostly about.

You can write one sentence to summarize each paragraph in a story.

You can write one sentence to summarize a portion of dialogue in a story.

Answer the items about the story you read.

1. Who are the characters in the story?
   * Sean, Riley, Mom, and Dad are the characters.
2. What is the conflict in the story?
   * The family can't find a good spot to camp with the RV, and they must keep moving the RV.
3. Write a paragraph to summarize the events in the story.
   * The family was excited about camping in the mountains with an RV. They had to register for the campsite. Riley and Sean had to help set up camp. Dad and Mom realized that there wasn't electricity and they had to move the RV. They packed everything back in the RV. They parked but then had to move again twice more. Then they got a flat tire, but at least they had electricity. They decided to fix the flat tire the next day and start a campfire and rest for the night.

© Evan-Moor Corp. • EMC 2426 • Reading Comprehension Fundamentals 117

Page 118

Name ______________________

Fiction
Summarize
Review

Answer the items.

1. Explain how to summarize a story.
   * Write the most important details from the story. You can summarize each paragraph or portions of dialogue.
2. How can reading a summary help people to better understand a story?
   * It can help them focus on the most important details from the story.
3. Why do you think it's best to leave minor details out of a summary?
   * If it's minor, it shouldn't be in the summary because the summary should be short. Minor details may distract from the important ones.

Read the paragraph. Then summarize it.

4. Mason and Sowra were standing in the crowd, waiting to see their dad jump out of the plane, along with a bunch of other skydivers. This wasn't his first jump, but they were as excited as ever. They always loved watching him skydive. After about an hour of waiting, they could see the plane approaching in the distance. Then, people started jumping out! Their dad was wearing a bright neon green skydiving suit, so the children couldn't miss him. As Sowra watched her dad flatten out his body and spread out his limbs, she couldn't help but think of a flying squirrel. Mason was taking pictures with his digital camera. After a few seconds, which felt like an eternity, the children's dad opened up his parachute. He glided down to the earth smoothly. He looked so happy. Eventually, he landed in a nearby field, laughing heartily as he rolled up inside his parachute on the ground. He gave the children tight hugs when he saw them.
   * Mason and Sowra watched their dad skydive. They saw him flatten his body in the air, open his parachute, and land smoothly. They hugged him.

118 Reading Comprehension Fundamentals • EMC 2426 • © Evan-Moor Corp.

Page 119

Name ______________________

Fiction
Make Inferences
1

You can **make inferences** as you read a story. When you make an inference, you use background information and clues in the text to figure out details that the author does not state directly. This is an example of an inference:

What I read: Gilbert goes to work each day, where he puts on an apron and specializes in making soups, roasts, and desserts.

Inference I can make: Gilbert is a chef.

Read the sentence. Then mark the sentence that tells an inference you can make.

1. Indra wishes she could order the dessert with peanut butter, but she doesn't want to end up with a rash, so she orders the vanilla pudding instead.
   Ⓐ Indra doesn't like peanut butter.
   ● Indra is allergic to peanuts.
2. When Jose looked at his dinner and frowned, his mom shook her head and said, "See, I told you we'd be eating soon."
   ● Jose ate a snack just before dinner.
   Ⓑ Jose doesn't like what's being served.

Read the sentences. Then write an inference you can make.

3. Mom handed the spoon to Marco and told him to mix the batter slowly; otherwise, it would splatter all over the place. After mixing for a moment, Marco looked at the counter and groaned.
   * Marco mixed the batter too fast, and it splattered on the counter.
4. When Dad was making pancakes, Emily asked if she could crack open the eggs for the batter. She cracked open two eggs and let them plop into the bowl. Then she asked her dad a question. "Hey, Dad, it's okay if some eggshells are in the pancakes, right?" "Let's just make a new batch of pancake batter," said Dad.
   * It is not safe or not good to have eggshells in pancakes.

© Evan-Moor Corp. • EMC 2426 • Reading Comprehension Fundamentals 119

Page 120

Name ______________________

Fiction
Make Inferences
2

You can **make inferences** as you read a story. When you make an inference, you use background information and clues in the text to figure out details that the author does not state directly. You can make inferences about characters, settings, events, and pictures.

Example: When you read a story and figure out on your own why a character probably acted a certain way, you are making an inference.

Read the paragraph. Then answer the questions.

Commander Boltworth landed his spacecraft on the surface of the planet. His navigator, Rex, stood up and said, "I'll make sure there's oxygen since I don't need to breathe in order to survive." Rex rolled out onto the icy surface. He lifted his metallic arm and opened a small hatch in his hand that had a thermometer-like tip. He took air samples and reported back that it was safe for Boltworth to come out. The commander stepped out cautiously and shivered. A group of beings that appeared alien stood nearby. They were about three feet tall. They were black and white with pointy beaks and wings. They waddled when they walked. When the commander tried to speak to the beings, they just ignored him. The commander was confused. "Earth is supposed to have intelligent life," he said. "Where is it?"

1. What inference can you make about Rex? Tell how you made this inference.
   * He is a robot. He says he doesn't need oxygen. He doesn't walk; he rolls. He has a metallic arm.
2. What inference can you make about Commander Boltworth? Tell how you know this.
   * He is not a human. He's an alien. He landed on Earth in a spaceship. He tries to talk to penguins.
3. What are the "beings that appeared alien"? Explain how you made this inference.
   * They are penguins. Boltworth landed in a place that's icy, like where penguins live. The description of the beings is consistent with penguins.

120 Reading Comprehension Fundamentals • EMC 2426 • © Evan-Moor Corp.

Page 122

Name ______________________

Fiction
Make Inferences
3

A Visit to the Family Farm

When you **make inferences** as you read, you figure out details that are not provided in the story. You can use background knowledge, clues in the text, and visual information to make inferences.

You can make inferences about the following things:

characters' traits and emotions

plot and setting

reasons that certain things happen in the story

Answer the questions about the story you read.

1. What is Summer's hobby? Explain why you think so.
   * She likes art. She has paintings, paintbrushes, and sketch books in her room.
2. Why do you think that Tanner says they couldn't do the same biking activity in the city?
   * The city probably doesn't have a steep hill with bumps and bushes.
3. How does Tanner feel about the dinner? Explain why you think so.
   * Tanner doesn't like it at all. The picture shows that he's unhappy. He pushes food aside and pretends to eat it for a while.
4. Why do you think Tanner stuffs food in his mouth when Uncle Travis looks at him?
   * He doesn't want to hurt Uncle Travis's feelings because Uncle Travis worked hard on the dinner.
5. How does Phoebe feel about the dinner? Explain why you think so.
   * She likes it. She gets a second helping.

122 Reading Comprehension Fundamentals • EMC 2426 • © Evan-Moor Corp.

***** These answers will vary. Examples are given.

Page 123

Name ______________________

Fiction
Make Inferences
Review

Answer the items.

1. Explain what an inference is.
* It's something the author doesn't directly state but you are able to figure out on your own.
2. Explain how your own background knowledge can help you make inferences as you read a story.
* If I can relate to a situation described in a story, I can infer other details about it.
3. How is making an inference different from guessing?
* Inferences require background knowledge and clues from the text. Guesses do not.
4. State the story elements or details that you can make inferences about.
* You can make inferences about setting, character traits, plot, and characters' feelings.

Read the paragraph. Then write an inference you can make.

5. Whenever students forget their P.E. uniforms, Mr. Sop, the P.E. teacher, makes them sit on the bleachers for the entire class period. Today, Suzy brought homework to do as she sits on the bleachers.
* Suzy forgot her P.E. uniform today.
6. Morgan was babysitting her little brother, Ryan, who was only six years old. She asked Ryan if he was hungry, and he said, "No, I snacked on some trail mix a little while ago." Later, Morgan saw an opened package of trail mix on the table. It said that the ingredients were chocolate chips, peanuts, raisins, cashews, and sunflower seeds, but Morgan didn't see any chocolate chips in the package at all. She saw all the other ingredients in the mix, though.
* Ryan ate all of the chocolate chips in the trail mix.

© Evan-Moor Corp. • EMC 2426 • Reading Comprehension Fundamentals 123

Page 124

Name ______________________

Fiction
Predict
1

When you **predict** as you read a story, you analyze details in the story to try to determine what will happen later. You use your own background knowledge and clues in the text to make predictions.

Sometimes, you may not accurately predict what happens later. Any prediction is a good prediction if it is based on details in the text.

Read the paragraph. Then answer the questions.

Brad was obsessed with taking photos. Everywhere he went, he saw scenes and images that he wanted to snap photos of. When Brad found out that his school had Camera Club, which met every Thursday, he decided to go to one of the meetings. The club's director, Mrs. Arias, told Brad that he needed to have his own digital camera, the only requirement for joining. Brad already knew that he wanted a Zakawn-P680, the most awesome camera being sold. He also knew that it was going to cost at least $100 and that he had only $47 saved up from his allowance money. When he got home that day, Brad said, "Can you get the camera for me, Mom? I don't have enough money."

"Well, Brad," she said, "I have told you for months that I am willing to increase your allowance if you are willing to take on more chores around the house, but you've never wanted to take me up on my offer. Why don't you start doing more chores now?"

"But, Mom," he argued, "I want the camera right now! I don't want to wait until I've done chores and saved up enough money! I'm begging you to get the camera now."

1. How do you think Brad's mom is going to respond? Explain why you think so.
* I think she will offer to increase Brad's allowance again and tell him to save up for the camera.
2. What do you think Brad will do if his mom responds how you predicted? Explain why.
* He won't take her offer because he hasn't when she's offered before. He won't get the camera.
3. What would you do if you were in Brad's situation? Explain why.
* Answers will vary.

124 Reading Comprehension Fundamentals • EMC 2426 • © Evan-Moor Corp.

Page 126

Name ______________________

Fiction
Predict
2

Off the Trail!

When you **predict** as you read a story, you analyze details in the story and state what you think is likely to happen later. You use your own background knowledge and clues in the text to make predictions. The following types of details may provide clues that help you make predictions:

certain habits of characters | **certain problems or conflicts**
the story's title | **characters' spoken words or thoughts**

Answer the questions about the story you read.

1. Did the title help you predict what the story would be about? Explain why or why not.
* Yes. I predicted the characters would get lost. Trails usually help you to avoid getting lost.
2. What clues in the story may have helped you predict that Emerson and his dad would lose the trail?
* The boulder field was far from the trail. Emerson's dad was reluctant to leave the trail.
3. Emerson loves to climb boulders. How does this detail help you make predictions about the story?
* Because he loves climbing boulders, you can predict that he'd leave the trail to climb one.
4. What do you think will happen the next time Emerson and his dad go hiking?
* I think they will stay on the trail and remember to continue climbing upward.
5. Did anything in the story help you predict how they'd solve their problem? Explain.
* Yes. Dad said that he walked up a hill when he got lost before, so I predicted they'd walk up.

126 Reading Comprehension Fundamentals • EMC 2426 • © Evan-Moor Corp.

Page 127

Name ______________________

Fiction
Predict
Review

Answer the items.

1. Explain how you make predictions as you read.
* I use clues and details in the text, and I think about what I know about the topic already.
2. How does analyzing a story help you predict?
* When you look closely at separate details in the story, it gives you a lot of clues.
3. How do the characters' actions and words in a story provide clues that help you make predictions?
* They like doing certain things, which is a clue about what they may choose to do later. They say things that tell about their worries for the future.
4. How does your own background knowledge help you make predictions as you read?
* When you know about a topic because you've been in a similar situation, it helps you predict.
5. How is a prediction different from a guess?
* You don't always form a guess by using clues or knowledge. A prediction is more likely to happen.

Read the paragraph. Then write a prediction for something that will happen after.

6. After school, instead of doing homework, Denny went to the mall with his older sister. He was going to do his homework as soon as he got home, but his friend Josh came over to hang out. Denny decided to do his homework after dinner. But Mom served dinner later than usual, and Denny felt tired after eating. He decided to take a shower to wake himself up and do his homework assignment later, in pajamas.
* Denny will keep putting off the homework.

© Evan-Moor Corp. • EMC 2426 • Reading Comprehension Fundamentals 127

Page 128

Name ______________________

Fiction
Cause and Effect
1

When you think about **cause and effect** in a story, you analyze the events to determine the reasons why they happen. A **cause** is a reason why something happens. An **effect** is what happens as a result.

These are some ways cause and effect are shown in a story:

The setting or environment makes a character feel or act a certain way.
A character's actions cause certain events to happen.
An event in the story causes a reaction.

Read the sentence. Circle it if it's about a cause and an effect.

1. It was a perfect day to go to the beach and lie out in the sun.
2. (A huge wave crashed and sent Iggy tumbling in the wet sand.)
3. Miguel spent over an hour collecting shells and smooth stones.
4. (Ryu was upset after a wave rolled up the beach and destroyed his sand castle.)
5. (Poor Dad fell asleep on the beach, and now he has a painful sunburn!)

Match each cause with the correct effect.

6.

cause	effect
Tori stepped on a pointed rock.	Tori got knocked over.
Tori forgot to put a bandage on her injury.	Tori made some new friends.
Tori didn't see the wave coming.	The cut on Tori's foot became infected.
Tori wandered over to some other kids.	Tori's foot was injured.

Read the sentence. Circle the cause and underline the effect.

7. (The weather was perfect,) so <u>many families decided to go to the beach.</u>
8. <u>Mom set up an umbrella</u> because (the sun was scorching and bright.)

128 Reading Comprehension Fundamentals • EMC 2426 • © Evan-Moor Corp.

Page 129

Name ______________________

Fiction
Cause and Effect
2

When you think about **cause and effect** in a story, it helps you to better understand the plot of the story. Events in a story can cause other things to happen as a result. The plot of a story is made up of a long line of events that happen for a reason.

Read the paragraph. Then answer the items.

Dad insisted we leave two hours early for the airport because last year he left late for a business trip and missed his flight. We quickly packed all our luggage into the trunk and set out in the afternoon. There was a ton of traffic. Sitting in the car, I felt really anxious. Would we miss our flight? We got to the airport much later than Dad had hoped. Luckily, the lines weren't long, though, and we were in the terminal with plenty of time to spare. Mom realized that during the rush to pack, she'd forgotten her book. She went into a bookstore to get a new one. While she was in there, a voice announced that our flight was boarding. Mom came rushing out of the store. "No time for a book!" she cried. "Let's go!"

1. Explain what caused Dad to have the family leave two hours early.
* He missed a flight in the past because he had left late and didn't want it to happen again.
2. Write one effect that resulted from the family packing so quickly.
* Mom forgot her book.
3. What caused the narrator to feel anxious?
* The narrator was worried that the family would miss the flight because there was a ton of traffic.
4. What happened when the voice announced the flight was boarding? Tell why.
* Mom ran out of the store without a book. She didn't want to miss the flight.

© Evan-Moor Corp. • EMC 2426 • Reading Comprehension Fundamentals 129

Page 131

Name ______________________

Fiction
Cause and Effect
3

Giant Mutant Frog!

Analyzing **cause and effect** in a story can help you to better understand the story. When something happens in a story, it can cause other things to happen as a result. The plot of a story is made up of a long line of events that happen for a reason. These are some ways cause and effect are shown in a story:

The setting or environment makes a character feel or act a certain way.
A character's actions cause certain events to happen.
An event in the story causes a character to feel or act a certain way.

Answer the items about the story you read.

1. Explain what caused the children to work up an appetite.
* They did physical activity on the playground.
2. Explain what caused Teddy to drop the bottle and why Phan and Violet laughed at Teddy about it.
* He jumped because he thought a bee flew by him. They laughed because it was a butterfly.
3. Write two effects of the drink spilling into the pond.
* It made the pond bright blue. It seems to have made the animals in the pond gigantic.
4. How would the story be different if the friends sat at a picnic table that wasn't near the pond?
* The drink wouldn't have spilled into the pond. Then the frog wouldn't have become mutated.
5. How did the children's actions affect the frog? How did the frog react?
* The frog became gigantic and left the pond after it ate Violet's backpack.

© Evan-Moor Corp. • EMC 2426 • Reading Comprehension Fundamentals 131

Page 132

Name ______________________

Fiction
Cause and Effect
Review

Answer the items.

1. How does analyzing cause and effect help you to better understand a story?
* You look closely at the details in the story when you think about cause and effect. This helps you understand why things are happening.
2. In your own words, explain what a cause is and what an effect is.
* A cause is the reason something happens, and an effect is a result or an outcome.
3. Explain how cause and effect helps to create events in the plot of a story.
* Many events in a story could be either a cause or an effect. One action often leads to another.

Read the paragraphs. Then answer the item.

4. "Imogen, stop feeding the raccoons in the backyard!" demanded Dad, pointing to some slices of bread sitting on the back porch. "It's not a joke. The more you do it, the more they'll hang around." Imogen liked seeing the raccoons in the backyard, though.

"But, Dad," she argued, "I only throw food that nobody in this house is going to eat. So, isn't it better to give it to the raccoons than to waste it?"

"I see your reasoning, Imogen, but you're actually doing more harm than good to the raccoons." Imogen frowned because she didn't understand, so Dad continued. "When you feed them, they stop trying as hard to get food on their own. More raccoons will show up, and they'll expect you to feed them. When you don't, they may go hungry." Imogen finally understood. She agreed to no longer feed the raccoons.

That evening, she looked onto the back porch. There were five more raccoons than usual out there. "Oh no, what have I done?" Imogen thought to herself.

Write one cause from the story. Then write its effect.
* Imogen throws food outside to feed the raccoons. More raccoons show up in the backyard as a result.

132 Reading Comprehension Fundamentals • EMC 2426 • © Evan-Moor Corp.

Page 133

Name ______________________

Fiction
Compare and Contrast
1

When you **compare and contrast** elements in a story, it helps you to better understand the story. To compare (analyze similarities) and contrast (analyze differences), you must carefully consider the details in the story. You can compare and contrast different stories. You can compare and contrast characters in a story. Look at these details:

characters' traits | **characters' spoken words and thoughts**
characters' actions | **characters' struggles**

Read *Story 1* and *Story 2*. Then answer the items.

Story 1

Krag gulped as he spotted the danger ahead. He was heading back home to his family's cave after a two-day hunting journey when a Tyrannosaurus rex popped into view. The dinosaur hadn't seen Krag yet, but there were no boulders for Krag to hide behind in this open land. Worried that the T. rex would smell the meat he was carrying and attack, Krag stood motionless, considering leaving the food behind.

Story 2

Mitchell rushed to make it to the bakery before it closed at six o'clock. His mom had ordered a birthday cake last week for his dad's surprise party, which was tonight. Mitchell parked in front of the bakery five minutes before closing time. Then he noticed Mrs. Namu, his neighbor, standing in front of the bakery. She was nice, but she was very talkative, and he knew he'd never make it inside on time if she stopped him to chat. He sat in the car for a minute, frozen and confused, wondering what to do.

1. Write three sentences that compare the main characters from Story 1 and Story 2.
* They both deal with a stressful situation and don't act. They're both bringing food to their families. They want to avoid something or someone.
2. Write one important way that the stories are different.
* Story 1's setting is fantasy, and story 2's is realistic.

© Evan-Moor Corp. • EMC 2426 • Reading Comprehension Fundamentals 133

✱ These answers will vary. Examples are given.

Page 134

Name ____________ Fiction — Compare and Contrast — 2

When you **compare and contrast** elements within a story, you analyze details that show similarities and differences. These are elements that you can compare and contrast in a story:

characters

events

settings or places described

Read the paragraph. Then answer the items.

Nora went to the art museum with her dad. They walked through cool air-conditioned corridors, which felt great compared to the sweltering, humid summer air outdoors. The art museum was crowded with people. There were so many beautiful paintings and statues, Nora didn't know where to look. Although Nora and her dad had to weave their way around lots of bodies, it was a calm environment because everyone was so quiet, with their eyes fixed upon the art. "Ready to go?" Nora's dad asked after a few hours of strolling around. Nora nodded, and they headed outside, where Nora immediately felt beads of sweat dripping down her neck and forehead. The busy sidewalk was packed with people rushing in opposite directions. It reminded Nora of a highway, except there were speeding pedestrians instead of speeding cars. Buses and cars on the street swooshed by continuously. Colorful signs, flashing traffic lights, and bright cones confused Nora, and she didn't know what her eyes should focus on. She just stayed close to her dad as they weaved among the other pedestrians. She hoped the walk home would be fast.

1. Contrast the settings inside and outside of the museum.
✱ The museum is cool, calm, and quiet. Outside it is hot, loud, and busy.

2. Compare the settings inside and outside the museum.
✱ They are both very crowded. They both have lots of objects to look at.

3. Write one way that Nora acts similarly inside and outside of the museum.
✱ She doesn't know where to look.

134 Reading Comprehension Fundamentals • EMC 2426 • © Evan-Moor Corp.

Page 136

Name ____________ Fiction — Compare and Contrast — 3

Thinking About Nepal

When you **compare and contrast** elements within a story, you analyze details that show similarities and differences. These are elements that you can compare and contrast in a story: **character**, **setting**, and **events** in the plot.

You can use visual information to help you compare and contrast elements.

Answer the items about the story you read.

1. Write four words from the story that describe hiking in Nepal but do not describe hiking near the narrator's home.
✱ challenging, breathtaking, peaks, rivers

2. Write four words from the story that describe hiking near the narrator's home but do not describe hiking in Nepal.
✱ flat, concrete, neat, bicyclists

3. How does the narrator use size to describe how he feels in each setting?
✱ He feels tiny in the Himalayas, but he feels like a giant among the squirrels near his home.

4. Contrast the feelings the narrator has in each setting.
✱ Near home, he feels that the hike is ruined. In Nepal, he feels like an explorer.

5. How does the visual information demonstrate the differences between the two settings described in the story?
✱ The photos show what the text describes. They show a concrete trail and beautiful peaks.

136 Reading Comprehension Fundamentals • EMC 2426 • © Evan-Moor Corp.

Page 137

Name ____________ Fiction — Compare and Contrast — Review

Answer the items.

1. Explain how to compare and contrast elements in a story.
✱ You have to analyze the story's details and look for descriptions of similarities and differences.

2. How can visual information help you to compare and contrast details in a story?
✱ It shows more details, so you can see similarities or differences possibly not provided in the text.

3. When you compare and contrast details in a story, how does this help you to better understand the story?
✱ You think about the details you read. It may give you explanations for certain events in the story.

Read the paragraph. Then answer the items.

Last year, Mr. Gold's sixth-grade class decided to play a friendly prank on Mrs. Dool's fifth-grade class. The sixth graders replaced all of the markers in the fifth-grade classroom with markers that were dried out and didn't work anymore. For an entire school day, the fifth graders tried to use the old markers. Then the students became fed up! This year, Mrs. Dool wanted her students to prank the sixth graders. The fifth graders hid a tablet in Mrs. Dool's classroom. At certain times during the day, the fifth graders played a weird old song from a playlist saved on the tablet. Until the sixth graders found the tablet, they had to listen to the weird songs throughout the day! This prank lasted for three entire school days. It was hilarious!

4. Write two details from the story to compare the two pranks.
✱ Both of the pranks were harmless. In both pranks, objects were put in classrooms.

5. Write two details from the story to contrast the two pranks.
✱ The marker prank lasted only one day, not three. The tablet prank involved technology.

© Evan-Moor Corp. • EMC 2426 • Reading Comprehension Fundamentals 137

Page 138

Name ____________ Fiction — Dialogue — 1

A **dialogue** is a conversation that takes place between characters in a story. Dialogue can provide significant details about the story.

Ask these questions as you analyze a story's dialogue:

Does the dialogue provide details about the setting?

Does the dialogue provide details about the characters?

Does the dialogue provide details about the plot?

Read the dialogue. Then answer the questions.

Dad scratched his head. "What row was it?" he asked.
"Try to remember," Mom said. "These bags are getting heavy."
"It's definitely parked near the spot where people return the carts," Jia said.
"But I see three of those, " said Mom.

1. Based on the dialogue, where do you think the story takes place?
✱ It's in the parking lot of a grocery store.

2. Who are the characters, and how do they know each other?
✱ There are two parents and their daughter.

3. What is the conflict in the story?
✱ They can't remember where the car is parked.

Read the dialogue. Then answer the item.

4. "Don't forget the paper plates and napkins," Kelly said. "Oh, and ice."
"You don't need to be bossy, Kelly," Fitz said. "Mom gave *me* the list."
"Just because you're in college, it doesn't mean you can't forget things," Kelly said.
"Let's just get this done," Fitz said. "The guests will be at our house soon."

Explain who Kelly and Fitz are and what they're doing.
✱ They are siblings. They are buying groceries for some kind of celebration at their house.

138 Reading Comprehension Fundamentals • EMC 2426 • © Evan-Moor Corp.

Page 140

Name ____________ Fiction — Dialogue — 2

Family Fun Challenge!

A **dialogue** is a conversation that takes place between characters in a story. Dialogue can provide significant details about the story.

Dialogue may provide details about the following:

character traits	reasons for characters' actions
setting	conflicts or challenges characters face
plot	characters' plans or intentions

Answer the items about the story you read.

1. Write three character traits that describe Marcus Starr.
✱ vain, demanding, talkative

2. What does the dialogue at the beginning tell you about the story?
✱ It suggests that a television show is about to be filmed. It describes the set, with lots of colors and contraptions for a physical challenge.

3. What does Marcus compare Jake Brenson to? Why does Marcus do this?
He compares him to a ninja. Jake probably moved quickly and avoided getting bonked.

4. Why does Julie Kim think that her mom is "freaking out"?
Mrs. Kim looked scared and was screaming the whole time she was on the ropes.

5. Write one important detail from the story that the dialogue provides.
✱ The Kim family won the $10,000.

140 Reading Comprehension Fundamentals • EMC 2426 • © Evan-Moor Corp.

Page 141

Name ____________ Fiction — Dialogue — Review

Answer the items.

1. Explain what dialogue is.
✱ It is a conversation that takes place between characters in a story.

2. Explain how dialogue can provide significant information about characters in a story.
✱ Things characters say can reveal traits that describe them, such as "generous" or "selfish." Dialogue can show characters' plans, too.

3. Explain how dialogue can provide significant information about plot.
✱ It can show what characters plan. Conflict is part of plot, and dialogue can tell more about the problems characters face or events in the story.

Read the dialogue. Then answer the items.

"If you borrowed my yoga mat, it's fine!" Ruby said sternly. "Just be honest!"
"I didn't borrow it," insisted Joaquin. "You don't believe your own brother? I don't even do yoga, you know that."
"I know you use my yoga mat as a foot pillow, Joaquin! I've seen y... " Ruby paused. "Hey, do you hear that thumping noise?" Joaquin and Ruby went into their sister Liv's room. "Hey! Don't use my yoga mat to squish a spider!" Ruby shrieked.

4. Describe the conflicts that the characters struggle with in the story.
✱ Ruby thinks Joaquin took her mat. Joaquin is upset that Ruby accuses him. Liv sees a spider.

5. Explain how the dialogue provides significant details in the story.
✱ It provides the relationship for Joaquin and Ruby. It provides the plot events and setting.

© Evan-Moor Corp. • EMC 2426 • Reading Comprehension Fundamentals 141

Page 142

Name ____________ Fiction — Idioms — 1

An **idiom** is a phrase or an expression. It is a form of figurative language, which has a meaning that is not literal. Use the context of the surrounding words and phrases to figure out the meaning of an idiom. Here is an example of an idiom in a sentence:

It's raining cats and dogs, so we won't go for a walk today.

The idiom is underlined. It means that it's raining a lot.

Read the pair of sentences, which contains an underlined idiom. Write what you think the idiom means. Then explain why you think so.

1. AJ was much quieter than usual. His mom couldn't tell what was on his mind, so she said, "A penny for your thoughts?"
✱ I think it means "what are you thinking?" AJ's mom can't tell what's on his mind.

2. "The ball is in your court," Erin said. "I don't care what movie we watch."
✱ I think it means "it's up to you." Erin says she doesn't care, so the choice is up to someone else.

3. "What if the doctor says I need a shot?" Paul asked, clearly worried. "We'll cross that bridge when we get to it," Mom said.
✱ I think it means "we'll deal with that problem if we need to." She doesn't deal with it now.

4. "I wish I could go," Kwon said with a cough. "But I'm feeling under the weather."
✱ I think it means "I don't feel well." Kwon coughs.

5. Priya's brother ate the last cookie and then lost the book she'd let him borrow. When he broke her phone, it was the last straw, and she lost her temper.
✱ I think it means it was the last problem she was willing to put up with. She lost her temper after.

142 Reading Comprehension Fundamentals • EMC 2426 • © Evan-Moor Corp.

Page 143

Name ____________ Fiction — Idioms — 2

An **idiom** is a phrase or an expression that has a figurative meaning, or a meaning that is not literal. If you take an idiom's meaning literally, it will not make sense.

Example: When a woman says she's **in over her head**, she doesn't mean she's underwater. She means that she can't handle everything that needs to be done.

Read the paragraph, which contains underlined idioms. Then answer the questions.

Leo was in a pickle. He had a big test coming up, and he hadn't made time to study. The night before the test, he decided that he needed to put his nose to the grindstone. He read his books and his notes. He looked at old homework assignments and quizzes and studied as much as he could.

1. **in a pickle**
What do you think this idiom means? Explain why you think so.
✱ It means "in trouble." Leo had a test but didn't study at all, so he was worried.

2. **put his nose to the grindstone**
What do you think this idiom means? Explain why you think so.
✱ It means "focus and work hard." After Leo chose to do what the idiom says, he worked hard.

Read the paragraph. Then answer the question.

Francine begged her brother Alfie to be quiet so she could study for her test, but he wouldn't cooperate with her at all. First, he played a song on his recorder. Then, he turned the television volume up really high. He thought it was funny. Later, Alfie was trying to listen to a song on his phone, and he asked Francine to quiet down. But she made more noise. "See, you're getting a taste of your own medicine," said Francine.

3. **a taste of your own medicine**
What do you think this idiom means? Explain why you think so.
✱ It means "you get treated how you treat others." Alfie refused to quiet down, so Francine did, too.

© Evan-Moor Corp. • EMC 2426 • Reading Comprehension Fundamentals 143

Page 145

Name ____________ Fiction — Idioms — 3

Our Pet Gator

An **idiom** is a phrase or expression. When you read an **idiom**, you don't take the meaning literally. Use the context of other words and sentences to figure out the meaning of an idiom.

Authors use idioms to add humor to the story.

Authors also use idioms to make the narrator and characters' dialogue sound natural. Many people use idioms when they speak.

Answer the questions about the story you read.

1. Which idiom means "everything possible"?
Ⓐ on cloud nine
Ⓑ leaps and bounds
● the whole nine yards
Ⓓ out on a limb

2. Pop said the people who had Cletus first must have bitten off more than they could chew. What did he mean by that? Explain how you know.
✱ He meant that they took on more responsibility than they could handle. They just gave up when they realized they couldn't care for Cletus.

3. **on cloud nine**
What do you think this idiom means? Explain why you think so.
✱ If you're on cloud nine, it means you're happy. Cletus looks like he's smiling and floating happily.

4. **we went out on a limb**
What do you think this idiom means? Explain why you think so.
✱ It means that we took a risk or an uncertain step to do something.

© Evan-Moor Corp. • EMC 2426 • Reading Comprehension Fundamentals 145

* These answers will vary. Examples are given.

Page 146

Name ______ Fiction — Idioms — Review

Answer the questions.

1. What is an idiom?
* It's an expression that is not meant to be taken literally.

2. How do idioms make the dialogue in a story realistic?
* People often use idioms as they speak, so it's realistic when characters use idioms, too.

Read the pair of sentences. Then write **yes** or **no** to tell whether or not it has an idiom.

3. Chris's dog, Sue, is very energetic, and she always wants Chris to pay attention to her. Chris often takes Sue on extra long walks so she will run out of steam. yes

4. Piper met her cousin Junior for the first time at the family reunion. But Piper found Junior to be quite rude, so the cousins got off on the wrong foot. yes

5. Brandon had received a gift card from his grandparents, which he could use at his favorite store. But then he lost the card, and he was extremely disappointed. no

Read the paragraph. Then answer the question.

6. Melanie's mom and dad were both working on Tuesday night, so Melanie was going to be home alone. Melanie's mom made a lasagna ahead of time and told Melanie that she just needed to heat it up for dinner. Melanie cut a square of lasagna and put it on a plate, but she didn't want to eat lasagna by itself. So Melanie went the extra mile and cut up some vegetables for a salad. She also toasted some bread rolls.

went the extra mile
What do you think this idiom means? Explain why you think so.
* It means that she put forth a little more effort to get the result she wanted.

146 Reading Comprehension Fundamentals • EMC 2426 • © Evan-Moor Corp.

Page 147

Name ______ Fiction — Symbolism — 1

In a story, **symbolism** is anything that stands for something else, such as a big idea or something that is happening in the world. An animal, object, or color can be a symbol. Details in the story help to show what the symbol stands for.

When looking for symbolism in a story, ask yourself these questions:

Does the story draw a comparison between an animal, object, or color and an important idea?

Does the story mention a certain animal, object, or color more than once?

Does a particular animal, object, or color appear at important parts of the story?

Read the story. Then answer the items.

Sir Kensington was the bravest knight in the land. He owned a magnificent sword and had a fierce lion painted on his armor. One day, the king summoned Sir Kensington. The knight came right away. Chest puffed out, he strode past a large statue of a lion and entered the throne room. The king told him that a dragon was terrorizing the kingdom, and that he needed a brave knight to put a stop to it. Sir Kensington held his head high. "Your Majesty, I shall defeat the dragon!" As the knight rode off to fight the dragon, a sense of fear swept over him. How big and fierce would this dragon prove to be? Looking up, Sir Kensington noticed a strange cloud. "That cloud looks like a lion!" he gasped. With renewed courage, he galloped forward.

1. In the story, a ______ is a symbol.
Ⓐ sword
Ⓑ cloud
Ⓒ knight
● lion

2. What details in the story show that this symbol stands for bravery and courage?
* The knight has renewed courage after he sees the lion cloud. He has a lion on his armor because knights are supposed to be brave.

3. Why is the symbol important to the story?
* It helped Sir Kensington feel courageous.

© Evan-Moor Corp. • EMC 2426 • Reading Comprehension Fundamentals 147

Page 149

Name ______ Fiction — Symbolism — 2

Disaster Relief

When an author uses **symbolism**, the author uses an animal, object, color, or image to represent something else, such as a big idea or something happening in the world. An author uses symbolism to draw a connection between the symbol and what it represents. Details in the story support this connection.

When looking for symbolism in a story, ask yourself these questions:

Does the story draw a comparison between an animal, object, or color and an important idea?

Does the story mention a certain animal, object, or color more than once?

Answer the items about the story you read.

1. Explain what the two patches on the mom's uniform represent.
* They're both American flags, but one of them is backwards. Together, they resemble a real flag flying in the breeze.

2. What does a bald eagle symbolize in the story? Explain how details support this.
* It symbolizes freedom. The narrator says there is nothing more free than a soaring bald eagle. It can spread its wings. It has the entire sky.

3. Why do you think the Founding Fathers chose a bald eagle instead of a turkey to be a national symbol for America?
* America values freedom, and the bald eagle flies high, like a free bird. The turkey is more limited.

4. Why does the sight of the soaring bald eagle make the narrator feel proud of her mom?
* The eagle makes her realize that her mom is serving a country that values freedom.

© Evan-Moor Corp. • EMC 2426 • Reading Comprehension Fundamentals 149

Page 150

Name ______ Fiction — Symbolism — Review

Answer the items.

1. Explain what symbolism is.
* It's an animal, object, color, or image that represents an idea or something else in a story.

2. How can recognizing symbolism in a story help you to better understand the story?
* It helps you understand the important idea that the author is trying to emphasize.

3. Write one question you can ask yourself when you're thinking about symbolism in a story.
* Is an animal, object, or color mentioned a lot?

4. Explain why authors use symbolism in a story.
* They use it to highlight an important idea.

Read the paragraph. Then answer the question.

5. "Look at that spider, Mac," said Grandma. Mac paused the movie to look up at the corner of the room where Grandma was pointing. He appeared disgusted.
"Oh, gross," he said, "let's get rid of it, quick."
"It's spinning and weaving its home," said Grandma. "It's entitled to make its own place in this world, isn't it?" Mac shrugged as Grandma continued. "It's chosen where to spin its web. It's chosen how tightly and how strongly to weave the strings. It's even chosen how big to make the web. Every choice the spider makes about the web, and each new string it weaves affects its life. It affects how much food it catches and how safe it will be." Mac didn't understand. "We all of us, big or small, weave our lives with our choices. Every choice we make is an important one, even if it seems insignificant."
Mac finally understood Grandma's point. "And now, Grandma, can we make the choice to continue our movie?" he said with a grin. Grandma nodded.

What do you think the spider web could represent in this story? Explain why.
* It could represent the choices people make. Grandma says "every choice we make."

150 Reading Comprehension Fundamentals • EMC 2426 • © Evan-Moor Corp.

Page 151

Name ______ Fiction — Historical Fiction — 1

A **historical fiction** story takes place in the past. Some of the events, characters, or settings may have been real, but the story is fictional.

These are important things to remember about historical fiction:

The setting is real or realistic.

The characters do things that people really did in the past.

The story provides factual details about how people lived in the past.

Read the pair of sentences. Circle it if it could be from a historical fiction story.

1. (circled) Nigel saw the newspaper article and gasped. Two brothers had just flown the world's first airplane!

2. Shali was writing a report on the Wright Brothers. She searched the internet for information and was amazed by what she found out.

3. (circled) It was 1919, and Mason needed a way to earn money. Having been a pilot during World War I, he began traveling around the country, performing aerial stunts for crowds.

Read the paragraph. Then answer the items.

A young journalist named Emmet stood among the crowd, which bristled with excitement. The strange man who'd arrived in Monday's stagecoach stood at the top of the hill, hoping to be the first person to fly. Strapped to his back was a pair of wings that looked just like those of a bird. He ran, flapped, and leaped! For a brief moment, Emmet thought he had the scoop of the century. That feeling quickly faded away, though, as the man tripped, stumbled, and rolled down the hill. Emmet sighed and went into the telegraph office to wire the disappointing story to the newspaper.

4. What details suggest that this story is historical fiction?
* The man arrived in a stagecoach. Emmet sends a telegraph.

5. Write one thing that might be different if the story's setting were the present time.
* Emmet would email the story with his computer.

© Evan-Moor Corp. • EMC 2426 • Reading Comprehension Fundamentals 151

Page 153

Name ______ Fiction — Historical Fiction — 2

His Majesty's Sense of Humor

A **historical fiction** story takes place in the past. Even though the story may seem true, it's fictional. These things are common in historical fiction:

The story mentions objects or things that people used in the past.

The story is about things that were realistic in the past.

The story gives details about things people did in the past.

Answer the items about the story you read.

1. What details suggest that this story takes place in the past?
* Everyone gets news by announcements in village squares. Being a jester is a job. The fastest way for Will to get to the castle was by horseback.

2. How did jesters get paid?
* They got food and a place to live. If they were really talented, they could earn money, too.

3. Write two details from the story that might be different if the story took place today.
* Will would audition for a talent show instead of a job for a king. Will would have found out that the king needed a jester on the Internet.

4. Write one way that royal jesters of the past are similar to comedians today.
* They both work to make people laugh.

5. If you were a king or a queen hundreds of years ago, would you have hired a jester? Explain why or why not.
* Answers will vary.

© Evan-Moor Corp. • EMC 2426 • Reading Comprehension Fundamentals 153

Page 154

Name ______ Fiction — Historical Fiction — Review

Answer the items.

1. Explain what makes a story a historical fiction.
* If a story is set in the past and provides realistic details about life in the past, it's historical fiction.

2. How is historical fiction different from other genres?
* Historical fiction is always set in the past and is realistic. Characters may have been real people.

3. Is it possible to learn facts about the past from reading a historical fiction story? Explain your answer.
* Yes. The story may tell about objects people used or how they did things. You can learn facts about the time period, daily life, clothing, and more.

Read the paragraphs. Then answer the item.

4. Maximus drove home as fast as he possibly could. He parked in the driveway and took the big box out of the trunk. He couldn't wait to take it inside to surprise his family. "Papa!" his children and wife shouted when he walked through the door.
"This is a surprise for you all," he said. Maximus took the object he'd just bought out of the box. He took the wire and plugged it into the wall. Then he adjusted the antennas and turned a dial. The flat surface started to make sounds and show pictures. "It's one of these new things called a television!" he said.
His family loved the surprise. "It's too bad all the pictures are black and white," said Maximus's son. "I wish the television could show things in color." After the family had watched television for an hour, Maximus's wife said she was going to heat up the leftovers from yesterday for tonight's dinner. "I'll put the leftovers in the oven now, so it should be all heated up in about a half an hour," she said.
"I'm so hungry, I wish there was a way to heat it up faster," said Maximus's son.

Write two details from the story that show that it is historical fiction.
* They heat food in an oven and don't know about microwaves. Their TV is only black and white.

154 Reading Comprehension Fundamentals • EMC 2426 • © Evan-Moor Corp.

Page 155

Name ______ Fiction — Realistic Fiction — 1

A **realistic fiction** story is about events that can actually happen. The setting is usually in the present and in a place that could be real. The details in a realistic fiction story are consistent with conditions in the real world.

This is a description of a realistic fiction story:

A boy has to miss his best friend's birthday party because he has the flu.

This is a description of story that is not realistic fiction:

A boy has to miss his best friend's birthday party because he has transformed into a giant bug.

Read the pair of sentences. Circle the pair that is from a realistic fiction story.

1. (circled) Min looked out the car's window at the big bear lumbering through the woods. "I wonder what he's thinking," Min thought.

2. A large bear drank some water from the stream. A strange feeling came over the bear and, to his shock, he suddenly knew how to speak Russian, Japanese, and English.

3. (circled) Jose did a research report on grizzly bears. He wrote about their diet, habitat, behavior, appearance, and other aspects of their lives.

Read the pair of sentences. Then state whether or not it is from a realistic fiction story. Explain your answer.

4. All of the bear leaders got together at a conference. They were discussing a persistent problem that their communities had been dealing with: humans invading their territories.
* This is not realistic fiction. Bears do not actually have conferences and discuss problems.

5. The nature expert had spent five days alone in the woods when he stumbled upon a baby bear that had fallen into a hole. She could hear the baby bear whimpering and decided to help the poor creature out, as it was probably weak, hungry, and thirsty.
* This is realistic fiction. A nature expert could really save a baby bear. A bear could fall into a hole.

© Evan-Moor Corp. • EMC 2426 • Reading Comprehension Fundamentals 155

Page 157

Name ______ Fiction — Realistic Fiction — 2

A Common Language

A **realistic fiction** story is about things that can actually happen. Even though it's a fictional story, it is believable. These are important details to remember about realistic fiction:

The events usually take place in the present time.

The characters have problems that real people deal with.

The characters' actions and dialogue are realistic and believable.

Answer the items about the story you read.

1. Describe in detail Caneze's problem in the story. Can real people have this problem?
* Caneze feels that she can't get to know her grandpa because they don't speak the same language. Different people within a single family can actually speak different languages.

2. Write three details from the story that suggest that this story takes place in the present.
* Caneze uses her phone to text. There are video games. Grandpa uses the Internet and a laptop.

3. How does Caneze feel at first when she's alone with her Grandpa? Are her feelings realistic? Explain why or why not.
* She feels awkward. It's realistic because many people feel awkward around new people.

4. Explain why this story is realistic fiction.
* The details and dialogue are realistic. The events could really happen. It takes place in the present.

* 5. Have you ever been in a situation similar to Caneze's? yes no

© Evan-Moor Corp. • EMC 2426 • Reading Comprehension Fundamentals 157

* These answers will vary. Examples are given.

Page 158

Name ____________ Fiction Realistic Fiction **Review**

Answer the items.

1. Explain what makes a story realistic fiction.
* It's a story that has accurate details about the world. It's about things that can really happen.

2. How is realistic fiction different from other genres?
* In realistic fiction, settings and events are in the present. All of the events could really happen.

3. Write about a problem that a character might have in a realistic fiction story.
* A character loses his backpack, which has his lunch, P. E. uniform, and textbooks in it.

4. Write about a problem that a character would not have in a realistic fiction story.
* A character uses a time machine to travel to the year 1832 but forgets his backpack in that year.

Read the paragraph. Then answer the item.

5. Wida was getting ready for school when she saw something that seriously concerned her in the mirror. "Oh my goodness, I have a gray hair!" she exclaimed to herself. "No way, I'm only twelve years old!" She took some tweezers and plucked out the gray hair, and she tried not to think about it again for the rest of the day. At school, though, she couldn't forget it. She told all her friends about the gray hair at lunch. As her friend Tammy was listening, her eyes became fixed on Wida's head. "What are you looking at, Tammy?" Wida asked. "Not another gray hair?" Tammy nodded. Now Wida was really freaking out. At dinner that night, she told her mom, who was a nurse, the whole story. Her mom said that this was nothing to worry about at all and that it was actually not that unusual. Wida felt relieved.

Write two details from the story that show that it is realistic fiction.
* The problem Wida has is believable and possible. The events seem to take place into the present.

158 Reading Comprehension Fundamentals • EMC 2426 • © Evan-Moor Corp.

Page 159

Name ____________ Fiction Myth **1**

A **myth** is a fictional story about supernatural events, or events that could not happen in the real world. A myth has characters with supernatural powers, such as gods, goddesses, and monsters. A myth often has a hero. These are additional details to remember about a myth:

- The setting is ancient.
- It can take place on Earth or in a place similar to Earth.
- It may explain how something was created or why something in the world is a certain way.
- It is told as if it is historical fact, even though it is not true.

Read the paragraph. Then answer the questions.

Now we have only one sun above Earth, but long ago, ten suns lived above Earth. They took turns going across the sky, one at a time. One day, however, they decided to stay in the sky together. Blinding light filled the sky. The heat dried wells and burned fields. At the same time, three monsters appeared in the land. Emperor Yao was miserable seeing his usually peaceful empire in such turmoil. He called upon Yi, the world's greatest archer, to help. Yi pulled back the string and let his first arrow fly. A flash filled the sky, and one of the suns was gone. One-by-one, Yi shot down eight more suns until there was just one left in the sky. Then he set out to defeat the monsters. One monster had an enormous tooth, which Yi shattered with an arrow. Next, Yi defeated a giant monster bird, and finally, he destroyed a vicious sea monster that had been terrorizing fishing villages. The empire was once again at peace.

1. Who is the hero in the story? Explain how you know.
* It is Yi. He gets rid of the extra suns in the sky. He defeats the monsters.

2. What details make this story a myth?
* It has supernatural beings. It has a hero. It has multiple suns in the sky, which is supernatural.

3. What does this myth explain about the world?
* It explains why there is only one sun in the sky.

© Evan-Moor Corp. • EMC 2426 • Reading Comprehension Fundamentals 159

Page 161

Name ____________ Fiction Myth **2**

Bellerophon and Pegasus

A **myth** is a fictional story about supernatural events, or events that could not happen in the real world. A myth has characters with supernatural powers, such as gods, goddesses, and monsters. A myth often has a heroic figure. These are additional details to remember about a myth:

- It can take place on Earth or in a place similar to Earth.
- It may have a lesson or a moral.
- It is told as if it is historical fact, even though it is not true.

Answer the items about the story you read.

1. Write one way that the setting is similar to Earth.
* It has cities and temples.

2. What makes Bellerophon the heroic figure in the story?
* He tames Pegasus. He defeats the Chimaera. He is wise.

3. Write two details from the story that demonstrate that it is a myth.
* There are gods and goddesses. There are supernatural beings, such as Pegasus.

4. What does the moral at the end of the story mean?
* It means that the punishment is worse for those who are very proud. Too much pride can cause you to become miserable.

5. Do you think that Bellerophon is a supernatural being? Explain why or why not.
* Yes. He may be the son of Poseidon. He received a bridle from Athena. He survived a big fall.

© Evan-Moor Corp. • EMC 2426 • Reading Comprehension Fundamentals 161

Page 162

Name ____________ Fiction Myth **Review**

Answer the items.

1. Mark the story idea that could be used to write a myth.
   - Ⓐ Everyone in the village was preparing for the New Year's feast. In a few hours, the village would be ringing in the new year and the turn of the century: the year 1900!
   - Ⓑ Buddy was excited and nervous because he was about to start taking driving lessons. He had never driven a space shuttle before, but now that he was twelve years old, it was time that he learned. The driving age for space vehicles had been lowered to twelve back in the year 2091.
   - Ⓒ Vera had never tried to order a gift online before, but she received an e-gift for her birthday, so she decided to give it a try.
   - ● Demula, who is a woman by day and a statue by night, has only forty days to travel to the goddess Shakna's temple and ask for help. Demula's village had recently been attacked by giant flies.

2. Write three details to remember about myths.
* They often have a hero. They may have a lesson. They have supernatural events and characters.

Read the paragraph. State whether or not it is a myth. Then explain why or why not.

3. Hundreds of years ago, when there were no flavors, the Cookers used to leave their castles in the sky to visit the people living on the planet below. The Cookers loved the people, and they thought of the people as their pets. The Cookers made all of the food that the people ate. The Cookers were giants, and they'd bring arm loads of food from their castles. All of the food was beige, and it all tasted like water. The people were always happy to receive the food, and they had never eaten anything else. They had a good relationship with the Cookers, until one day, when a person decided to start cooking his own food. The person used some plants that grew on the planet. The person sprinkled and chopped and grated ingredients. When this person tasted the food, his eyes grew wide. He loved the food he had made and vowed to never eat the Cookers' food again. He started sharing the food he cooked with the other people, and they all made the same vow. The Cookers became furious. They decided to never bring food down from the sky to the people on the planet ever again.
* It's a myth. The events and Cookers are supernatural. It explains why there are flavors.

162 Reading Comprehension Fundamentals • EMC 2426 • © Evan-Moor Corp.